Scarcity or Abundance?

Scarcity or Abundance?

A Debate on the Environment

Norman Myers & Julian L. Simon

W. W. Norton & Company / New York / London

Julian Simon's Chapter 2 reprinted from *The Public Interest,* No. 101 (Fall 1990), pp. 89–100. © 1990 by National Affairs, Inc. Portions of Julian Simon's Chapter 3 appeared in different form in the *New Scientist,* and portions of Chapter 4 appeared in different form in the *Washington Journalism Review.*
All reprinted by permission.

Printed in the United States of America
First Edition

The text of this book is composed in Caslon 540, with the display set in Univers Extra Condensed. Composition and manufacturing by The Maple-Vail Book Manufacturing Group.
Book design by Chris Welch.

Library of Congress Cataloging-in-Publication Data
Myers, Norman.
Scarcity or abundance? : a debate on the environment / by Norman Myers and Julian Simon.
p. cm.
1. Environment sciences—Philosophy. 2. Environmental degradation. 3. Man—Influence on nature. I. Simon, Julian Lincoln, 1932– . II. Title.
GE40.M94 1991.
363.7—dc20 93-27995

ISBN 0-393-03590-5

W. W. Norton & Company, Inc.
500 Fifth Avenue, New York, N.Y. 10110
W. W. Norton & Company Ltd.
10 Coptic Street, London WC1A 1PU

1 2 3 4 5 6 7 8 9 0

Contents

List of Tables and Figures

NORMAN MYERS

Editor's Note

For the purposes of this book, each author wrote a "pre-debate" statement, which could not be substantively altered after their exchange. The debate then took place in New York City on October 14, 1992, before a live audience at the Kellogg Conference Center of Columbia University's School of International and Public Affairs. It was moderated by Dean John Ruggie, who provides a foreword. After the debate, the authors had several months to write a "post-debate" statement, in which they present their final arguments in response both to the debate proceedings and their opponent's opening statement.

This chronological organization allows readers to follow the debate much as they might jury proceedings, where they can judge for themselves which of the distinguished debaters is more persuasive.

Foreword

One Earth, Two Worlds

Now that the fear of global nuclear holocaust has receded, it is difficult to imagine any issues of greater significance for planetary survival than those debated in this book. It is also difficult to imagine two more different views of that prospect than those expressed by our two authors, Julian Simon and Norman Myers.

The first tells a story of environmental plenty if not bliss, of progressive improvement in the human condition. The reassurance voiced by Franklin Delano Roosevelt in his inaugural address, "that the only thing we have to fear is fear itself," aptly captures Simon's message. Human ingenuity and institutional adaptation in the long run are the most powerful forces of all, he insists, prompting opportunity and the search for solutions.

The second tells a story of ecological degradation that is potentially catastrophic in its effects. It is a few seconds before midnight, and the erosion if not collapse of planetary life-support systems, species extinction, and the material as well as spiritual impoverishment of humankind are but ticks of the clock away. "We are now playing God," Myers concludes, and will pay the price unless we cease and desist.

What accounts for these radically different views about what is, presumably, the same "real world"? The reasons are many and varied, and include the use of different assumptions in model construction, different baselines for trend data, different guesses in place of poor or non-existent data, different methods of extrapolation, as well as errors of commission and omission on the part of the analysts. A very different kind of reason, however, is that, to some degree, our two authors are not assessing the same "real world" at all.

Their difference in world views goes beyond the fact that Simon tends to focus on increases in material measures, such as minerals availability, grain harvests, or the life expectancy of populations, whereas Myers focuses on the sustainability of biogeophysical systems and their complex feedback loops. The underlying ontology of their worlds also differs. Simon's world is composed of palpable and infinitely divisible units, existing within a field of discrete events. In contrast, Myers's world is made up of indivisible wholes, linked together by cycles and conjunctures that are subject to butterfly effects. If Simon's dominant metaphor is mechanical, Myers's is organic. If Simon is virtually whiggish in his commitment to the idea of human betterment, Myers conjures up the *Weltschmerz* of the Romantic movement at the height of the Industrial Revolution.

Humankind does not now know whether Simon is right, or Myers. We must come to know. Our collective existence could hang in the balance. The debate between our two authors sparked extensive controversy and discussion when it took place at Columbia University's School of International and Public Affairs. The School and W. W. Norton, joint organizers of the debate, hope and believe that it will have a similar effect among the public at large.

John Gerard Ruggie
DEAN, SCHOOL OF INTERNATIONAL AND PUBLIC AFFAIRS
COLUMBIA UNIVERSITY, NEW YORK
FEBRUARY 1994

Preface

Julian Simon

There's lots of good news, and it's getting even better. My half of this book contains solid evidence that several "environmental" matters which may scare you really are not to be feared; they are not what the public thinks them to be.

These are the purposes of my side of the debate: First, to tell important truths because it is fun to tell and hear them (as long as one's interests are not threatened). Second and more serious, to show you that when you develop new technology, build new goods, and expand the scope of our creative activities, you are on the side of the angels—you are promoting human improvement, and the quality of life. Our economic activities generally create more than they destroy. Hence we should encourage freedom and enterprise rather than fettering opportunity and throttling down the rate of progress. Productive people and organizations should walk tall with pride and get on with their jobs, rather than skulk around with a guilty conscience at befouling our environment.

The topics I deal with here are a small set of the conventional "green" beliefs that are massively contradicted by the scientific evidence. If these data make you question the common wisdom about how our society is doing in these *particular* cases, perhaps you will also review your thinking about the *entire set* of related issues, and recognize that across the board our human situation is getting better rather than getting worse. Perhaps you will also consider that if the issues discussed—which in the recent past were considered insuperable problems—turned out to be non-problems after we had time to gather the facts about them, it is not unlikely that the same fate will occur to the more recently publicized "green" issues—the ozone layer, the greenhouse effect, acid rain, and their kin—which we have not yet had time to understand thoroughly.

My work on population economics has evolved organically over the decades. Therefore, this book draws heavily upon previous articles and books—especially *The Economics of Population Growth* (1977), *The Ultimate Resource* (1981), *Population Matters* (1990), and *Population and Development in Poor Countries* (1992). Indeed, there are at least two sentences in this book that were first written in 1969 and have continued to appear in successive evolutions of this set of ideas—just as there are vestiges in our bodies of some much less developed species that existed long eons before us. This does not mean that we are just made-over amoebae or monkeys, and this book is not a makeover of any previous book, but it is the outgrowth of them. And in turn the forthcoming revision of *The Ultimate Resource* will contain new material from this volume. Additional citations and references to the professional literature and other documentation may be found in my technical books and articles.

Henning Gutmann's intellectual and publishing entrepreneurship is the cause of this book, for which I thank him. I also appreciate Aaron Wildavsky's permission to use our joint work in the third section. The rest of my many intellectual debts are noted in the front matter to my earlier books.

Preface

Norman Myers

In my contributions to this book I want to show that while there is much downside news in the environmental arena, *we still have much to play for*. Our prospect depends upon three key factors. First, do we have a firm enough grip on the basic science, both the ecology and the economics? Second, do we recognize the implications of environmental ruin for us—for our lifestyles, our values, our ways of viewing both one another and our world? Third, and most important of all, do we have the heart as well as the brains to set about building the new world that is still available to us? Nothing less will do than to devise fresh outlooks for all of us in whatever part of our one Earth. In face of the momentous challenge—surely the greatest since we left the primordial cave—can we keep our eye on the potential vision in prospect, a vision of a world transformed, a world of expanded options, a world where we enjoy peace with each other through peace with the Earth (and vice versa)? Can we muster the courage—no other word for it—to become all we can be, and do it for the first time ever?

For sure, it will be no easy venture. It will be demanding

and exhilarating. We shall feel so deeply involved we shall have little time to ask if it is enjoyable. Those of us who are on wavelength, let's make waves. Above all, let's not quack with the flock. The prospect will demand a personal conviction on the part of each and every one of us that we can indeed measure up to the challenges ahead—challenges that will be big enough to make us feel ten feet tall along the way.

You, the reader, will encounter two radically different views in this book of the outlook for our human species, our Earth, and our world. You could hardly face a more momentous judgment, given what is at stake. In my opinion, the prospect amounts to a "heaven forbid" versus a "golden age" outcome. Since we are going to have to redesign our world anyway (read on), we might as well shoot for the world we truly want.

All this applies especially to students—surely one of the greatest of the world's resources. During the course of my teaching forays at Berkeley, Cornell, Utrecht, and dozens of other universities, students invariably show me that youth is not wasted on the young. Many of them know the Dire Straits secret: Hearts that can think and brains that can feel. Their idealism reminds me that the finest attribute of humans is not ability to calculate, it is capacity to care. Students care like crazy: for the world around them, for long-suffering Earth, for our future. Keep on with your caring, students, and keep on motivating the oldsters like myself until you can get your own hands on the levers of decision. I gain an emphatic boost from your reactions—so why not do as many students have done on reading my other books, and send me a note to say how far you agree with what you read here. Keep me on track with what you make of it all, what you believe, and what you feel about what is much more your prospect than mine.

While preparing what follows, I have received valuable comments from a host of friends and colleagues. In particular, I am delighted to thank Martha Campbell, Dr. Herman Daly, Dr. David Duthie, Dr. Anne H. Ehrlich, Professor Paul R. Ehrlich, Dr. Mario Giampietro, Lindsey Grant, Dr. Carl Haub, Rick Heede, Hal Kane, Amory Lovins, Professor David Pimentel,

David Takacs, and Professor Edward O. Wilson. Most of all, I have enjoyed the splendid support of my Research Associate, Jennie Kent, who has supplied ideas, insights, and analyses, plus inspiration of numerous sorts.

The germ idea for this book came from my Norton editor, Mary Cunnane. She has encouraged me from start to finish of a taxing task. Much the same applies to my literary agent, Ginger Barber: supportive as ever. Thanks too to another Norton editor, Henning Gutmann, who has guided the project all the way along.

Pre-Debate Statement

Julian Simon

1

Introduction

Is a big wheat harvest a good thing? Sometimes we read headlines such as "Good harvest, bad news"—the bad news being for wheat farmers, who face low prices. On balance a big harvest surely is better for society as a whole than a small harvest. Still, the headline is negative, as if a bad thing has happened.

Is the trend of black infant mortality rates discouraging? Take a look at Figure 1-1 and make your judgment, please. My own judgment is that the overall picture is good for blacks as well as for the community as a whole, because many fewer babies are dying nowadays than in earlier years and many fewer parents need to grieve. Unless you focus only on the *relative* positions of the two groups, there seems slim basis for judging the situation as bad, unless you enjoy being morally indignant.

This is the point of these examples: viewing the same facts, one person may be optimistic while the other is pessimistic. The contradiction often happens because persons judge from different points of view. Frequently the root of the difference is the length of the period you focus on—the short run or the

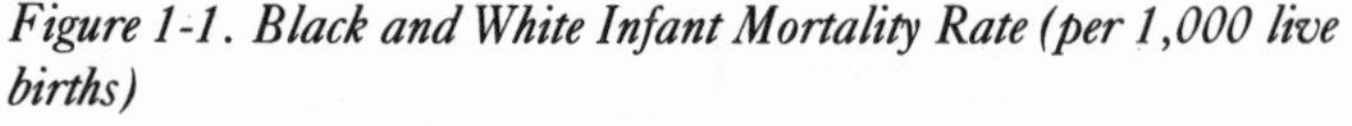

Figure 1-1. Black and White Infant Mortality Rate (per 1,000 live births)

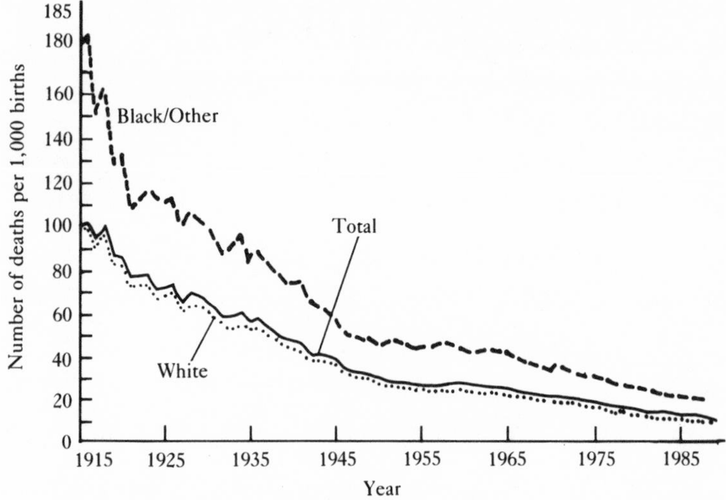

Source: U.S. Dept. of Commerce Bureau of the Census, *Historical Statistics of the United States: Colonial Times to 1970* (GPO, Washington, D.C., 1976); U.S. Dept. of Commerce Bureau of the Census, *Statistical Abstract of the United States* (GPO, Washington, D.C., various years).

long run. For many issues—and especially issues related to economic and population growth—the long-run effect is the opposite of the short-run effect. More people are an economic benefit in the long run, though they are a burden in the short run.

My central proposition here is simply stated: Almost every trend that affects human welfare points in a positive direction, as long as we consider a reasonably long period of time and hence grasp the overall trend.

In this introduction, I will first review some important absolute trends in human welfare. To repeat, my thesis is that just about every important measure of human welfare shows improvement over the decades and centuries.

LET'S START WITH some trends and conclusions that have long represented the uncontroversial settled wisdom of the economists and other experts who work in these fields, except for the case of population growth. On that latter subject, what you read below was a minority viewpoint until sometime in the 1980s, at which point the mainstream scientific opinion shifted almost all the way to the position set forth here.

Length of Life

The most important and amazing demographic fact—the greatest human achievement in history—is the decrease in the world's death rate. In Figure 1-2 we see that it took thousands

Figure 1-2. Life Expectancy Rates

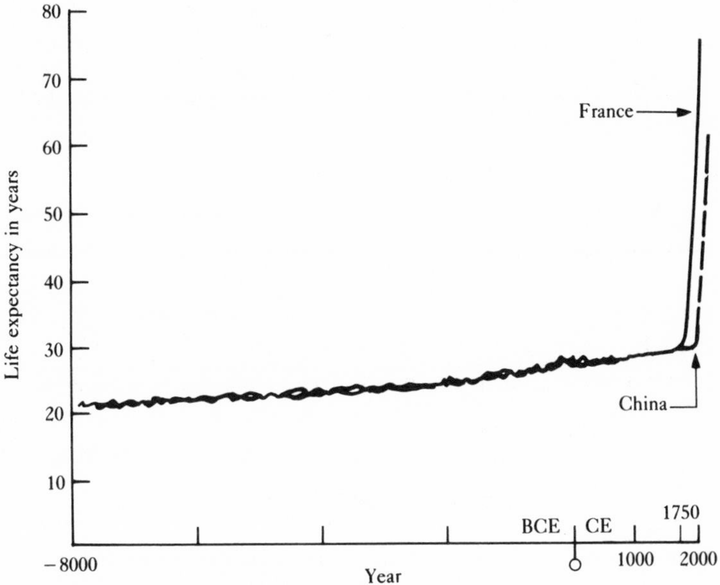

Source: Stylized and drawn by the author.

Figure 1-3. Life Expectancy Rates: Female Expectation of Life at Birth

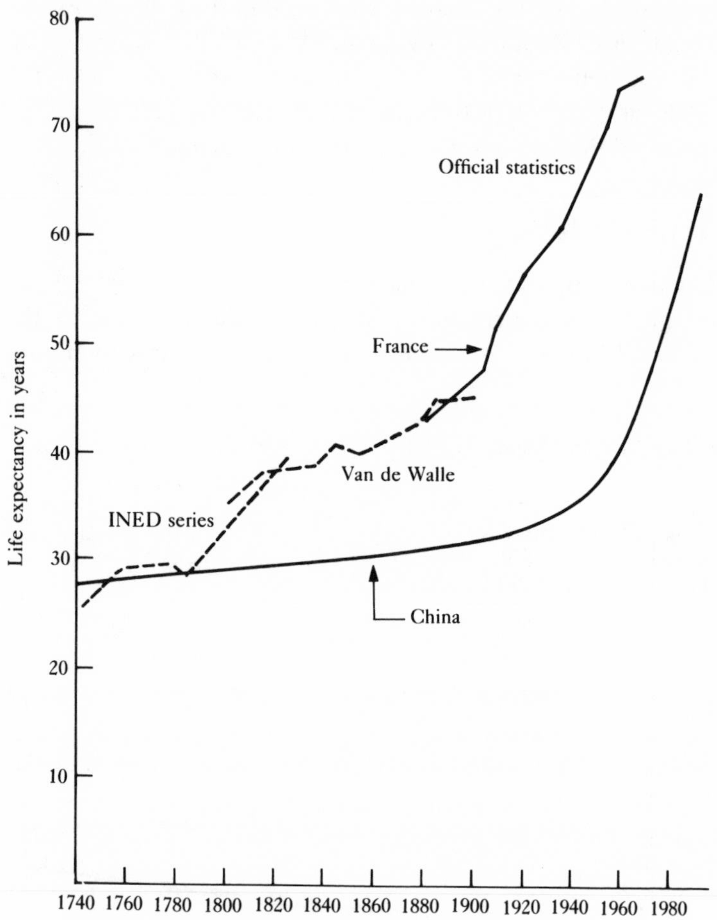

Source: Compiled by the author.

of years for life expectancy at birth to increase from just over twenty years to the high 20s. Then, in just the past two centuries, the length of life you could expect for your newborn child in the advanced countries jumped from perhaps thirty years to about seventy-five years (see Figure 1-3). It is this decrease in

Figure 1-4. Agricultural Labor Force in Great Britain, 1600–present

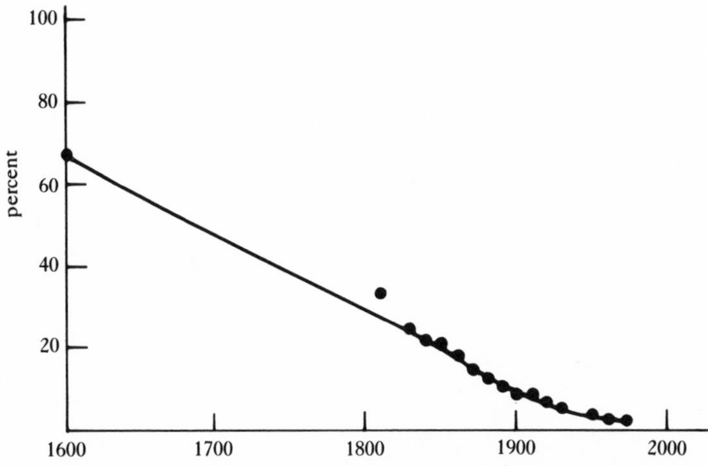

Sources: Phyllis Deane, "Great Britain," in *The Fontana Economic History of Europe: The Emergence of Industrial Societies, Part One,* edited by Carlo M. Cipolla (Fontana, London, 1970), various pp.; Brian Mitchell, *European Historical Statistics: 1750–1970,* abridged edn. (Columbia Univ. Press, New York, 1978), p. 61.

the death rate that is the cause of there being a larger world population nowadays than in former times. Is this not the greatest change that humankind has ever experienced?

Then, starting well after World War II, the length of life one could expect in the *poor* countries leaped upward by perhaps fifteen or even twenty years, caused by advances in agriculture, sanitation, and medicine. Are not these trends remarkably benign?

Agricultural Labor Force

The best simple measure of a country's standard of living is the proportion of the labor force that works in agriculture. If almost everyone works at farming, there can be little production of non-agricultural goods. In Figure 1-4 we see the astonishing decline over the centuries in the proportion of the population working in agriculture in Great Britain to only about one person in fifty, and the same story describes the United States. This has enabled us to increase our consumption per person by a factor perhaps of 20 or 40 over the centuries.

Raw Materials

During all of human existence, people have worried about running out of natural resources—flint, game animals, what have you. Amazingly, all the evidence shows that exactly the opposite has been true. Raw materials—all of them—are becoming more available rather than more scarce. Figures 1-5a and 1-5b

Figure 1-5a. Copper Prices Indexed by Wages

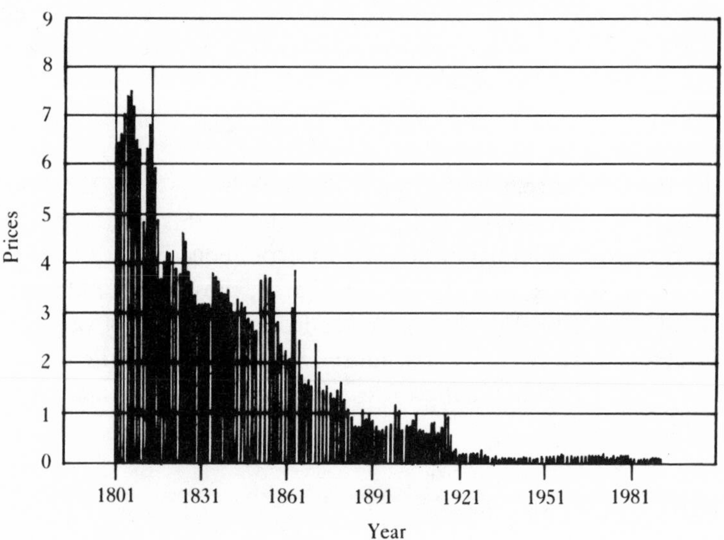

Source: U.S. Dept. of Commerce Bureau of the Census, *Historical Statistics of the United States: Colonial Times to 1970;* U.S. Dept. of Commerce Bureau of the Census, *Statistical Abstract of the United States* (various years).

Figure 1-5b. Copper Prices Indexed by CPI

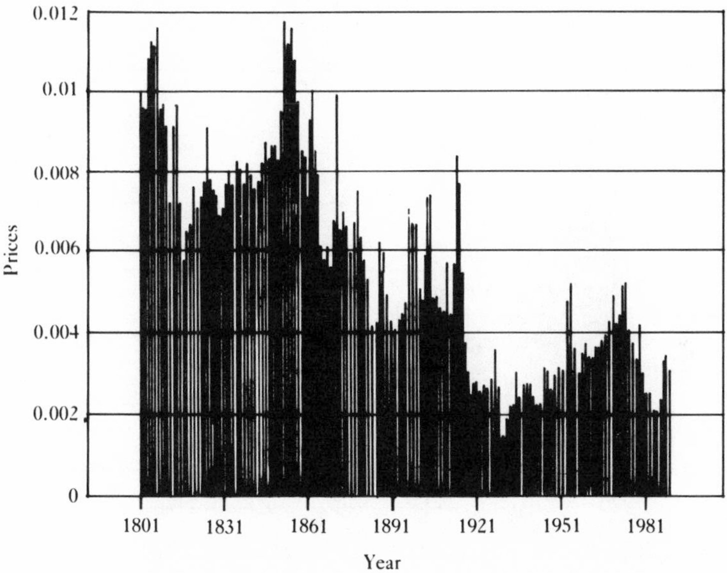

Source: U.S. Dept. of Commerce Bureau of the Census, *Historical Statistics of the United States: Colonial Times to 1970;* U.S. Dept. of Commerce Bureau of the Census, *Statistical Abstract of the United States* (various years).

clearly show that natural resource scarcity—as measured by the economically meaningful indicator of cost or price for copper, which is representative of all raw materials—has been decreasing rather than increasing in the long run, with only temporary exceptions from time to time. In the case of copper, we have evidence that the trend of falling prices has been going on for a very long time. In the eighteenth century BCE in Babylonia under Hammurabi—almost 4,000 years ago—the price of copper was about 1,000 times its price in the United States now, relative to wages. And there is no reason why this downward trend might not continue forever.

The trend toward greater availability includes the most coun-

Figure 1-6a. Wheat Prices Indexed by Wages

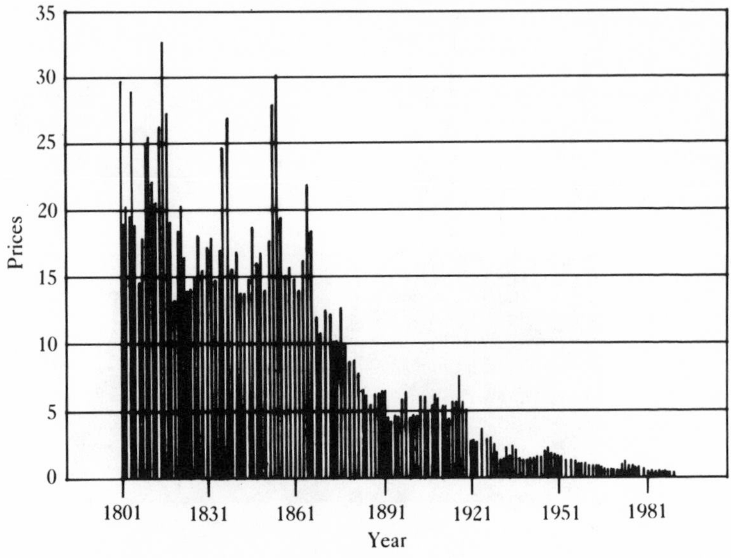

Source: U.S. Dept. of Commerce Bureau of the Census, *Historical Statistics of the United States: Colonial Times to 1970;* U.S. Dept. of Commerce Bureau of the Census, *Statistical Abstract of the United States* (various years).

terintuitive case of all—oil. The price rises in crude oil since the 1970s did not stem from increases in the cost of world supply, but rather cartel political action. The production cost in the Persian Gulf still is perhaps 25–75 cents per barrel (1993 dollars). Concerning energy in general, there is no reason to believe that the supply of energy is finite, or that the price of energy will not continue its long-run decrease forever. I realize that it seems strange that the supply of energy is not finite or limited, but if you want a full discussion of the subject, I hope that you will consult another of my books.*

*See *The Ultimate Resource* (1981, or 2nd edition, forthcoming), chapters 1–3.

Figure 1-6b. Wheat Prices Indexed by CPI

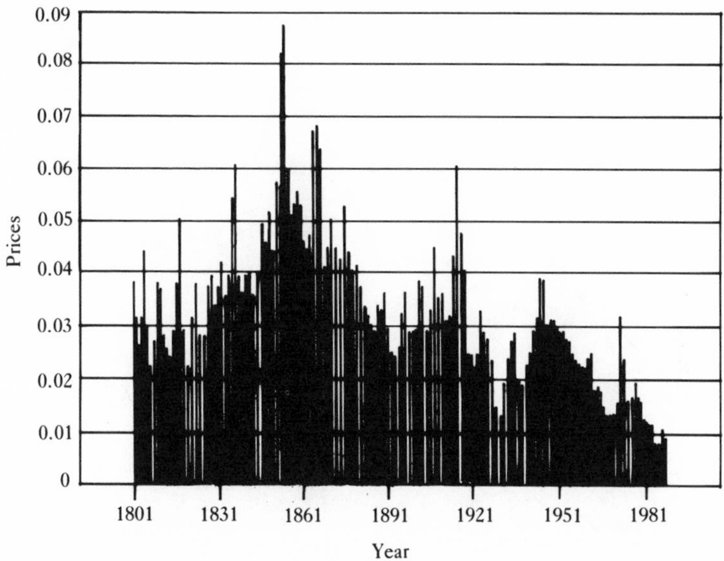

Source: U.S. Dept. of Commerce Bureau of the Census, *Historical Statistics of the United States: Colonial Times to 1970;* U.S. Dept. of Commerce Bureau of the Census, *Statistical Abstract of the United States* (various years).

Food

Food is an especially important resource. The evidence is particularly strong for food that we are on a benign trend despite rising population. The long-run price of wheat relative to wages, and even relative to consumer products, is down, due to increased productivity. (See Figures 1-5 and 1-6.)

Famine deaths have decreased during the past century even in absolute terms, let alone relative to population, which pertains particularly to the poor countries. Food consumption per person is up over the last thirty years (see Figure 1-7). Africa's food production per person is down, but by 1993 few people still believe that Africa's suffering has anything to do with a

Figure 1-7. Index of World Food Production Per Capita, 1951–1990 (1948–52 = 100)*

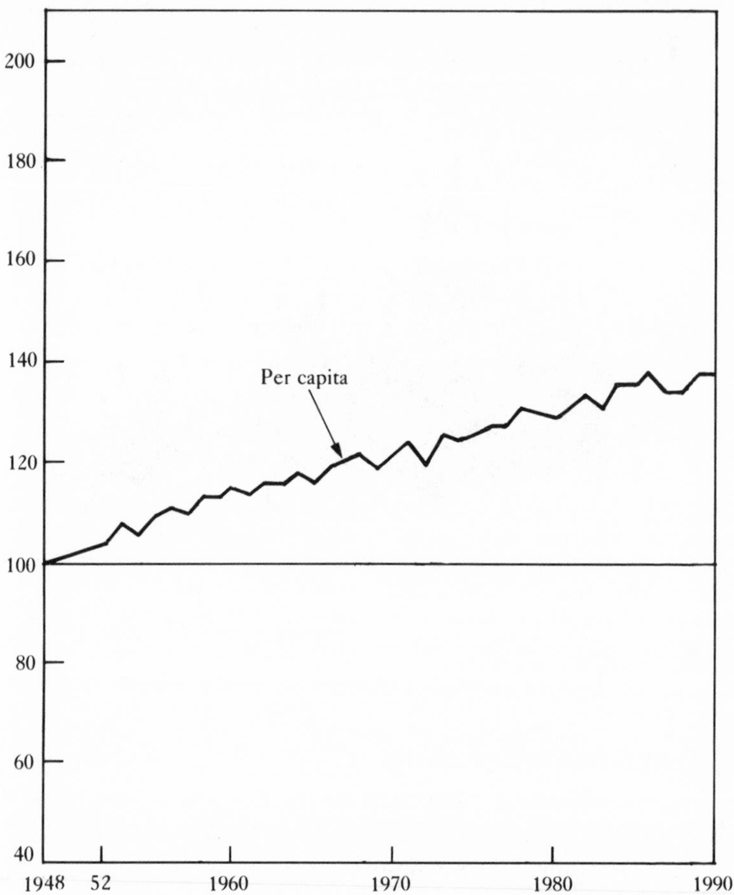

*Data from U.S. Dept. Agr., Econ. Res. Ser., *World Indices of Agricultural and Food Production* (various issues); *ibid., World Agricultural Trends and Indicators* (various issues); FAO, *Quarterly Bulletin of Statistics* (various issues); and *ibid., Production Yearbook* (various issues).

shortage of land or water or sun. Hunger in Africa clearly stems from civil wars and the collectivization of agriculture, which periodic droughts have made more murderous.

Human Life and Labor

There is only one important resource which has shown a trend of increasing scarcity rather than increasing abundance—human beings. Yes, there are more people on Earth now than ever before. But if we measure the scarcity of people the same way that we measure the scarcity of other economic goods—by how much we must pay to obtain their services—we see that wages and salaries have been going up all over the world, in poor as well as rich countries. The amount that you must pay to obtain the services of a manager or a cook has risen in India, just as the price of a cook or manager has risen in the United States over the decades. The increases in the prices of people's services are a clear indication that people are becoming more scarce economically even though there are more of us.

Cleanliness of the Environment

Ask an average roomful of people if our environment is becoming dirtier or cleaner, and most will say "dirtier." The irrefutable facts are that the air in the United States (and in other rich countries) is safer to breathe now than in decades past. The quantities of pollutants have been declining, especially particulates which are the main pollutant. The proportion of sites monitoring water of good drinkability in the United States has increased since the data began in 1961. Our environment is increasingly healthy, with every prospect that this trend will continue. (See the data in Figures 1-8.)

Figure 1-8a. National Ambient Concentrations of Pollutants

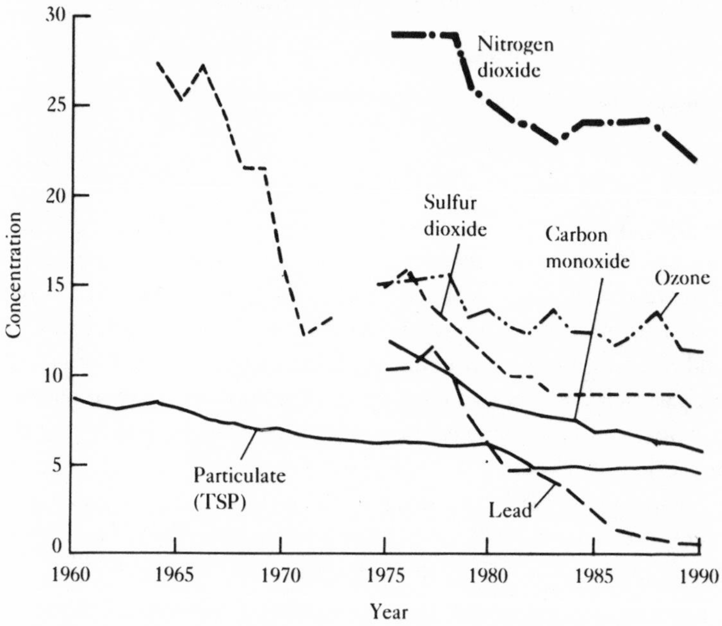

Source: Council on Environmental Quality, Environmental Quality, 22nd Annual Report, 1992, p. 276; Council on Environmental Quality, Environmental Quality, 1981, 12th Annual Sulfur 1964 thru 1972: EPA (1973).

Population Growth

The effects of population growth are discussed at some length in section 2; this has been the central issue in all my work for decades.

Species Extinction

Species extinction is discussed at some length in section 3, because it is the core of my debate opponent's best-known professional work, and I have replied to his central assertion.

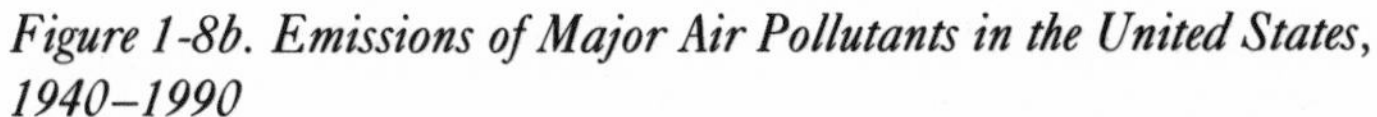

Figure 1-8b. Emissions of Major Air Pollutants in the United States, 1940–1990

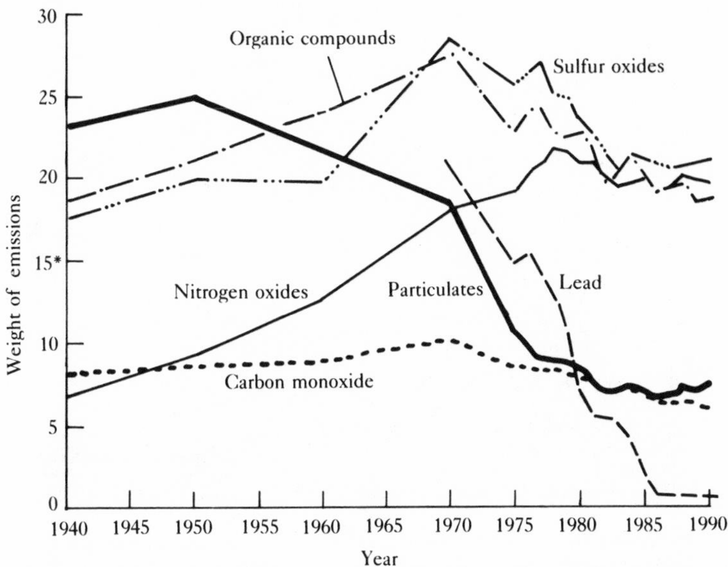

*In millions of metric tons per year, except lead in ten thousands of metric tons per year, and carbon monoxide in 10 million metric tons per year.

Source: Council on Environmental Quality, Environmental Quality, 22nd Annual Report, 1992, p. 273.

The Vanishing Farmland Crisis

The supposed problem of farmland being urbanized has now been entirely discredited, out-and-out disavowed by those who created the scare. This saga serves to illuminate many similar environmental issues, and therefore it is discussed in detail in section 4.

Figure 1-8c. Air Quality Trends in Major Urban Areas (number of days worse than the PSI index level), 1973–1989

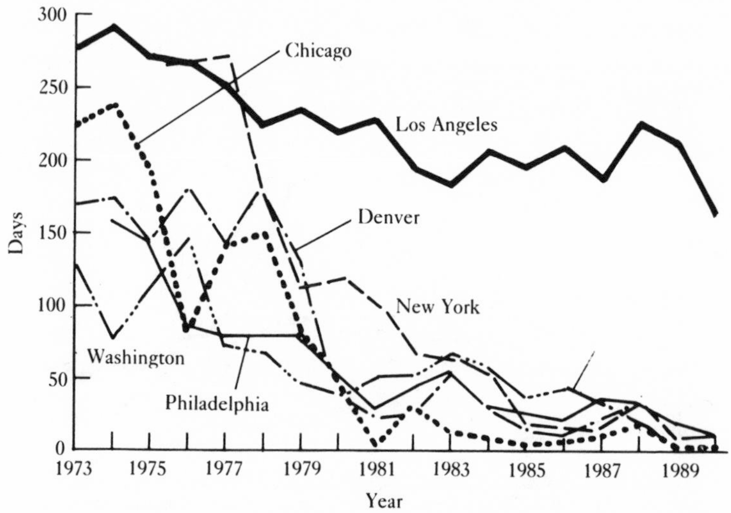

Source: Council on Environmental Quality, Environmental Quality, 22nd Annual Report, 1992, p. 277; Council on Environmental Quality, Environmental Quality 1981, 12th Annual Report, 1981, p. 244.

The Greenhouse Effect, the Ozone Layer, and Acid Rain

What about the greenhouse effect? The ozone layer? Acid rain? I'm not a technical expert on the atmosphere. I can say with confidence, however, that on all of these issues there is major scientific controversy about what has happened until now, why it happened, and what might happen in the future. All of these scares are recent, and there has not yet been time for complete research to be done and for the intellectual dust to settle. There may be hard problems here, or there may not.

Even more important for people is that no threatening trend in *human welfare* has been connected to those phenomena. There has been no increase in skin cancers from ozone, no

Figure 1-8d. Phosphorus Loadings to the Great Lakes (percent of target level), 1976–1989

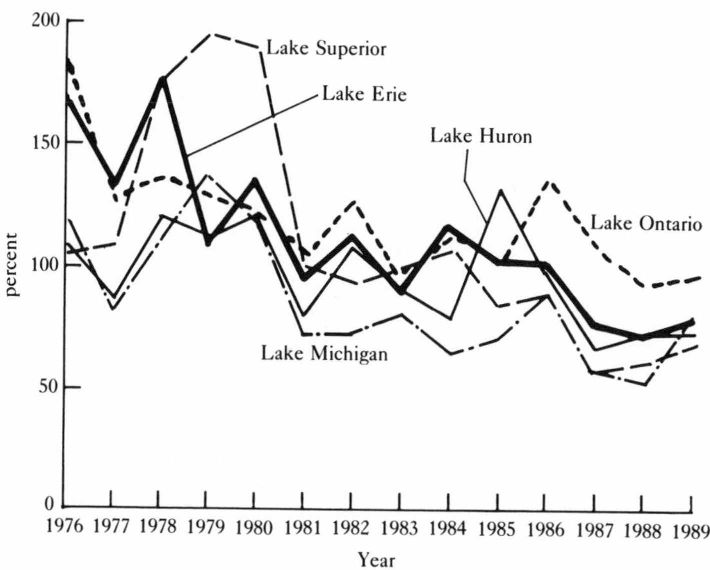

Source: Council on Environmental Quality, Environmental Quality, 22nd Annual Report, March 1992.

damage to agriculture from a greenhouse effect, and at most slight damage to lakes from acid rain. It may even be that a greenhouse effect would benefit us on balance by warming some areas we'd like warmer, and by increasing the carbon dioxide to agriculture.

Perhaps the most important aspect of the greenhouse–ozone–acid rain complex, and of their as-yet-unknown cousin scares which will surely be brought before the public in the future, is that we now have large and ever-increasing capabilities to reverse such trends if they are proven to be dangerous, and at costs that are manageable. Dealing with greenhouse–ozone–acid rain would not place an insuperable constraint upon

Figure 1-8e. DDT Levels in the Great Lakes (parts per million in whole fish samples), 1965–1983

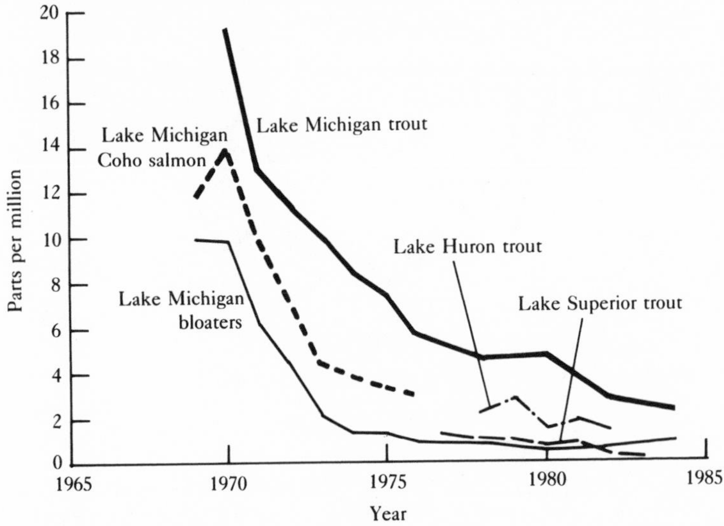

Source: Council on Environmental Quality, Environmental Quality, 17th Annual Report, 1986, p. C-44, 45.

growth, and would not constitute an ultimate limit upon the increase of productive output or of population. So we can look these issues squarely in the eye and move on. Section 5 discusses the atmospheric issues.

Section 6 discusses why people believe false bad news about resources and environment, and ends with a brief conclusion.

Are These Predictions Sure Enough to Bet On?

I am so sure of all these upbeat statements that I offer to bet on them, my winnings going to fund new research. Here is the offer: You pick (a) any measure of human welfare—such as life

Figure 1-8f. PCB Levels in the Great Lakes, 1972–1990

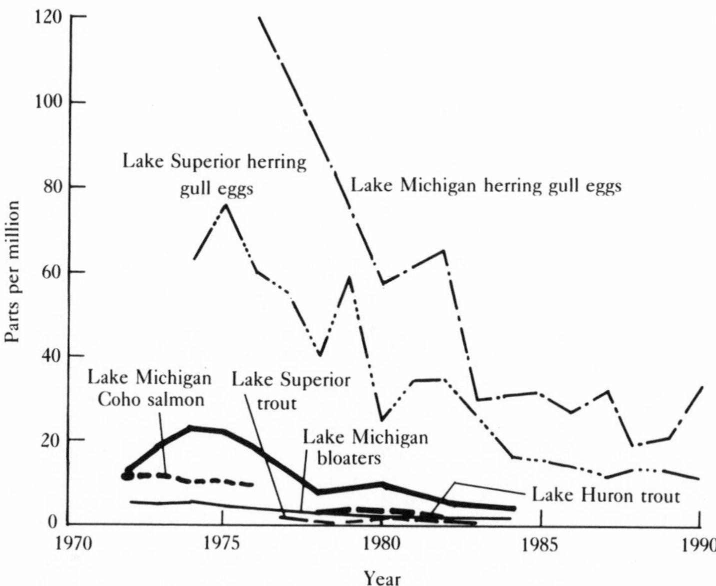

Source: Council on Environmental Quality, Environmental Quality, 17th Annual Report, 1986, p. C-44, 45; Council on Environmental Quality, Environmental Quality, 22nd Annual Report.

expectancy, infant mortality, the price of aluminum or gasoline, the amount of education per cohort of young people, the rate of ownership of television sets, you name it; (b) a country (or a region such as the developing countries, or the world as a whole); (c) any future year, and I'll bet a week's or a month's pay that that indicator shows improvement relative to the present while you bet that it shows deterioration.

Figure 1-8g. Dieldrin Levels in the Great Lakes, 1969–1990

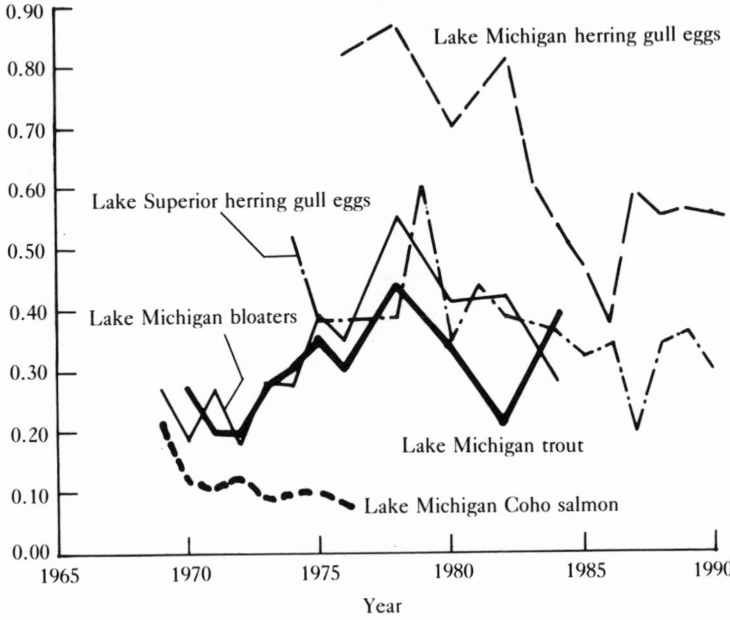

Source: Council on Environmental Quality, Environmental Quality, 17th Annual Report, 1986, p. C-45; Council on Environmental Quality, Environmental Quality, 22nd Annual Report, 1992.

2

Population Growth Is Not Bad for Humanity

Once again there is widespread hysteria about the world having too many people, and too many babies being born. But it is now well established scientifically that population growth is not the bogey that conventional opinion and the press believe it to be. In the 1980s a revolution occurred in scientific views toward the role of population growth in economic development. The economics profession has turned almost completely away from the previous judgment that population growth is a crucial negative factor in economic development. There is still controversy about whether population growth is even a minor negative factor in some cases, or whether it is beneficial in the long run. But there is no longer any scientific support for the earlier view which was the basis for U.S. government policy and then the policies of other countries.

Erroneous belief about population growth has cost dearly. In poor countries, it has directed attention away from the factor that we now know is central in a country's economic development, its economic and political system. And in rich countries, misdirected attention to population growth and its supposed consequence of natural resource shortages has caused waste through such programs as now-abandoned synthetic-fuel programs, and the useless development of airplanes that would be appropriate for an age of greater scarcity.

Anti-natalist U.S. foreign policy is dangerous politically, too, because it risks being labeled racist, as happened in India when Indira Gandhi was overthrown because of her sterilization program. Furthermore, misplaced belief that population growth slows economic development provides support for inhumane programs of coercion and the denial of personal liberty in one of the most sacred and valued choices a family can make—the number of children that it wishes to bear and raise—in such countries as China, Indonesia, and Vietnam.

The Revolution in Population Economics

Concerning the view that population growth is a crucial negative factor in economic development, the "official" turning point came in 1986 with the publication of a book by the National Research Council (NRC) and the National Academy of Sciences (NAS) entitled *Population Growth and Economic Development.* This report almost completely reversed the previous report on the same subject from the same agency. The 1971 report said that "[A] reduction in present rates of population growth is highly desirable from many points of view, because high fertility and rapid population growth have seriously adverse social and economic effects. . . . [p. 1] Rapid population growth slows down the growth of per capital incomes in less developed countries [p. 2]." It then proceeded to list supposed ill effects upon savings, investment, food supplies, unemployment, modernization, technological change, industrialization, social areas, education, health and child development, and the environment.

Compare the 1986 NRC-NAS report. On the subject of the greatest worry, raw materials, it concluded: "The scarcity of exhaustible resources is at most a minor constraint on economic growth [p. 16] . . . the concern about the impact of rapid population growth on resource exhaustion has often been exaggerated [p. 17]." And it was calm about most of the other effects that caused alarm in the 1971 report. The general conclusion goes only as far as, "On balance, we reach the qualitative conclusion that slower population growth would be beneficial to economic development for most developing countries. . . . [p. 17]." That is, in 1986, the NRC-NAS report found forces operating in both positive and negative directions; its conclusion does not apply to all countries; and the size of the effect is not known even where it is believed to be present.

This is a major break from the past monolithic characterization of additional people as a major drag upon development across the board. And since then the mainstream economic reviews of the subject have moved even further from the old warnings. In fact, for almost as long as the Malthusian idea has been the core of U.S. theory about foreign aid, starting in the 1960s, there has been a solid body of statistical evidence that contradicts the conventional wisdom about the effects of population growth—data which falsify the ideas that support U.S. population policy toward less developed countries. By now perhaps two dozen competent statistical studies have accumulated covering the few countries for which data are available over the past century, and also the many countries for which data are available since World War II, and almost all are in full agreement. The basic method is to gather data on each country's rate of demographic growth and its rate of economic growth, and then to examine whether—looking at all the data in the sample together—the countries with high demographic growth rates have economic growth rates lower than average, and countries with low demographic growth have economic growth faster than average.

The clear-cut consensus of this body of work is that faster demographic growth is *not* associated with slower economic growth. On average, countries with whose populations grew faster did not grow slower economically. That is, there is no basis in the statistics for the belief that faster demographic growth causes slower economic growth.

Additional strong evidence comes from pairs of countries that have the same culture and history, and had much the same standard of living when they split apart after World War II—East and West Germany, North and South Korea, and China and Taiwan (see Table 2-1). In each case the centrally planned communist country began with less population "pressure," as measured by density per square kilometer, than did the market-directed non-communist country. And the communist and non-communist countries in each pair also started with much the same birth rates and population growth rates. Data for other interesting countries are included, also. The market-directed economies have performed vastly better economically than the centrally-planned countries. Income per person is higher. Wages have grown faster. Key indicators of infrastructure such as telephones per person show a much higher level of development. And indicators of individual wealth and personal consumption, such as autos and newsprint, show enormous advantages for the market-directed enterprise economies compared to the centrally-planned, centrally-controlled economies. Furthermore, birth rates fell at least as early and as fast in the market-directed countries as in the centrally-planned countries, for better or for worse.

These comparative data provide solid evidence that an enterprise system works better than does a planned economy. For our purposes here, this powerful explanation of economic development cuts the ground from under population growth as a likely explanation. And under conditions of freedom, demographic growth poses less of a problem in the short run, and brings many more benefits in the long run, than under conditions of government planning of the economy.

Table 2-1. Demographic and Economic Growth: Selected Countries, 1950–83

	Population Density and Growth											
	East Germany	*West Germany*	*North Korea*	*South Korea*	*China*	*Taiwan*	*Hong Kong*	*Singapore*	*USSR*	*USA*	*India*	*Japan*
Population per Sq. Km., 1950	171	201	76	212	57	212	2236	1759	8	16	110	224
% Change in Pop., 1950	1.2	1.1	−7.8	0.1	1.9	3.3	−10.4	4.4	1.7	1.7	1.7	1.6
% Change in Pop., 1955	−1.3	1.2	3.5	2.2	2.4	3.5	4.9	4.9	1.8	1.8	1.9	1.0
% Change in Pop., 1960	−0.7	1.3	3.0	3.3	1.8	3.1	3.0	3.3	1.8	1.7	2.0	0.9
% Change in Pop., 1970	−0.1	1.0	3.0	2.4	2.4	2.2	2.2	1.7	1.0	1.1	2.2	1.3
% Change in Pop., 1983	−0.3	−0.2	2.1–2.6	1.4–1.6	1.3–1.6	1.8	1.5	1.2	0.7–0.9	0.9	2.1–2.2	0.6

Source: Population per square km.: United Nations Educational, Scientific, and Cultural Organization, *UNESCO Yearbook* (1963), pp. 12–21. Percentage change in population: U.S. Department of Commerce, *World Population* (1978); and United Nations, Report on *World Population* (1984).

Table 2-1. Demographic and Economic Growth: Selected Countries, 1950–83 (Continued)

	Real Income Per Capita											
	East Germany	*West Germany*	*North Korea*	*South Korea*	*China*	*Taiwan*	*Hong Kong*	*Singapore*	*USSR*	*USA*	*India*	*Japan*
Real GDP per capita, 1950[a]	1480	1888	n.a.	n.a.	300	508	n.a.	n.a.	1373	4550	333	810
Real GDP per capita, 1960	3006	3711	n.a.	631	505	733	919	1054	2084	5195	428	1674
Real GDP per capita, 1970	4100	5356	n.a.	1112	711	1298	2005	2012	3142	6629	450	4215
Real GDP per capita, 1980	5532	6967	n.a.	2007	1135	2522	3973	3948	3943	8089	498	5996
Real GNP per capita, 1959[b]	Same as W. Germ.	2943	Same as S. Korea	193	n.a.	417	1053	n.a.	n.a.	7447	217	649
Real GNP per capita, 1960	n.a.	3959	n.a	473	n.a.	429	979	1330	n.a.	8573	220	1403
Real GNP per capita, 1970	6584	6839	556	615	556	868	1807	2065	4670	10769	219	4380
Real GNP per capita, 1982	9914	11032	817	1611	630	2579	5064	5600	5991	12482	235	9774

[a]Figures for real gross domestic product (GDP) per capita are based on 1975 international prices.
[b]Figures for real gross national product (GNP) per capita are based on 1981 constant U.S. dollars.

Sources: Real GDP per capita: Robert Summers and Alan Heston, "Improved International Comparisons of Real Product and Its Composition: 1950–1980," *Review of Income and Wealth* (June 1984): pp. 207–62. Real GNP per capita: International Bank for Reconstruction and Development (IBRD), *World Tables* (1980). GNP deflator: Council of Economic Advisers (1986, Table B 3).

Life Expectancy and Infant Mortality

	East Germany	*West Germany*	*North Korea*	*South Korea*	*China*	*Taiwan*	*Hong Kong*	*Singapore*	*USSR*	*USA*	*India*	*Japan*
Life Expectancy at Birth, 1960	68	69	54	54	53	65	65	64	68	70	43	68
Life Expectancy at Birth, 1982	73	74	65	68	67	73	76	73	69	75	55	77
Infant Mortality, 1960	39	34	78	78	165	32	37	35	33	26	165	30
Infant Mortality, 1982	12	12	32	32	67	18	10	11	28	11	94	7

Source: IBRD, *World Development Report* (1985), pp. 260–261.

Table 2-1. Demographic and Economic Growth: Selected Countries, 1950–83 (Continued)

Industrialization and Urbanization												
	East Germany	*West Germany*	*North Korea*	*South Korea*	*China*	*Taiwan*	*Hong Kong*	*Singapore*	*USSR*	*USA*	*India*	*Japan*
% Labor Force in Agric., 1960	18	14	62	66	n.a.	n.a.	8	8	42	7	74	33
% Labor Force in Agric., 1980	10	4	49	34	69	37 (1978)	3	2	14	2	71	12
% Urbanized, 1960	72	77	40	28	18	58	89	100	49	70	18	63
% Urbanized, 1982	77	85	63	61	21	70 (1980)	91	100	63	78	24	78

Sources: Labor force in agriculture: IBRD, *World Development Report* (1985), pp. 258–259. Urban population: IBRD, *World Development Report* (1985), pp. 260–261.

	Education and Consumption											
	East Germany	*West Germany*	*North Korea*	*South Korea*	*China*	*Taiwan*	*Hong Kong*	*Singapore*	*USSR*	*USA*	*India*	*Japan*
Higher Education Enrollment, 1960	16	6	n.a.	5	n.a.	n.a.	4	6	11	32	3	10
Higher Education Enrollment, 1982	30	30	n.a.	22	1	n.a.	12	10	21	56	9	31
Newsprint per Person, 1950–54	3.5	5.1	n.a.	0.6	n.a.	0.9	4.3	n.a.	1.2	35.0	0.2	3.3
Newsprint per Person, 1982	9.6	21.5	0.1	5.8	1.2	n.a.	16.4	32.1	4.5	44.1	0.4	24.0
Telephones per 100 Pop., 1983	20.6	57.1	n.a.	14.9	0.5	25.8	38.2	36.7	9.8	76.0	0.5	52.0
Autos per 100 Pop., 1960	0.9	8.2	n.a.	0.1	0.005	0.1	1.0	4.2	0.3	34.4	0.1	0.5
Autos per 100 Pop., 1970	6.7	24.1	n.a.	0.2	0.008	n.a.	2.8	7.2	0.7	43.9	0.1	8.5
Autos per 100 Pop., 1984	18.9	41.3	n.a.	1.1	0.010	3.1	4.6	9.3	3.9	55.5	0.2	22.8

Sources: Higher education: IBRD, *World Development Report* (1985), pp. 266–267. Newsprint: *UNESCO Yearbook* (1963), pp. 400–409. Telephones: U.S. Department of commerce, *Statistical Abstract* (1986), p. 845. Automobiles: Motor Vehicle Manufacturers Association of the U.S. Inc., *World Motor Vehicle Data* (various years).

How Does Malthusianism Go Wrong?

How can the persuasive common sense embodied in the Malthusian theory be wrong? To be sure, in the short run an additional person—baby or immigrant—inevitably means a lower standard of living for everyone; every parent knows that. More consumers mean less of the fixed available stock of goods to be divided among more people. And a larger number of workers laboring with the same fixed current stock of capital implies that there will be less output per worker. The latter effect, known as "the law of diminishing returns," is the essence of Malthus's theory as he first set it out. But if the resources with which people work are not fixed over the period being analyzed, then the Malthusian logic of diminishing returns does not apply. And the plain fact is that, given some time to adjust to shortages, the resource base does not remain fixed. People create more resources of all kinds. When horse-powered transportation became a major problem, the railroad and the motor car were developed. When schoolhouses become crowded, we build new schools—more modern than the old ones. Extraordinary as it seems, natural resource scarcity—that is, the cost of raw materials, which is the relevant economic measure of scarcity—has tended to decrease rather than to increase over the entire sweep of history, as we saw in Figures 1-3 and 1-4. This trend is at least as reliable as any other trend observed in human history. And demographic growth has speeded the process rather than hindered it. The most extraordinary aspect of the resource-creation process is that temporary or expected shortages—whether due to population growth, income growth, or other causes—tend to leave us even better off than if the shortages had never arisen, because of the continuing benefit of the intellectual and physical capital created to meet the shortage. It has been true in the past, and therefore is likely to be true in the future, that we not only need to solve our problems, but we need the problems that accompany the growth of population and income.

The same process occurs with the supplies of non-material resources. The data show that societies with relatively high proportions of youths somehow find the resources to educate their children roughly as fully as do countries at similar income levels with lower birth rates. Outstanding examples of high rates of education in the face of relatively large numbers of children include the Philippines, Costa Rica, Peru, Jordan, and Thailand.

Nor does it make sense to reduce population growth because of the supposedly increasing pollution of our air and water; we saw that our air and water are becoming cleaner rather than dirtier (see Figure 1-8).

Section 1 showed the extraordinary decrease in the world's death rate in terms of increases in life expectancy. Let's now put it differently. In the early nineteenth century the planet Earth could sustain only 1 billion people. Ten thousand years ago, only 4 *million* could keep themselves alive. Now, 5 *billion* people are living longer and more healthily than ever before. This increase in the world's population represents our triumph over death.

I would expect lovers of humanity to jump with joy at this triumph of human mind and organization over the raw forces of nature. But many people lament that there are so many humans alive to enjoy the gift of life. They even approve the brutal coercive population-control programs in China.

The most important benefit of population size and growth is the increase it brings to the stock of useful knowledge. Minds matter economically as much as, or more than, hands or mouths. The progress of civilization is limited largely by the availability of trained workers. The main fuel to speed the world's progress is the stock of human knowledge. And the ultimate resource is skilled, spirited, hopeful people, exerting their wills and imaginations to provide for themselves and their families, thereby inevitably contributing to the benefit of everyone.

Skilled and creative people require, however, an appropriate economic and political framework that provides incentives for working hard and taking risks, enabling their talents to flower and come to fruition. The key elements of such a framework are respect for property, fair and sensible rules of the market that are enforced equally for all, and the personal liberty that accompanies economic freedom. In the absence of such a framework, the short-run costs of population growth are greater, and the long-run benefits fewer, than in free societies.

What Should Our Outlook Be?

The doomsayers of the population-control movement offer a vision of limits, decreasing resources, a zero-sum game, conservation, deterioration, fear, and conflict—concluding with calls for more governmental intervention in markets and family affairs. Should that be our vision? Or should our vision be that of those who look optimistically upon people as a resource rather than as a burden—a vision of receding limits, increasing resources and possibilities, a game in which everyone can win, building, the excitement of progress, and the belief that persons and firms, acting spontaneously in the search of their individual welfare, and regulated only by rules of a fair game, will produce enough to maintain and increase economic progress and promote liberty? And what should be our mood? The population restrictionists say we should be sad and worry. I and many others believe that the trends suggest joy and celebration at our newfound capacity to support human life—healthily, and with fast-increasing access to education and opportunity all over the world. I believe that the population restrictionists' handwringing view leads to despair and resignation. My "side's" view leads to hope and progress, in the reasonable expectation that the energetic efforts of humankind will prevail in the future—as they have in the past—to increase worldwide our numbers, our health, our wealth, and our opportunities.

3

The Statistical Flummery About Species Loss*

Species extinction came to scientific prominence in 1979 with my debate opponent Norman Myers's book *The Sinking Ark*. It then was brought to an international public and onto the U.S. policy agenda by the 1980 *Global 2000 Report to the President* (U.S. CEQ, 1981). These still are the canonical texts. *Global 2000* forecast extraordinary losses of species between 1980 and 2000. "Extinctions of plant and animal species will increase dramatically. Hundreds of thousands of species—perhaps as many as 20 percent of all species on earth—will be irretrievably lost as their habitats vanish, especially in tropical forests," it said.

The actual data on the observed rates of species extinction are wildly at variance with Myers's and following statements, and do not provide support for the various policies suggested to deal with the purported dangers. Furthermore, recent scientific and technical advances—especially seed banks and genetic engineering, and perhaps electronic mass testing of new

*This section is drawn from work done with Aaron Wildavsky.

drugs—have reduced the importance of maintaining a particular species of plant life in its natural habitat. But the bandwagon of the species extinction issue continues to roll with ever-increasing speed.

Society properly is concerned about possible dangers to species. Individual species, and perhaps all species taken together, constitute a valuable endowment, and we should guard their survival just as we guard our other physical and aesthetic assets. But we should strive for as clear and unbiased an understanding as possible in order to make the best possible judgments about how much time and money to spend in guarding them, in a world in which this valuable activity must compete with guarding and supporting other valuable aspects of civilization.

Species Loss Estimates

The standard forecast for loss of species comes from Alan Lovejoy:

> What then is a reasonable estimate of global extinctions by 2000? In the low deforestation case, approximately 15 percent of the planet's species can be expected to be lost. In the high deforestation case, perhaps as much as 20 percent will be lost. This means that of the 3–10 million species now present on the earth, at least 500,000–600,000 will be extinguished during the next two decades. (*U.S.*, 1980, II, p. 331)

The basis of any useful projection must be some body of experience collected under some range of conditions that encompass the expected conditions, or that can reasonably be extrapolated to the expected conditions. But none of Lovejoy's references contain any scientifically impressive body of experience. The only published source given for his key table is Myers's 1979 book. This is Myers's summary:

As a primitive hunter, man probably proved himself capable of eliminating species, albeit as a relatively rare occurrence. From the year A.D. 1600, however, he became able, through advancing technology, to over-hunt animals to extinction in just a few years, and to disrupt extensive environments just as rapidly. Between the years 1600 and 1900, man eliminated around seventy-five known species, almost all of them mammals and birds—virtually nothing has been established about how many reptiles, amphibians, fishes, invertebrates and plants disappeared. Since 1900 man has eliminated around another seventy-five known species—again, almost all of them mammals and birds, with hardly anything known about how many other creatures have faded from the scene. The rate from the year 1600 to 1900, roughly one species every 4 years, and the rate during most of the present century, about one species per year, are to be compared with a rate of possibly one per 1000 years during the "great dying" of the dinosaurs.

Since 1960, however, when growth in human numbers and human aspirations began to exert greater impact on natural environments, vast territories in several major regions of the world have become so modified as to be cleared of much of their main wildlife. The result is that the extinction rate has certainly soared, though the details mostly remain undocumented. In 1974 a gathering of scientists concerned with the problem hazarded a guess that the overall extinction rate among all species, whether known to science or not, could now have reach 100 species per year. . . .

Let us suppose that, as a consequence of this man-handling of natural environments, the final one-quarter of this century witnesses the elimination of 1 million species—a far from unlikely prospect. This would work out, during the course of 25 years, at an average extinction rate of 40,000 species per year, or rather over 100 species per day. The greatest exploitation pressures will not be directed at tropical forests and other species-rich biomes until towards the end of the period. That is to say, the 1990s could see many more species accounted for than the previous several decades. But already the disruptive processes are well underway, and it is not unrealistic to suppose that, right now, at least one species is disappearing each day. By the late 1980s we could be facing a situation where one species becomes extinct each hour. (*The Sinking Ark*, 1979, pp. 4–5)

We may extract these key points from the above summary quotation:

1. The estimated extinction rate of known species is about *one every four years* between the years from 1600 to 1900.

2. The estimated rate is about *one a year* from 1900 to the present.

3. Some scientists (in Myers's words) have "hazarded a guess" that the extinction rate "could now have reached" 100 species per year. That is, this number is simply conjecture; it is not even a point estimate but rather an upper bound. The source given for the "some scientists" statement is a staffwritten news report. (It should be noted that the subject of this guess is different than the subject of the estimates in [1] and [2], because the former includes mainly or exclusively birds or mammals whereas the latter includes all species. While this difference implies that [1] and [2] may be too low a basis for estimating the present extinction rate of all species, it also implies that there is even less statistical basis for estimating the extinction rate for species other than birds and mammals than it might otherwise seem.)

4. This guessed upper limit in (3) is then increased and used by Myers, and then by Lovejoy, as the basis for the "projections" quoted above. In *Global 2000* the language became "are likely to lead" to the extinction of between 14 percent and 20 percent of all species before the year 2000. (*U.S.*, 1980, II, p. 328) So an upper limit for the present that is pure guesswork has become the basis of a forecast for the future which has been published in newspapers to be read by hundreds of millions of people and understood as a scientific statement.

The two historical rates stated by Myers, together with the yearly rates implied by Lovejoy's estimates, are plotted together in Figure 3-1. It is clear that the Lovejoy extrapolation has no better claim to belief than a rate that is, say, one hundredth as

Figure 3-1. Myers-Lovejoy Estimates of Species Extinction and Their Extrapolations to the Year 2000

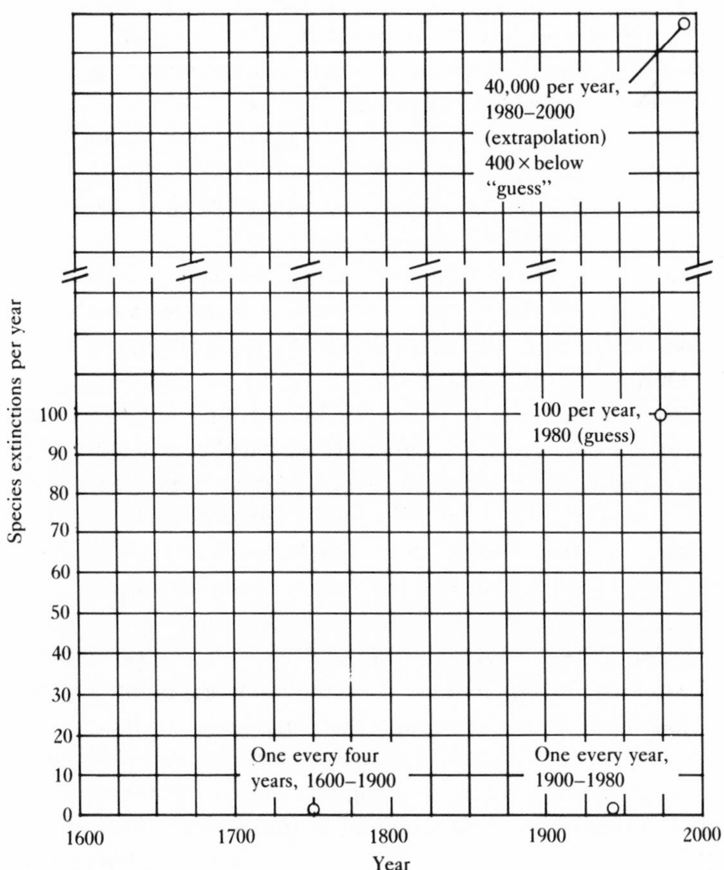

Source: See text.

large. Indeed, looking only at the two data points alone, many forecasters would be likely to project a rate close to the past rate, nowhere near Lovejoy's estimate, on the basis of the common wisdom that in the absence of additional information, the best first approximation for a variable tomorrow is its value today, and the best second approximation is that the variable will change at the same rate in the future that it has in the past.

Projected change in the amount of tropical forests implicitly underlies the differences between past and projected species loss rates in Lovejoy's extrapolation. But to connect this element logically, there must be systematic evidence relating an amount of tropical forest removed to a rate of species reduction. The only available evidence runs against this theory. Ariel Lugo details the situation in Puerto Rico, where "human activity reduced the area of primary forests by 99%, but, because of coffee shade and secondary forests, forest cover was never below 10 to 15%. This massive forest conversion did not lead to a correspondingly massive species extinction, certainly nowhere near the 50% alluded to by Myers." (1989, p. 28)

During the 1980s there was increasing recognition that the rate of species loss really is not known. Indeed, as of 1989 Myers himself wrote, "Regrettably we have no way of knowing the actual current rate of extinction in tropical forests, nor can we even make an accurate guess" (1989, p. 102) And Paul Colinvaux (1989) refers to the extinctions as "incalculable." One would think that this absence of knowledge would make anyone leery about estimating future extinctions.

Nevertheless, Myers continues, "But we can make substantive assessments by looking at species numbers before deforestation and then applying the analytical techniques of biogeography. . . . According to the theory of island biogeography, we can realistically reckon that when a habitat has lost 90% of its extent, it has lost half of its species" (1989, p. 43). This is mere speculation, however. And, as noted above, Lugo (1989) found disconfirming evidence in Puerto Rico. Yet the conservationists go right on pressing for expensive public policies on the unproven assumption that the number of species being extinguished is huge.

(Too late for inclusion in this pre-debate statement—the rules rigidly prevented any addition afterwards—there appeared a book published by the World Conservation Union (IUCN), edited by Whitmore and Sayer, containing a variety of articles which support what I say here about numbers of extinctions. Excerpts from those articles may be found in my post-debate statement, point 6.)

Many biologists privately agree that the extinction numbers are quite uncertain. But they go on to say the numbers do not matter scientifically. The policy implications would be the same, they say, even if the numbers were different even by several orders of magnitude. But if so, why mention any numbers at all? The answer, quite clearly, is that these numbers do matter in one important way: they have the power to frighten the public in a fashion that smaller numbers would not. I find no scientific justification for such use of numbers.

Some have said: But was not Rachel Carson's *Silent Spring* an important force for good even though it exaggerated? Maybe so. But the books are not yet closed on the indirect and long-run consequences of ill-founded concerns about environmental dangers. And it seems to me that, without some very special justification, there is a strong presumption in favor of stating the facts as best we know them, especially in a scientific context, rather than in any manipulation of the data, no matter how well intended.

The Risks from Species Loss

Let's look backwards and wonder: What kinds of species may have been extinguished when the settlers clear-cut the Middle West of the United States? Could we be much the poorer now for their loss? Obviously we do not know the answers. But it seems hard to even *imagine* that we would be enormously better off with the persistence of any such imagined species. This casts some doubt on the economic value of species that might be lost elsewhere.

Still, the question exists: How should decisions be made, and sound policies formulated, with respect to the danger of species extinction? I do not offer a comprehensive answer. It is clear that we cannot simply save all species at any cost, any more than we can save all human lives at any cost. Certainly we must make some informed estimates about the present and future social value of species that might be lost, just as we must estimate the value of human life in order to choose rational policies about public health services such as hospitals and surgery. And just as with human life, valuing species relative to other social goods will not be easy, especially because we must put values on some species that we do not even know about. But the job must be done somehow.

We must also try to get more reliable information about the number of species that might be lost with various forest changes. This is a very tough task, too.

Lastly, any policy analysis concerning species loss must explicitly evaluate the total cost of protective actions—for example, the cost of cessation of foresting in an area. And such a total cost estimate must include the long-run indirect costs of reduction in economic growth to a community's education and general advancement.

Preserving the Amazon and other areas in a state of stability might even have counterproductive results for species diversity, according to a recent body of research. Natural disturbances, as long as they are not catastrophic, may lead to environmental disturbance and to consequent isolation of species that may "facilitate ever-increasing divergence," as Colinvaux tells us. Colinvaux goes on to suggest that "the highest species richness will be found not where the climate is stable but rather where environmental disturbance is frequent but not excessive." (1989) This is another subtle issue which must be taken into account.

Discussing Matters with the Conservationists

Why is there such an enormous gulf between what you hear from the conservationists and what you are reading here?

1. In the case of species extinction, as with many other public issues, there is a tendency to focus only upon the bad effects

of human activities, and to exclude from consideration the possible good effects—for example, the increase in species due to human activities. (Lugo, 1989, pp. 28–30)

2. Conservation biologists' goals with respect to species diversity are not clear. Sometimes they emphasize the supposed economic benefits of species diversity, and sometimes non-economic goals. This vagueness of goals makes it very difficulty to compare the worth of a species-saving activity against another value.

3. Many biologists consider the interests of humans and of other species to be opposed.

Conclusion

There is now no prima facie case for any expensive species-safeguarding policy without more extensive analysis than has been done heretofore. The existing data on the observed rates of species extinction are almost ludicrously inconsistent with the doomsters' claims of rapid disappearance, and they do not support the various extensive and expensive programs they call for. Furthermore, recent scientific and technical advances—especially seed banks and genetic engineering—have diminished the importance of maintaining species in their natural habitat. But the question deserves deeper thought, and more careful and wide-ranging analysis, than has been given it until now.

I do not suggest we ignore extinctions. Rather, we should be as informed as possible. We should separate the available facts from the guesswork and the purposeful misstatements, in order to improve the public decision-making process. And society should take into account—but in a reasoned fashion—the economic and non-economic worths of species, in light of our values for human and non-human aspects of nature and other aspects of life on Earth. It is important that we think as clearly as we can about this problem that is indeed difficult to think about sensibly.

4

The "Urban Sprawl" and Soil Erosion Scam

This section tells the saga of the most conclusively discredited political-environmental fraud of recent times. This case may serve as a model of many similar issues for which the full story has not come to light, and in which there does not exist a public confession by the official agency involved that the original scare was entirely false.

The heart of this issue is that many persons, in the name of "environmentalism," want to prevent other people from building houses on farmland near them. Under the guise of preventing future food shortage, they mobilize the powers of public authority to attain their private goals. That is, the famine-protection claims are simply a smoke screen for property owners who want a bucolic view, we can infer. But whatever the motives, this phony scare campaign steals taxpayers' money and prevents young couples from getting the housing they want.

As I was preparing this debate, the following appeared on September 10, 1992, in the *Washington Post:* "State Preservation Program Stems Loss of Farmland to Development . . . The easement program was enacted . . . not only to curb development . . . but also to help keep the state partially self-sufficient in food production. . . . Loss of farming . . . also means more food must be imported from out of state, which can drive prices up." (pp. Md 1, 7)

These and similar programs in a score of other states are justified with the proposition that the United States is losing farmland at an unprecedented rate—that population growth produces urban sprawl, that highways pave over "prime farmland" and recreational land, and that the farmland is needed to stave off hunger in the future. Those assertions have now been wholly disproven—and acknowledged to be so by the U.S. Department of Agriculture (USDA), which originally raised the alarm. That is, even the original purveyors of the false facts about the "vanishing farmland crisis" agree that the widely reported scare was without foundation. For more details, see Easterbrook (1986) and Simon (1990).

The relevant data are as follows:

Table 4-1. Major Uses of Land, United States, 1987

	(Millions of Acres)
Cropland[1]	399
Grassland pasture and range[2]	656
Forestland[3]	648
Special uses[4]	271
Urban and other land[5]	291
Total land area	2265

[1] Total cropland, excluding cropland used only for pasture.

[2] Grassland and other non-forested pasture and range, including cropland used only for pasture.

[3] Excludes forestland in parks and other special uses of land.

[4] Includes uses specified in source.

[5] Urban areas, miscellaneous uses not inventoried, and land having little surface use such marshs, swamps, bare rock areas, desert, and tundra.

Source: Thomas Frey, "Land Use Trends in the United States," in Julian L. Simon, ed., *The State of Humanity* (Basil Blackwell, Boston, forthcoming).

Table 4-1 shows that of the 2.3 billion acres in the United States as of 1987, all the land taken up by cities, highways, nonagricultural roads, railroads, and airports amounts to only 82 million acres—just 3.6 percent of the total. (Frey, forthcoming) Clearly there is very little competition between agriculture on the one side, and cities and roads on the other.

Concerning the trends: from 1920 to 1987, land in urban and transportation uses rose from 29 million acres to 82 million acres—a change of 2.3 percent of the total area of the United States. (Frey, forthcoming) During those fifty-four years, population increased from 106 million to 244 million people. Even if this demographic trend were to continue—in fact, population growth has slowed down—there would be an almost unnoticeable impact on U.S. agriculture (see Table 4-2).

About 1980, headlines like these began to appear in the newspapers: "The Peril of Vanishing Farmlands" *(The New York Times)*, "Farmland Losses Could End U.S. Food Exports" *(Chicago Tribune)*, "Vanishing Farmlands: Selling Out the Soil" *(Saturday Review)*, and "As World Needs Food, U.S. Keeps Losing Soil to Land Developers" *(Wall Street Journal)*. The new stories asserted that the urbanization-of-farmland rate had jumped by a multiple of 3 from the 1960s to the 1970s—from less than 1 million acres per year to 3 million acres per year. This assertion was wholly untrue, as we shall see. Indeed, even the original purveyors of the false facts have 'fessed up and now agree that the widely reported scare was without foundation.

Several scholars—including William Fischel, Clifford Luttrell, Fraser Hart, and myself—found that the 3-million-acres-a-year rate was most implausible, in light of various sets of data from other sources and given the nature of the surveys from which the National Agricultural Land Study (NALS) estimate was drawn. We also got help from H. Thomas Frey, a geographer who had been the keeper of the urbanization and other land-use data for the Economic Research Service of the USDA for many years. All sides agreed that in 1967 the total urban and built-up area in the United States (excluding highways, railroads, and airports) was between 31 and 35 million acres. It was also agreed that the rate of urbanization was slower in the 1960s

Table 4-2. Major Uses of Land, 48 Contiguous States, 1900–87

Land Use (million acres)	*1900*	*1910*	*1920*	*1930*	*1940*	*1950*	*1959*	*1969*	*1978*	*1982*	*1987*
Cropland[1]	319	347	402	413	400	409	393	384	395	404	399
Used for crops	—	324	374	379	363	387	359	333	369	383	331
Idle	—	23	28	34	37	22	34	51	26	21	68
Grassland pasture and range[2]	831	777	730	719	717	700	695	689	660	659	654
Forestland[3]	600	600	602	601	608	612	614	603	583	567	558
Urban and other land	153	179	169	170	180	183	200	221	259	266	285
Special use areas[4]	—	—	—	—	—	90	95	102	114	119	128
Miscellaneous areas[5]	—	—	—	—	—	93	105	119	145	147	157
Total land areas[6]	1903	1903	1903	1903	1905	1904	1902	1897	1897	1896	1896

— = Not available

[1] Total cropland, excluding cropland used only for pasture.

[2] Grassland and other non-forested pasture and range including cropland used only for pasture.

[3] Excludes forestland in parks and other special uses of land.

[4] Includes uses specified in source.

[5] Urban areas, miscellaneous uses not inventoried, and land having little surface use such as marshes, swamps, bare rock areas, desert, and tundra.

[6] Changes in total land area are due to changes in methods and materials used in remeasurements and to increase in the area of artificial reservoirs.

Source: Frey, "Land Use Trends in the United States," in Simon, ed., *The State of Humanity* (forthcoming).

than in the 1950s. Yet the Department of Agriculture's National Agricultural Lands Study said that over the ten years from 1967 to 1977, there was a 29-million-acre increase in urban and built-up land.

That is, over the course of more than two centuries, in the process of reaching a population of about 200 million people, the United States built towns on between 31 and 35 million acres. NALS now asserted that suddenly in the course of another ten years, and with a population increase of only 18 million people, the urban and built-up areas increased by 29 million acres (almost none of it due to transportation)—a near doubling.

To put it differently, the long-run trend in the decades up to 1970 was about 1 million acres of total land urbanized per year—not increasing but rather constant or slowing. The Soil Conservation Service in conjunction with NALS then announced that the rate jumped to between 2 and 3 million acres yearly from 1967 to 1975 or 1977 (depending on which version you read).

There were two bases given for the 3-million-acre number, and NALS shifted from one to the other when either was criticized: (1) A small sample re-survey of part of the 1967 "inventory" of sampled farms, done by the Soil Conservation Service. (A similar inventory had previously been done in 1958.) (2) The 1977 sample inventory. Seymour Sudman and I (1982) then showed that there were so many flaws that both sources should be considered totally unreliable. The flaws included a huge error that put the right numbers in the wrong columns for huge chunks of Florida.

Various government agencies were mobilized by the USDA to rebut our criticisms, but we successfully rebutted them. Then the scare seemed to die down a bit, but not before the private American Farmland Trust was organized in 1980 from former employees of NALS. Annually it now spends a couple of million dollars a year to "protect" the United States from the danger of vanishing farmland, and gets money from the United Fund charity drives.

Then the bombshell: In 1984, the Soil Conservation Service (SCS) officially issued a paper by Linda Lee that completely reversed their own earlier scare figures and confirmed the estimates of the critics. The accompanying press release made it super-clear that the former estimates were now being retracted. "[T]he acreage classified as urban and built-up land was 46.6 million acres in 1982, compared to 64.7 million acres reported in 1977." Please read that again. It means that whereas in 1977 the SCS had declared that 64.7 million acres had been "lost" to built-upon land, just five years later SCS admitted that the actual total was 46.6 million acres. That is, the 1977 estimate was fully *50 percent too high*, a truly amazing error for something so easy to approximate and check as the urbanized acreage of the United States.

With unusual candor, the USDA press release added: "The 1982 data, which correlate closely with data from the 1980 U.S. Census of Population [the census was not available at the time of the argument described above, but later fully corroborated Frey's estimates based on prior data], are considered accurate because of the availability of better maps, more time for data collection, many more sample points, and better quality control." It continued: "The 1977 estimate thus appears to have been markedly overstated."

Even earlier, an "official" Congressional Research Service report (Dunford, 1983) had reported the situation correctly: "National Agricultural Lands Study indicated that almost three million acres of agricultural land was annually converted to relatively irreversible nonfarm uses between 1967 and 1975. . . . Subsequent analyses and more recent empirical evidence have not supported these results. . . . In conclusion, the most recent reliable information indicates that the conversion of farmland to urban and transportation uses occurred at about half the rate indicated in the National Agricultural Lands Study." (p. CRS-v) "The putative figure of 3 million acres per year from the NALS has been repudiated by subsequent analyses and more recent empirical evidence." (p. CRS-10) This 1983 report completely confirmed the criticisms that others and I leveled at the NALS claims. Table 4-3 shows the estimates from NALS and three subsequent estimates from other official sources. And Figure 4-1 shows a revealing graph drawn from a recent official program; the falsity of the 1977 National Resources Inventory estimate, which the Department of Agriculture continued to defend for long, is immediately apparent.

The entire "crisis" was hokum. This was not a regrettable but understandable exaggeration of a real problem, but a nonproblem manufactured by the Department of Agriculture and some members of Congress out of whole cloth under the guise of concern about food production for the starving world. The crisis was created for the benefit of (a) the so-called environ-

Table 4-3. Estimated Rates of Urbanization

Study	*Period Covered*	*Average Annual Expansion in Urban Area (million acres)*
National Agricultural Land Study[1]	1967–75	2,875
Economic Research Service	1970–80	740–1,000
Bureau of the Census	1970–80	1,276
1987 NRI[2]	1982–87	726
Second Resources Conservation Appraisal[3]	1977–82	900–1,100

1. USDA, 1982. Based on 1967–75 Potential Cropland Study (Dideriksen, *et al.*, 1977).
2. USDA, 1989.
3. USDA, 1990. Based on comparison of 1977–82 NRI (USDA, 1982) and Census urban area data.

Source: Marlow Vesterby, Ralph E. Heimlich, and Kenneth S. Krupa. *Urbanization of Rural Land in the United States* (U.S. Department of Agriculture, Agricultural Economic Report, September 1991).

mentalists, and (b) people who own homes that abut on areas which might be developed into housing developments, and whose vistas and ambience might thereby be affected. The connection between the farmland scare and prevention of housing construction has been documented for California by Frieden (1979).

But what about the *fertility* of the land used for human habitation and transportation? Even if the total quantity of land used by additional urban people is small, perhaps the new urban land has special agricultural quality. One often hears this charge, as made in my then-home town in the 1977 City Council election: The mayor "is opposed to urban sprawl because 'it eats up prime agricultural land.' " But in fact, as new cropland is created, and some old cropland goes out of use, the overall effect—for example, between 1967 and 1975, the period at which the scare was directed—is that the average quality of cropland in the United States has improved.

The idea that cities devour "prime land" is a particularly clear example of the failure to grasp economic principles. Let's take the concrete (asphalt?) case of a new shopping mall on the outskirts of Champaign-Urbana, Illinois. The key economic idea is that the mall land has greater value to the economy as a shopping center than it does as a farm, wonderful though this Illinois land is for growing corn and soybeans. That's why the

Figure 4-1. Measures of Urban Area, 1958–1987

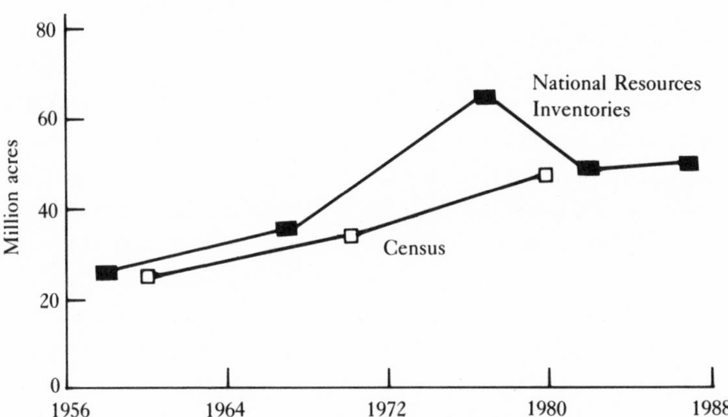

Note: The National Resources Inventories (NRI) includes developed uses outside urban areas delineated by the census. Inaccurate mapping of urban boundaries in 1977 resulted in an overestimate of urban area, which was corrected in the 1982 NRI (Lee, 1984).

These problems, and failure to record actual changes in land uses over time, made existing data unusable. USDA's Economic Research Service instead used another technique proven in previous studies that is better suited to studying questions about land use changes.

Source: U.S. Department of Agriculture, *Agriculture Information Bulletin* No. 629, August 1991.

mall investors could pay the farmer enough to make it worthwhile for him or her to sell. A series of corny (yes, yes) examples should bring out the point.

If, instead of a shopping mall, the corn-and-soybean farmer sold the land to a person who would raise a new exotic crop called, say, "whornseat," and who would sell the whornseat abroad at a high price, everyone would be delighted. The land clearly would be more productive raising whornseat than corn, as shown by the higher profits the whornseat farmer would make as compared with the corn-and-soybean farmer, and as also shown by the amount that the whornseat farmer is willing to pay for the land.

A shopping mall is similar to a whornseat farm. It seems different only because the mall does not use the land for agriculture. Yet economically there is no real difference between the mall and a whornseat farm.

Both ignorance and mysticism enter importantly into conventional thinking about farmland. For example, one hears that "Once it's paved over, it's gone for good." Not so. Consider the situation in Germany, where entire towns are moved off the land for enormous strip-mining operations. After the mining is done, farmland is replaced, and the topsoil that is put down is so well enriched and fertilized that "reconstituted farmland now sells for more than the original land." Furthermore, by all measures the German stripmined area is more attractive and environmentally pure than before. (Raymond, 1984, p. 246)

It is relevant that the press did nothing to uncover the scam, or even to report it when it had been revealed. Even the press release reversal and "confession" did not evoke coverage, though the original scare story was a front-page headliner for the *Chicago Tribune* and a cover story for news magazines.

Nor did the farmland crisis then vanish for lack of factual support. The false news continues to reverberate, as noted above.

Soil Erosion

Soil erosion is a related and parallel story. The scare that farmlands are blowing and washing away is a fraud upon the public similar to the urbanization fraud.

In the early 1980s there was a huge foofarah about the terrible dangers of farmland being ruined. In a January 11, 1983, speech to the American Farm Bureau Federation, the President of the United States said, "I think we are all aware of the need to do something about soil erosion." The headline on a June 4, 1984, *Newsweek* "My Turn" article typified how the issue was presented: "A Step Away from the Dust Bowl." (It may or may not be coincidence that the soil erosion scare took off just about the time that the paving-over scare seemed to peter out in the face of criticism.) More recently we have such statements as that of U.S. Vice President Albert Gore, Jr., about how "eight acres' worth of prime topsoil floats past Memphis every hour," and that Iowa "used to have an average of sixteen inches of the best topsoil in the world. Now it is down to eight inches" (1992, 1). My opponent Mr. Myers makes much of supposed soil erosion in his discussion here and elsewhere.

But the aggregate data on the condition of farmland and the rate of erosion do not support the concern about soil erosion. The data suggest that the condition of cropland has been improving rather than worsening. Theodore W. Schultz (1984), the only agricultural economist to win a Nobel Prize, and Leo V. Mayer (1982) of the USDA, both wrote very forcefully that the danger warnings were false. Schultz cited not only research but also his own lifetime recollections starting as a farm boy in the Dakotas in the 1930s. Figure 4-2 shows data from soil condition surveys which make clear that erosion has been lessening rather than worsening since the 1930s. But even a Nobel laureate's efforts could not slow the public-relations juggernaut that successfully coopted the news media and won the minds of the American public.

The USDA press release of April 10, 1984, cited above contained a second quiet bombshell confession: "The average

Figure 4-2. Trends in Soil Erosion in the United States, 1934–present

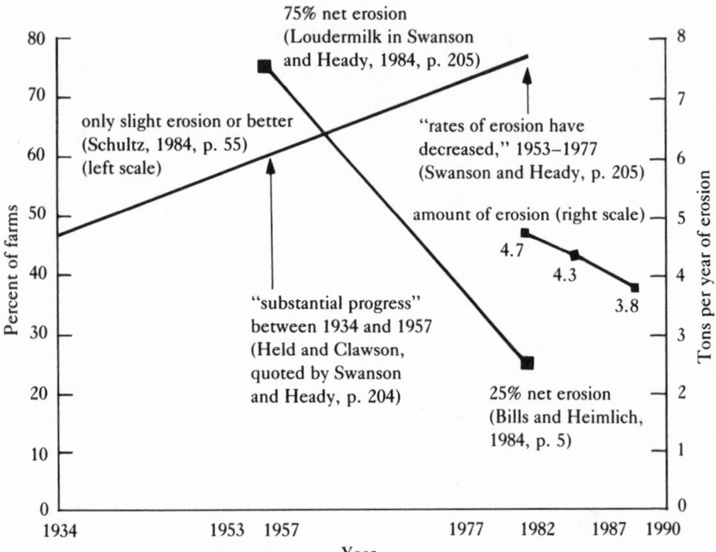

Source (for amount of erosion data): Ralph E. Heimlich, "Soil Erosion and Conservation Policies in the United States," in Nick Harley, ed., *Farming and the Countryside: An Economic Analysis of External Costs and Benefits* (C.A.B. International, 1991), pp. 59–90.

annual rate of soil erosion on cultivated cropland dropped from 5.1 tons per acre to 4.8 tons per acre." That is, erosion was *lessening rather than getting worse*, exactly the opposite of what NALS had earlier claimed. But newspapers and television either did not notice or did not credit these criticisms. Even after the USDA admitted that the newer data clearly show that the danger was not as claimed, nothing appeared in print (to my knowledge) to make the public aware of this new non-danger and of how the public was misled.

The main bad effect of soil erosion is not damage to farmland, but rather the clogging of drainage systems, which then need costly maintenance; the latter is many times as costly as the former. (Swanson and Heady, 1984)

5

Atmospheric Issues

The ozone layer, acid rain, and the supposed greenhouse effect and global warming are salient in public thinking, and hence call for mention here. I am not an atmospheric scientist, and on the technical issues I can only refer you to recent reliable scholarly assessments. I shall try to put these issues in some reasonable perspective, however.

The Greenhouse Effect and Global Warming

For full background, please see Landsberg (1984), Michaels (1992), Balling (1992), Elsaesser (forthcoming), and Idso (1989).

My *guess* is that global warming will simply be another transient concern, barely worthy of consideration ten years from now in a book like this one. Consider that, when I first addressed environmental matters in the late 1960s and 1970s, the climatological issue of major public concern was still global *cooling*. These quotations (cited in Bray, 1991) illustrate the prevailing thinking about climate in the early 1970s, only a decade before the scare about *warming* began in earnest:

> National Oceanic and Atmospheric Administration, noted in 1976: The media are having a lot of fun with this situation. Whenever there is a cold wave, they seek out a proponent of the ice-age-is-coming school and put his theories on page one. . . . Whenever there is a heat wave . . . they turn to his opposite number, [who predicts] a kind of heat death of the earth.
>
> The cooling has already killed hundreds of thousands of people in poor nations. It has already made food and fuel more precious, thus increasing the price of everything we buy. If it continues, and no strong measures are taken to deal with it, the cooling will cause world famine, world chaos, and probably world war, and this could all come by the year 2000.
>
> —Lowell Ponte, *The Cooling* (1976)

> The facts have emerged, in recent years and months, from research into past ice ages. They imply that the threat of a new ice age must now stand alongside nuclear war as a likely source of wholesale death and misery for mankind.
>
> —Nigel Calder, former editor of *New Scientist* and producer of scientific television documentaries, "In the Grip of a New Ice Age," *International Wildlife* (July 1975)

> At this point, the world's climatologists are agreed. . . . Once the freeze starts, it will be too late.
>
> —Douglas Colligan, "Brace Yourself for Another Ice Age," *Science Digest* (February 1973)

> I believe that increasing global air pollution, through its effect on the reflectivity of the earth, is currently dominant and is responsible for the temperature decline of the past decade or two.
>
> —Reid Bryson, "Environmental Roulette," in John P. Holdren and Paul R. Ehrlich, eds., *Global Ecology: Readings Toward a Rational Strategy for Man* (1971)

Bryson went so far as to tell the *New York Times* that, compared to the then-recent period, " 'There appears to be nothing like it [in warmth] in the past 1,000 years," implying that cooling was inevitable. (*New York Times* Staff, 1975, p. 170)

Indeed, many of the same persons who were then warning about global *cooling* are the same climatologists who are now warning of global *warming*—especially Stephen Schneider, one of the most prominent of the global-warming doomsters.

It is interesting to reflect on the judgments that would be made now of past decisions if the world had followed the advice of the climatologists who only fifteen years ago urged the world to take immediate steps to head off the supposed cooling threat.

Should we not be glad that governments did not act upon the anti-cooling advice they were given back then? Does this not call into question the warming forecasts? And does this not detract further from the credibility of the doomsaying environmental spokesmen, who have been systematically wrong in every prediction that they have made during the past three decades, and who are now up in arms about global warming?

Curiously, within days after drafting the above paragraph, there appeared a newspaper story (*Washington Post,* May 19, 1992, A3) entitled "Volcano Reverses Global Warming: Scientists Expect Mean Temperature to Drop 1 Degree Over 2–4 Years." The event in question was the eruption in June 1991 of Mount Pinatubo in the Philippines. Then within a few days more there appeared a scholarly article finding that smoke particles may lead to cooling rather than warming, as had previously been assumed (Penner, Dickinson, O'Neill, 1992).

Whether or not the climate models will be right about Mount Pinatubo, and about the cooling effect of smoke particles, is in question, of course. The problem here, as with the global-warming issue generally, is that our planet contains many forces about which scientists as yet know very little, and which they can predict poorly if at all—for example, volcanic eruptions. It is an act of hubris and great imprudence to proceed as if there is solid tested scientific knowledge when—as is the case here—

a single article in a single journal can nearly reverse the basic conclusions.

This is what I glean about global warming from the references above, especially Balling (1992). Before the "concerned" reader concludes that the following treatment is simply a whitewash, however, it would be fair to examine the state of your own knowledge on the subject—what you know about technical facts, and the sources of the supposed information. The basis of most people's thoughts on the subject is simply newspaper and television stories by journalists who have never seriously read the relevant professional literature.

1. All climatologists agree that there has been an increase in atmospheric carbon dioxide in recent decades. But there is great disagreement about the implications (if any) for global temperature. In the late 1980s the range of thinking ran from those who believed that there will be warming of up to 7 degrees in the next midcentury to those who argued that the evidence is so mixed that one cannot predict any warming at all; by 1993, the top of the range had come down from 7 to 2 degrees. The high-end-estimate climatologists have also scaled back the estimates of possible rise in sea level from several feet to at most a few inches. Some climatologists even argue that present imperfect knowledge is also consistent with global *cooling* as a result of carbon dioxide buildup; they assert that it is possible that as scientists learn more, they might well decide that cooling is the more probable outcome.

2. Those who foresee much warming rely heavily on simulation models, believing them to be comprehensive and reliable. Those who foresee little or no warming mostly rely on the temperature data for the past century. Many of the skeptics of global warming believe that the simulation models lack solid theoretical basis and are built on shaky ad hoc assumptions. Skeptics also point to the absence of correlation between temperature and carbon dioxide buildup in the past.

3. Even those who predict warming agree that any likely warming would not be great relative to year-to-year variability,

and would be swamped by long-run natural variability over the millennia.

4. If warming does occur, it is likely to be uneven in time and place. More of the effect would be at night rather than by day, more in the low-sun season and less in the high-sun season, and more in the arctic regions than in the tropical parts of the world. It should be noted that these effects are less unwelcome than if the effects were in the opposite parts of the daily cycle and the planet's geography.

5. If there will be warming, it will occur over many decades, during which period there would be much time for economic and technical adjustment.

6. Any necessary adjustments would be small relative to the adjustments that we make during the year to temperature differences where we reside and as we travel. A trip from New York to Philadelphia, or spring coming a day or two earlier than usual, is not very different than the temperature gradient for any likely warming within the next century.

7. The necessary adjustments would be far smaller than the effects of the advent of air conditioning in any of the places in this world where that device commonly is found. The alterations that air conditioning—let alone central heating—make in the environment in which we spend our hours dwarf any alterations required by any conceivable global warming.

8. If there should be warming, and if one is worried about it, the clear implication is substitution of nuclear fission for the burning of fossil fuels. This would have other benefits as well, of course, especially the lives saved from air pollution and coal mining.

One can gauge the effectiveness of the mass media in creating public opinion on these subjects by the increase in just a single year in the proportion of the public that were "aware of the global warming issue"—from 59 percent in 1988 to 79 percent in 1989. (*The Washington Times*, November 3, 1989) There is no way that individuals can measure for themselves the extent of global warming. Hence their thinking is labile and easily influenced by television and newspapers. Then the politicians and the environmental activists who give scare stories to the press cite public opinion as a reason to change public policy.

Assessing global warming increasingly resembles assessing the likely availability of raw materials—speculative theory inconsistent with the historical data versus the historical data themselves. The alarm about the greenhouse effect seems to come from those who pay attention only to various theoretical models—just as the alarm about global cooling came only from theoretical models in the 1970s (and from some of the same persons who were alarmed then)—whereas those who focus on the historical record seem unconvinced that there have been unusual changes and are quite unworried about the future. With respect to natural resources, the conclusion is inescapable that those who have believed the historical record have been correct, and those who have believed theories without checking them against the record have been in error. Is it not likely that this would be the case with global warming, too?

Acid Rain

The acid rain scare has now been exposed as one of the great false alarms of our time. In 1980 the federal government initiated the huge National Acid Precipitation Assessment Program (NAPAP), employing 700 scientists and costing $500 million. The NAPAP study found—to the surprise of most of its scientists—that acid rain in the United States was far less threatening than it had been assumed to be at the onset of the study. It is mainly a threat to a few lakes—about 2 percent of the lake surface in the Adirondacks (Brookes, 1990, p. 2)—all of which could be made less acid with cheap and quick liming, and which were as acid as now in the years before 1860 when forests around them began to be cut and wood burned (which lowers acidity). In 1990 the Congress passed the Clean Air Act, which will have large economic consequences upon the nation, with the NAPAP findings unknown to most or all of the Congress; the NAPAP director expressed disappointment in 1990 that "the science that NAPAP performed . . . has been so largely ignored." (Ibid.) Indeed, the NAPAP findings were systematically kept from public view until the television program *60 Minutes* aired a broadcast on the scandal.

In Europe, the supposed effects of acid rain in reducing forests and tree growth have turned out to be without foundation; forests are larger, and trees are growing more rapidly, than in the first half of this century.

The acid rain scare re-teaches an important lesson: It is quick and easy to raise a false alarm, but to quell the alarm is difficult and slow. The necessary solid research requires considerable time. And by the time the research is complete, many people have a stake in wanting the scientific truth not to be heard—advocacy organizations who gain public support from the alarm; and bureaucrats who have a stake in not being shown to have been in error, and who already have built some empire on the supposed problem.

The Ozone Layer

> This unprecedented assault on the planet's life-support system could have horrendous long-term effects on human health, animal life, the plants that support the food chain, and just about every other strand that makes up the delicate web of nature. And it is too late to prevent the damage, which will worsen for years to come.
>
> —*Time*, February 17, 1992, quoted in *Media Watch*, (March 1992), p. 1

For a reliable scholarly assessment on which I rely, please see F. Singer (1989; forthcoming).

1. The ozone layer and its "hole" over Antarctica certainly deserve study. But this is very different than recommending

action. The best principle might be: "Don't do something. Stand there." As with other issues discussed here, it is important that the government not attempt to fix what is not broken.

2. Some long-run data are shown in Figure 5-1. These data show no trends that square with public scares.

3. Concern about the ozone hole is only recent. There has hardly been time for competent researchers to build a body of evidence on which to reliably judge what is happening. And scares come and go. The likelihood is very low that a scare that is only a few years old will turn out to be a truly difficult problem for society, given the record of scares and subsequent debunkings.

Indeed, the history of a closely related scare should give special pause to those who are inclined to take action about the

Figure 5-1. Total Atmospheric Ozone, 1926–1980, as Observed in Arosa, Switzerland

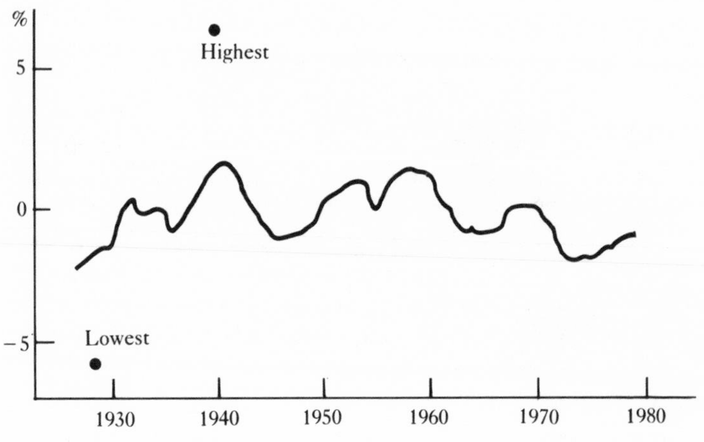

Source: H. E. Landsberg, "Global Climatic Trends." In Julian L. Simon and Herman Kahn, eds., *The Resourceful Earth: A Response to Global 2000* (Basil Blackwell, New York, 1984).

ozone layer: the saga of the supersonic airliners (Singer, 1989). In 1970, the alarm was raised that SSTs would emit water vapor that would destroy ozone. Before research work could even begin, critics of the SST urged that the planes be banned.

Then it turned out that the relevant emission was not water vapor but nitrogen oxides. And further research showed that, if anything, SSTs would *add* to the amount of ozone in the stratosphere. That scare is now dead and gone, but not without causing damage.

4. There is great controversy about the ozone layer, with some respected scientists arguing that there is nothing to worry about while some argue to the contrary. The press tends to report only on those scientists who utter warnings of catastrophe.

5. Volcanic ash and sunspots are cited as possible "natural" causes, along with the human-produced chlorofluorocarbons (CFCs). It has been noted that CFCs at the peak production level were only a quarter of a percent (.0025) of the amount of chlorine released every year by the sea, which implies that the effect of reducing human-produced CFCs is very questionable. (Ray, n.d.)

6. Even if the ozone layer should be thinning right now, it need not be a permanent thinning. If human intervention is causing the change, human intervention can reverse it.

7. Perhaps most important is that even if the ozone layer is thinning, it need not imply bad effects for humanity. The chief threat seems to be skin cancers. But the evidence on the geography or the time pattern of skin cancers over the years does not square with the thickness of the ozone layer. (Singer, 1989; forthcoming) And even if a thinner layer implies more skin cancer, all else equal, people can intervene in many ways—even with as simple a device as wearing hats more frequently.

Increased ultra-violet radiation stemming from decreased ozone also may have beneficial effects in reducing rickets disease, which results from too little sunlight and Vitamin D. (Elsaesser, 1990)

6

Final Matters

Can All This Good News Be True?

Hearers of the messages in this book are often incredulous, and ask, "But what about the other side's data?" There are no other data. I invite you to test for yourself this assertion that the conditions of humanity have gotten better. Pick up the Bureau of the Census's *Statistical Abstract of the United States* and *Historical Statistics of the United States* at the nearest library, and consult the data yourself (see the index for such topics as Pollution, Life expectancy, and the various individual natural resources, plus price indexes) on the measures of human welfare that depend upon physical resources, for the United States or for the world as a whole: Food production per person. Availability of natural resources as measured by their

prices. The cleanliness of the air we breathe and the water we drink in the United States. The amount of space per person in our homes, and the presence of such amenities as inside toilets and telephones. Most important, the length of life and the incidence of death. You will find that every single measure shows a trend of improvement rather than the deterioration that the doomsayers claim has occurred.

What Is the Mechanism Which Produces Progress Rather Than Deterioration?

It is crucial to include in our environmental and resource assessments not only the short-run effects of additional people and economic activity, which can be negative for a while, but also the positive long-run effects of the problems induced by the additional people and economic activity. It is this crucial adjustment mechanism that is too often left out of thinking on these matters.

The process goes like this: More people and increased income cause problems in the short run. These problems present opportunity, and prompt the search for solutions. In a free society, solutions are eventually found, though many people fail along the way at cost to themselves. In the long run the new developments leave us better off than if the problems had not arisen.

What Happens If We Should Not Continue to Make New Discoveries?

We now have in our hands—in our libraries, really—the technology to feed, clothe, and supply energy to an ever-growing population for the next 7 billion years. Most amazing is that most of this specific body of knowledge developed within the past hundred years or so, though it rests on knowledge that had accumulated for millennia, of course.

Indeed, the last necessary additions to this body of knowledge—nuclear fission and space travel—occurred decades ago. Even if no new knowledge were ever invented after those advances, we would be able to go on increasing forever, improving our standard of living and our control over our environment. The discovery of genetic manipulation certainly enhances our powers greatly, but even without it we could have continued our progress forever.

Pre-Debate Statement

Norman Myers

1

Introduction

If current predictions of population growth prove accurate and patterns of human activity on the planet remain unchanged, science and technology may not be able to prevent either irreversible degradation of the environment or continued poverty for much of the world. . . . Unrestrained resource consumption for energy production and other uses . . . could lead to catastrophic outcomes for the global environment. Some of the environmental changes may produce irreversible damage to the Earth's capacity to sustain life. The overall pace of environmental change has unquestionably been accelerated by the recent expansion of the human population. . . . The future of our planet is in the balance.

—U.S. NATIONAL ACADEMY OF SCIENCES AND BRITISH ROYAL SOCIETY, MAY 1992

We are at a watershed stage in human history because of environmental decline in conjunction with rapid population growth. Our planetary ecosystem faces unparalleled threat. What we do, or don't do, today will affect people into the future for hundreds if not thousands of generations. Recent patterns and trends of environmental abuse suggest they are going to have a hard time of it.

That's the bad news. The better news is that the full catastrophe still lies down the road. The best news is that much of it need not overtake us at all if we move with sufficient speed and foresight to head off the problems at the pass. No doubt about it: we still have time, though only just time, to get on top of many of our problems before they get on top of us. And if we measure up to what lies ahead, we shall surely feel we stand ten feet tall while confronting challenges of creative scope unknown to any previous generation.

All this supposes that our environmental prospect is indeed dire. There is much evidence, accepted by leaders on every side. Consider, for instance, the 1987 assertion of the World

Commission on Environment and Development, a United Nations body comprising luminaries from West and East, North and South.[1] They included politicians, economists, industrialists, bankers, lawyers, and others who make their way in the political arena or the competitive marketplace. They were cold-eyed analysts, with not a single eco-freak among them. Yet one of their reports included a statement of remarkable frankness:

> Humankind faces two great threats. The first is that of a nuclear exchange. Let us hope it remains no more than a diminishing prospect for the future. The second is that of environmental ruin worldwide—and far from being a prospect for the future, it is a fact right now.

Well might the commissioners have produced such a startling assertion. We face environmental decline of multiple sorts. In just the past year we have:

—*Lost 25 billion tons of topsoil,* enough to grow 9 million tons of grain and to make up the diets of at least 200 million hungry people.

—*Lost 150,000 square kilometers of tropical forest* (an area equivalent to Florida), which has cost us dear in terms of timber harvests, species habitats, watershed services, and climate stability. Tropical timber exports have declined from $8 billion in 1986 to $6 billion in 1991, and they are expected to plunge to $2 billion in the year 2000 or shortly thereafter.[2] Ten years ago, deforestation-derived flooding in the Ganges Valley alone was levying costs of $1 billion per year.[3]

—*Lost 60,000 square kilometers* (the size of West Virginia) to desertification so severe that these lands will not be able to grow food for decades at best. Desertification results in lost agricultural production worth $42 billion per year.[4]

—*Witnessed the extinction of tens of thousands of species,* some of which could have supplied new anti-cancer drugs such as two from the rosy periwinkle that now afford economic benefits to American society worth more than $400 million per year.

—*Further depleted the ozone layer in both the northern and southern hemispheres*, causing it to lose still more of its capacity to protect us from cancer- and cataract-causing radiation, which also attacks crop plants and marine food chains.

—*Taken a solid step toward a greenhouse-affected world*, which will cause profound environmental disruptions right around the Earth.

—*Taken on board Spaceship Earth another 93 million people*, equivalent to a "new Mexico."*

*Contrast all this with Simon's statement that "If [environmental and resource problems] mean that the situation of humanity is worse now than in the past, then the idea of a crisis—and all that follows from it—is dead wrong. In almost every respect important to humanity, the trends have been improving, not deteriorating." Note also, "[It is] an indubitable economic fact [that] natural resources are increasingly *less* important with each passing decade."

2

Biodiversity

Before going on to consider population and other big-picture aspects of our environmental predicament, let us consider a single issue, biodiversity—or, rather, bio-depletion, meaning the mass extinction of species under way. Unlike all other environmental problems, species extinction is irreversible. Evolution may eventually come up with replacement species offering numbers and variety to match today's array, but so far as we can discern from episodes of mass extinction and their "bounce-back" periods in the prehistoric past, the time required will be at least 5 million years, possibly several times longer.[1] If we allow the present mass extinction to proceed unchecked, we shall impoverish the biosphere for a period equivalent to at least 200,000 human generations, or twenty times longer than the period since humankind itself emerged as a species.

Species Extinction Rate

There is abundant evidence that we are into the opening phase of a mass extinction of species.[2] The National Academy of Sciences in conjunction with the British Royal Society declared in July 1992 that "the failure to sustain biodiversity [is] a matter of great concern, locally, regionally and internationally . . . a potential loss for everyone."[3]

In summary, the evidence for a mass extinction under way is as follows.* Earth's stock of species has been widely estimated to total a minimum of 10 million.[4] Some scientists believe the true total could well be 30 million, possibly 50 million, and conceivably 100 million.[5] Since many if not most of the additional species are considered to live in tropical forests, the real total is not a matter of mere speculation. (Tropical forests are taken here to mean tropical moist forests, being far richer in species than tropical dry forests.) These forests are where habitats are being lost fastest and where the great bulk of species extinctions is occurring. So, if the real total is 30 million species, the extinction rate will be almost three times higher than the rate postulated for a planetary total of only 10 million species. But for the sake of being cautious and conservative, let us accept a total of 10 million species. Roughly half of these spe-

*Authors of the references listed, together with other biodiversity experts, have published well over 100 papers demonstrating that a mass extinction is indeed under way. Yet in a letter to *The Washington Post*, August 7, 1991, Simon asserted that ever since the first account of the present mass extinction (i.e., Myers, *The Sinking Ark*, 1979), "Biologists have presented no new data to substantiate their assertions," and that "I (and colleagues) have documented the complete absence of evidence for the claims that species extinction is going up rapidly, or even going up at all. No one has refuted our documentation. Instead, proponents of the species-extinction scam simply ignore data that falsify their claims of impending doom. . . . A fair reading of the available data suggests a rate of extinction not even one-thousandth as great as the doomsayers scare us with . . . [through] pure guesswork." "If There's an Ark, It's Not Going Down." *Baltimore Sun*, June 11, 1992.

cies live in tropical forests, even though remaining forests now cover only 6 percent of Earth's land surface.

The forests are being destroyed at a rate of at least 150,000 square kilometers per year.*[6] In addition, an expanse as large again is being grossly disrupted through over-heavy logging and slash-and-burn cultivation, with much degradation and impoverishment of ecosystems and their species' life-support systems. But in the interests of being cautious and conservative again, let us consider only the first form of habitat loss, outright destruction of forests. The current loss of 150,000 square kilometers per year represents 2 percent of remaining forests. The annual loss increased by 89 percent during the 1980s, and if present patterns and trends of forest destruction persist with still more acceleration in the annual rate, the current amount of 2 percent may well double again by the year 2000.†

A current annual 2 percent rate of forest destruction does not mean that 2 percent of the forests' species are disappearing as well. Many species have wide distributions, sometimes extending for hundreds of thousands of square kilometers. Equally to the point, and by strong contrast with the situation

*This figure is based primarily on remote-sensing surveys, which constitute by far the most objective, comprehensive, and systematized form of documentation available, complete with time-series data. My 1992 paper, cited in the Notes, is the latest assessment of the issue, undertaken through the Remote-Sensing Centre of the European Commission in conjunction with NASA. Simon protests that my deforestation findings have always been far too high, sometimes several times too high. Yet he arrives at this conclusion by invoking no remote-sensing documentation of his own, and by misinterpreting my data through his own internal arithmetic, on one occasion getting a decimal place wrong by two places.

†The main UN agency concerned with forests, the Food and Agriculture Organization (FAO), has estimated that the average annual deforestation in tropical moist forests during the period 1981–90 was 122,000 square kilometers, reaching a level of 131,000 square kilometers in 1990. This latter figure was more than twice as much as FAO estimated for 1979, compared with my own estimate of an 89 percent increase during the 1980s. If we assume that the deforested amount has expanded in 1991 at the same annual rate, then the FAO estimate for 1991 would be 134,000 square kilometers—a figure only 11 percent less than my own estimate.

outside tropical forests, many other species enjoy restricted ranges, their entire populations confined to just a few tens of thousands of square kilometers;[7] many cloud-forest plants in tropical Latin America are endemic to isolated sites smaller than 10 square kilometers.[8] In the tropical forests of South America, 440 bird species (25 percent of the total) have ranges of less than 50,000 square kilometers, by contrast with eight species (2 percent of the total) with similarly restricted ranges in the United States and Canada.[9] On a single forested ridge in the western Andes of Ecuador, there used to be as many as ninety plant species endemic to the area, i.e., found nowhere else. Although no comprehensive scientific check has been made, one can realistically assume on the basis of plant / animal relationships elsewhere that the same habitat contained many times as many endemic animal species, mainly invertebrates. In the late 1980s, the ridge's forest was cleared for agriculture and the ninety plant species plus their associated animal species were summarily eliminated.[10]

How shall we translate a 2 percent annual rate of forest destruction into an annual species extinction rate? The analytic way ahead is revealed by the theory of island biogeography, a well-established theory with much supporting empirical evidence drawn from hundreds of on-ground analyses in many parts of the world.[11] The theory asserts that when a habitat loses 90 percent of its original extent, it can no longer support more than 50 percent of its original species.*

*Again, this rule is cautious and conservative. It depends critically upon the status of the remaining 10 percent of habitat. If this relict expanse is split into many small pieces (as is often the case with remnant tracts of tropical forests), a further "islandizing effect" comes into play, reducing the stock of surviving species still more. It is not clear how severe this additional depletion can be. Informed estimates suggest the 50 percent can readily be reduced to 40 percent, more generally to 30 percent, sometimes to 20 percent, and occasionally even to 10 percent (Wilson, 1992). Moreover, isolated remnants of forest become prone to additional depauperizing processes such as "edge effects," also to dessicating effects due to local climate change. So the calculation for island biogeography extinctions is strictly a *minimum* estimate.

The most broad-scale application of island biogeography to tropical deforestation and species extinctions has been presented by one of the authors of the original theory, Professor Edward O. Wilson of Harvard University.[12] He has calculated that with the current deforestation rate, and supposing there are only 10 million species on Earth, there is an annual loss of at least 27,000 species, or an average of 74 per day. Wilson frequently emphasizes, moreover, that this is an extremely optimistic calculation. If we employ a more "realistic" reckoning to take account of a number of other bioecological factors such as diseases, alien introductions, and over-hunting, the annual total will become a good deal larger. Widespread habitat destruction is taking place in other species-rich biomes as well, as Wilson and others have demonstrated, notably in Mediterranean-type zones (see below), coral reefs, wetlands, montane environments, and many islands. So the overall total can safely be reckoned to be at least 30,000 species per year.

This annual extinction rate is way above that of the "natural" rate of extinctions before the advent of the human era, considered to be roughly one species every four years.[13] So the present rate is at least 120,000 times higher.

For sure, Wilson's calculations for tropical forests represent a generalized mode of estimating the present extinction rate. It is applied at biome level, making little allowance for local circumstances. Fortunately we have a parallel set of calculations for local level too, in the form of a "hot spots" analysis relating to areas that (a) feature exceptional concentrations of species with exceptional levels of endemism, and (b) face exceptional threat of imminent habitat destruction. This approach reveals that fourteen hot spots in tropical forests contain more than 37,000 endemic plant species, or 15 percent of all plant species, in less than 311,000 square kilometers, or just 0.2 percent of Earth's land surface. These hot spots also contain a still higher though unquantified proportion of Earth's animal species.[14]

Five of the hot spots have already lost 90 percent or more of their original forest expanse, and the rest are expected (if recent land-use trends continue even without acceleration) to lose 90 percent by the end of the century or shortly thereafter. If we apply the 90 percent / 50 percent rule of island biogeography, these areas will lose at least half of their species within the foreseeable future; some will have lost a good share already. This in itself will constitute a mass extinction as great as any since the demise of the dinosaurs and associated species 65 million years ago. If we include four other hot spots, this time in Mediterranean-type zones, we find that 50,000 endemic plant species, or a full 20 percent of all plant species, face severe threat of habitat destruction in just 0.5 percent of Earth's land surface.[15]

A skeptic may still object that if extinctions are occurring in large numbers right now, why aren't they individually documented? How much precise evidence is there? To this, the pragmatic scientist responds that it is far easier to demonstrate that a species exists than that it does not. To achieve the first, all one has to do is to find a few specimens. To achieve the second with equal certainty, one would have to search every last locality of the species' range before being finally sure. This is all right for the purist. Unfortunately, we live in a world without sufficient scientists, funding and, above all, time to undertake a conclusive check. Given that we are witnessing a mass extinction of exceptional scope, should it not be sufficient to make a best-judgment assessment of what is going on—and in cases of uncertainty ("Has the species finally disappeared or is it still hanging on?"), assume that if a species has not been seen for decades, it should be considered to be extinct until it is proven to be extant?

This is the case with large numbers of species. Recall the ninety endemic plant species of the western Ecuador ridge, where outright deforestation of habitat has eliminated all natural vegetation. Yet the plants have not been declared officially extinct; conservation organizations generally require that a species fail to be recorded for fifty years before it can be designated *in memoriam*. In Peninsular Malaysia, a four-year search for 266 species of freshwater fish turned up only 122 of them, yet they are all officially regarded as still in existence.[16] In Lake Victoria, over half the former stock of 300 haplochromine fish species, all but one of them endemic, have not been seen for years; even though they are not officially considered extinct, this species extinction spasm ranks as the greatest extinction episode of vertebrate species in modern times.[17] Dozens more such instances can be cited, though we have scarcely made a start on documenting the total situation.[18]

Let us bear in mind, above all, that we are dealing with the irreversible loss of unique life forms. It is not always possible to detail the precise survival status of tens of thousands of threatened plant species and millions of animal species. In light of these factors, should the burden of proof not be shifted onto the shoulders of the skeptics, and have them prove their point rather than the reverse?*

This brings up a key question as concerns species extinctions (and the same applies to many other environmental issues). What is "legitimate scientific caution" in the face of uncertainty? Uncertainty can cut both ways. Some observers may object that in the absence of conclusive evidence and analysis, it is appropriate to stick with low estimates of species extinctions on the grounds that they are more "responsible." But how about the crucial factor of asymmetry of evaluation? A low estimate, ostensibly "safe" because it takes a conservative view of

*On the issue of ultimate certainty such as is demanded by a few skeptics, note a comment by Ehrlich on the arguments downplaying the loss of biodiversity: "Mostly they are equivalent to saying that people should not be overly concerned about the burning down of the world's only genetic library because the number of 'books' in it is not known within an order of magnitude, and fire modelers disagree on whether the planet's genetic library will be half consumed in a couple of decades, or whether that level of destruction might take 50 years. Apparently a few scientists would never call the fire department unless they could inform it of the exact temperature of the flames at each point in a holocaust." "Population Diversity and the Future of Ecosystems." *Science* 254 (1991): 175.

such limited evidence as is to hand in documented detail, may fail to reflect the real situation just as much as does an "unduly" high estimate that is more of a best-judgment affair, based on all available evidence with varying degrees of demonstrable validity. In a situation of uncertainty where not all parameters can be quantified to conventional satisfaction, let us not get hung up with what can be counted if that is to the detriment of what also counts. Undue caution can readily become recklessness; and as in other situations beset with uncertainty, it will be better for us to find we have been roughly right than precisely wrong.

So far we have considered only current extinctions. How about the future? Through detailed analysis backed by abundant documentation, Wilson considers we face the prospect of losing 20 percent of all species within thirty years and 50 percent or more thereafter.[19] Another long-standing expert in this area, Dr. Peter Raven, calculates that one sixth of all plant species, and, by implication, of all animal species, occur in the tropical forests of just three countries, Colombia, Ecuador, and Peru; and that these three countries appear likely to lose virtually all their forest cover within another three decades at most, hence their species communities will be largely eliminated. In a further and more extensive calculation, Raven believes that half of all species exist in tropical forests that will be reduced to less than one tenth of their present expanse within the same three decades ahead. So in accord with island biogeography, Raven concludes—and he stresses this is a conservative prognosis—that one quarter of all species will be eliminated during the next thirty years, and "fully half of total species may disappear before the close of the 21st century."[20] These estimates have been endorsed by the Club of Earth, which comprises scientists with a collective total of several hundred years of professional endeavor. The estimates are also in line with my own assessments and those of a number of other analysts.[21]

If we are indeed on track toward a biotic holocaust that will eliminate half of Earth's species within the foreseeable future, this will be a unique event in life's history since it will be due to the activities of a single species.* Fortunately humankind has the unique power not only to eliminate other species but to save other species as well—*and right now we have the chance to save them in their millions*. As we shall see below, we still have time to convert a profound problem into a glorious opportunity.

The Economics of Extinction

There are solid reasons of biology, ecology, genetics, evolution, aesthetics, and ethics for us to regret the loss of any species.[22] But since the world is run, in certain observers' eyes at least (and especially those of Julian Simon), by the conclusive wisdom of the marketplace, let us focus here on some commercial, financial, and other economic values of species.

There are hundreds of ways in which species and their genetic resources, especially those of tropical forests, contribute to our material welfare.[23] In the public health field, one in four medicines and pharmaceuticals owes its origin to germplasm materials or other key products of plant species. These products include antibiotics, analgesics, diuretics, tranquilizers, and a host of similar items.[24] The contraceptive pill stems from a plant of West Africa's forests. A child suffering from leukemia

*Cohen, J. I., J. T. Williams, D. L. Plucknett, and H. Shands. "Ex Situ Conservation of Plant Genetic Resources: Global Development and Environmental Concerns." *Science* 253:866–872. It is fundamentally mistaken to suppose, as does Simon in his article "If There's an Ark, It's Not Going Down," that we can adequately safeguard species in gene banks. These cater only for certain categories of plants, or no more than one percent of all species at best; and they are subject to numerous genetic and evolutionary problems. Nor is there conservation scope in the prospect that, as Simon postulates, "genetic recombination techniques now enable biologists to create new variations of species." Biologists are limited by the genetic variability available to them, and this essential resource is being ever more rapidly depleted.

in 1960 faced only one chance in five of remission, but today a child enjoys four chances in five thanks to two potent drugs derived from alkaloids of Madagascar's rosy periwinkle. These drugs, also used against Hodgkin's disease and a number of other cancers, generate commercial sales totaling more than $200 million per year in the United States alone, while the economic benefits to American society, in terms of worker-productivity saved, and so on, are estimated at $400 million a year. Worldwide, the commercial value of plant-based prescription drugs is $40 billion per year.[25] Three promising responses to AIDS derive from plant materials.

Similar benefits accrue to us in the fields of agriculture and industry, with values reckoned in the billions of dollars per year.[26] Yet we enjoy these diverse products after scientists have conducted intensive investigation of only one in 100 of tropical forests' 125,000 plant species, and a far smaller proportion of their millions of animal species—even though it is among the latter that we may eventually find most economic applications to support our material welfare.[27]

Plainly, species constitute an economic resource of exceptional value. A few observers object that before we engage in expensive campaigns to save species, we should look at the costs and benefits in terms of human welfare. (An emphatic skeptic of this sort is Simon, even though he offers no hint of economic analysis in his numerous writings on the species preservation issue.* Two pharmacognosy experts have calculated that projected extinctions of plant species in the United States during the last sixteen years of this century will cost Americans $3.3 billion per year in plant-based drugs foregone.[28] Yet the budget for saving millions of species in tropical forests

*He believes that "The evaluational task approaches, or surpasses, the limits of any existing human knowledge"—notwithstanding the abundant economic analyses in the professional literature. See Simon, J. L., and A. Wildavsky. "On Species Loss, the Absence of Data, and Risks to Humanity." In J. L. Simon and H. Kahn, eds., *The Resourceful Earth*, (Basil Blackwell, New York, 1984

through additional protected areas need be no more than $200 million per year.[29] Economic evaluation, including cost-benefit analysis, of numerous protected areas shows they offer substantial goods and services apart from biodiversity conservation, often enough to offset the costs of declaring these areas off limits to conventional development in the form of, for example, agriculture.[30]

3

The Population Factor

Let us now consider an issue that many people see as the biggest environmental problem of all: population. In this section we shall look both at rapid population growth in developing countries, and at the population impact of developed countries by virtue of their excessively consumerist lifestyles.

The Demographic Background

We are in the middle of an unprecedented expansion of human numbers. It took 10,000 lifetimes for the world's population to reach 2 billion people. Now, in the course of a single lifetime, that total is increasing to three times as many, and within another lifetime it could well double again.

Global population in 1993 amounted to 5.5 billion people. Of these, 4.3 billion are in developing nations and 1.2 billion in developed nations. The total is growing at a rate of 1.7 percent per year. The annual increase, now 93 million people, will not peak until 1998, with 98 million people. It is this factor, the annual increase in absolute numbers, that is also critical to the population prospect. Of the annual increase, more than 90 percent is in developing nations, and over half in Africa and southern Asia, which feature the majority of the world's 1.2 billion "poorest of the poor."* By definition, developing nations have limited capacity to cope with the environmental and economic consequences of ultra-rapid growth in human numbers, due to their low per capita incomes, unproductive agriculture, meager technology, and inadequate investment. Even if they had all these requisites, they would still be hardpressed. A country as organized as Switzerland with its clocklike precision of planning could hardly take on board twice as many people in a single generation, let alone do it time after time.

Given the record of the last two decades, it becomes increasingly hard to see how sub-Saharan Africa, for example, will experience a projected quintupling of human numbers within little over another century as long as gross environmental impoverishment continues to spread. Because of degradation of agricultural lands—chiefly soil erosion and desertification—agricultural productivity is expected to decline by one quarter between 1985 and 2010,[1] yet per capita food supply is already one fifth less than in 1960 and one person in three is severely malnourished. Those who consider that population growth may soon be pressing against or even exceed the environment's "carrying capacity" (see below) are inclined to be skeptical about demographic projections made in an "environmental vacuum."

In many respects, then, it is turning out that we have achieved economic advancement in the past at environmental cost to the future's potential for still more advancement—and even at the more serious cost of an actual decline in human welfare. Consider the case of Green Revolution agriculture,

*Note that these "poorest of the poor" are projected to increase to 1.3 billion in the year 2000 and 1.5 billion in 2025, in the absence of greatly expanded efforts to relieve their plight.

which enabled growth in grain production to keep ahead of growth in human numbers throughout the period 1950 to 1984. There have been a number of covert costs along the way, in the form of overloading of croplands leading to soil erosion, depletion of natural nutrients, and salinization of irrigation systems. These costs, while unnoticed or disregarded for decades, are now levying a price in terms of cropland productivity. One fifth of Pakistan's irrigated lands and one third of India's have become so salinized that they have lost most if not all of their fertility,[2] yet these two countries have often been proclaimed as Green Revolution successes.

At global level, food production is suffering sizable setbacks through environmental problems at a time when population growth continues to roar ahead. Soil erosion leads to an annual loss in grain output estimated at 9 million tons; and other problems, such as salinization and water logging of irrigated lands, at 3 million tons. In addition, there are various types of pollution damage to crops worth another 2 million tons.[3] So the total from all forms of environmental degradation comes to 14 million tons of grain output per year. This is to be compared with gains from increased investments in irrigation, fertilizer, and other inputs of 29 million tons per year. Thus environmental factors now cause the loss of almost half of all gains from technology-based and other advances in agriculture. Worse, the proportion has steadily risen in recent years, and seems set to expand still further within the foreseeable future. We can little afford this shortfall since we need an additional 28 million tons of grain output each year just to cater for the needs of population growth, let alone the demands of economic advancement and enhanced diets. While the gain in grain output is only around 1 percent each year, population growth remains at 1.7 percent (and in the developing world, with almost four fifths of the world's population, at 2.0 percent).*[4] We are not feeding hungry people more, we are feeding more hungry people.

This would not matter if population growth had been ade-

*Of the 1.2 billion people suffering absolute poverty, 800 million are chronically malnourished and 400 million are so undernourished they are

quately restricted way back. It hasn't, and we are left with a situation where we have already overshot the carrying capacity of the Earth, if only because of growing resource depletion. So, should we think not only in terms of resource shortages but of population "longages"? Fortunately there is a good-news aspect to the situation. Over 90 percent of developing world people now live in countries where population growth is considered too high for economic growth and is to be reduced with all due despatch.* To meet these aspirations, we shall need to double our outlays on family planning by the year 2000. Fortunately these outlays are trifling compared to the costs of an overpopulated world: the developed world citizen's share will work out at one penny per day.[5] Is this not a worthwhile investment to ensure that every child is a wanted child?†

---

semi-starving. During the past two decades, more than 200 million people have died of hunger-related causes, though Simon constantly dismisses the idea that there has been any starvation crisis at all.

*Contrary to the arguments frequently heard from Simon (in defiance of the expressed preferences of the great bulk of humankind) to the effect that population growth has always been a general economic benefit and will remain so. Among other supposed pluses, Simon considers that "Additional persons lead to an increase in worker output." See, for example, Simon's "Resources, Population, Environment: An Oversupply of False Bad News." *Science* 208 (1980): 1431–37; *Population Matters: People, Resources, Environment, and Immigration* (Transaction Press, New Brunswick, NJ, 1990); and *Population and Development in Poor Countries* (Princeton University Press, NJ, 1992.) If Simon's assertion were true, we should expect to find exceptional economic advancement among the millions of people packed into squatter settlements around Mexico City, and Ethiopia's affluence to be an order of magnitude ahead of Switzerland's.

†Simon favors population growth to the extent that he regularly insists there should be limited official support for family planning. In a *Fortune* article entitled "Population Panic" on May 21, 1990, he asserts, "The increase in the world's population represents our victory over death. You would expect lovers of humanity to jump with joy at this triumph of human mind and organization. Instead, [the doomsayers] lament that so many people are enjoying the gift of life." He does not comment on the 300 million couples who want no more children but are prevented from exercising this basic human right through lack of birth-control facilities. Nor does he spare a thought for the 40–60 million women who undergo

Carrying Capacity

Carrying capacity amounts to "the number of people that the planet can support without irreversibly reducing its capacity to support people in the future."[6] There is much evidence that human numbers with their consumption of resources, plus the technologies deployed to supply that consumption, are often exceeding carrying capacity already.

To illustrate, let us revisit the question of food production. The World Hunger Project has calculated that the planetary ecosystem could, with present agrotechnologies and with equal distribution of food supplies, *sustainably* support no more than 6 billion people even if they all lived off a vegetarian diet—and the 1993 global population is already 5.5 billion.[7] If humans derived 15 percent of their calories from meat and milk products, as do many people in South America, the total would decline to 4 billion. If they gained 25 percent of their calories from animal protein, as is the case with most people in North America, the Earth could sustainably support only 2.8 billion people.

True, these calculations reflect no more than today's food production technologies. Some observers protest that this underestimates the scope for technological expertise to keep on expanding carrying capacity. For sure, we must hope that many advances in agrotechnologies are still available to come on

---

abortions each year, a total that has increased as a result of reduced U.S. funding for international family planning—a measure strongly promoted by Simon. He also overlooks my unvarying support for reducing child mortality as a strictly humanitarian measure apart from its scope for supplying motivation for family planning (as long as parents watch a good number of their children die, they will remain indifferent to birth-control practices). Thanks to the latest medical technology, we have the means to save a whopping 100 million children during the 1990s at an annual cost of $400 million. If rich-nation citizens were to pick up the entire tab, it would work out per person at the equivalent of half a beer a year. What a splendid prospect, available to no human community in the past.

stream. But consider the population/food record over the past four decades. From 1950 to 1984, and thanks largely to breakthroughs in Green Revolution agriculture, there was a 2.6-fold increase in world grain output. This achievement, representing an average annual increase of almost 3 percent, raised per capita production by more than one third: a remarkable performance by any measure. But from 1985 to 1992 (1993 figures not published at the time this book went to press), there was far less annual increase, even though the period witnessed the world's farmers investing billions of dollars to increase output. Crop yields appeared to have "plateaued"; plant breeders and agronomists had (temporarily?) exhausted the scope for technological innovation. The 1992 harvest was little higher than that of 1985, yet there were an extra 626 million people to feed. While world population increased by 12.8 percent, grain output per person declined by nearly 9 percent.*[8]

As for the future, bear in mind that if ever there are 10 billion people to be fed adequately (the UN medium projection is 10 billion in 2050), we will have to produce nearly three times as many calories as today. To grow that much food, we will need to farm all the world's current croplands as productively as Iowa's best cornfields, or three times the present world average. Regrettably there are all too few new areas to be opened up to agriculture. Per capita cropland expanded at an annual rate of 0.5 percent per year throughout the period 1950–80, but since then the rate has averaged only half as much; and primarily because of population growth, the amount of per capita arable land has declined by 1.9 percent per year.[9] The additional cropland area needed to feed increasing human numbers in developing countries by 2050 is well over half as much again as the present expanse,[10] yet cropland availability per person is expected to decline in virtually all parts of the world, in some regions critically so (Figure 3-1). Similarly, the annual expansion of irrigated lands, which supply one third of our food from one sixth of our croplands, grew by 2 to 4 percent per year

*See note on page 71.

during 1950–80, but at only 1 percent per year since 1981.[11]

For a specific instance of carrying capacity, look at the case of Kenya. The 1993 population of 28 million people is projected to expand to 125 million by the time zero growth is attained at some stage in the twenty-second century. Yet even if the nation were to employ Western Europe's high-technology agriculture, it could support no more than 52 million people off its own lands[12]—and even if it were to achieve the two-child family forthwith, the population would still double because of demographic momentum (49 percent of Kenyans are age fifteen or under, meaning that disproportionately large numbers of potential parents are already in place). So Kenya will have to depend on steadily increasing amounts of food from outside to support itself. But in large part because of its high population growth rate—3.7 percent per year—Kenya's per capita economic growth in recent years has been less than 2 percent. Worse, Kenya's terms of trade have been declining throughout the 1980s until they are barely positive today, meaning the country faces the prospect of diminishing financial reserves to purchase food abroad. Its export economy will have to flourish permanently in a manner far better than it has ever achieved to date if the country is to buy enough food to meet its fast-growing needs. Worst of all, the country will have to undertake this massive challenge with a natural resource base from which forests have almost disappeared, watershed flows for irrigation agriculture are badly depleted, and much topsoil is gone with the wind.

Kenya shows many signs, then, of already being in an "overshoot" situation as concerns its carrying capacity. The best time to tackle the situation was during the far-back period when its population was only starting to grow rapidly—and when all seemed well in terms of its capacity to feed itself for a while. The source of its population/food dilemma was becoming entrenched. Other nations with currently satisfactory capacity to ensure their food supplies might ponder Kenya's experience. The main opportunity remaining for Kenya to relieve its situation lies with an immediate and vigorous effort to slow its population growth. Were the two-child family to be achieved in 2010 instead of the projected 2035, Kenya's ultimate population could be held to 72 million, 53 million (42 percent) less than expected.[13]

Carrying capacity can apply to economic and social factors as well, in conjunction with linkages to the environmental framework within which economies and societies operate. For a specific case, consider employment. Today, the developing world's workforce numbers just over 2 billion people. Of these, over one quarter are unemployed or grossly underemployed; their total exceeds the entire workforce of the developed world. By the year 2025, the developing world's workforce is projected to surge to well over 3 billion.[14] To supply employment for the new worker multitudes, let alone for those without work today (unemployment plus underemployment frequently runs as high as 40 percent in many developing countries), means that each year during the 1990s the developing world will have to create nearly 40 million new jobs. The United States, with an economy half as large again as the entire developing world's, often has trouble in generating another 2 million jobs each year.

Of course, we must be careful not to oversimplify the situation. Several other factors are involved in the population/environment relationship, notably negligent technology, inadequate investment, and faulty development policies. But population growth and environmental degradation are engaged in a multiple-linkage relationship, where one serves to compound the adverse impacts of the other.[15]

Population pressures are now so great in many if not most parts of the world that they are causing widespread degradation of natural resource stocks. The most comprehensive and systematized analysis to date is that of Paul Harrison, who has engaged in detailed documentation and methodical evaluation.[16] He concludes that population growth in developing countries has accounted for:

—*72 percent of expansion of arable lands during 1961–85*, leading to desertification, deforestation, and decline of many natural environments;

—*79 percent of deforestation during 1973–88*, leading to tens of thousands of species extinctions each year;

—*69 percent of increase in livestock numbers during 1961–85*, leading to soil erosion, desertification, deforestation, and methane (greenhouse gas) emissions; and

—*46 percent of growth in carbon dioxide emissions from fossil fuels during 1960–88*, carbon dioxide being the base that accounts for half of global-warming processes.

Many other analyses come up with similar findings, albeit with marginally different statistical conclusions.[17]

Note too that parallel population/environment relationships apply in developed nations. The average American family comprises two children. But when we factor in consumption of natural resources and compare the American lifestyle with the global average, the "real world" size of an American family is more like twenty to twenty-five children.

Environmental Discontinuities

Superoptimists believe that because things seem to have got better in the past, they can only do the same in the future.[18] Regrettably there is good reason to suspect the future will be far from a case of "the same as before, only more so and better so." Growth in human numbers, in conjunction with growth in human consumption and growth in environmentally adverse technology, often serves to build up a situation that generates an "overshoot" outcome. In turn, this outcome can precipitate a downturn in the capacity of environments to sustain human communities even at their erstwhile level. The phenomenon is known as an "environmental discontinuity." Technically speaking, it occurs when ecosystems have absorbed stresses over long periods without much outward sign of damage, till they eventually reach a disruption level at which the cumulative consequences of stress reveal themselves in critical proportions. A familiar example is acid rain. We should anticipate that as human communities continue to expand in numbers, they will exert increasing pressures on already overburdened ecosystems and natural resource stocks, whereupon environmental discontinuities will become more common.[19]

An instance has arisen in the Philippines, where the agricultural frontier closed in the lowlands during the 1970s. As a result, multitudes of landless people started to migrate into the uplands, leading to a buildup of human numbers at a rate far greater than that of national population growth. The uplands contain the country's main remaining stocks of forests, and they feature much sloping land. The result has been a marked increase in deforestation and a rapid spread of soil erosion.[20] In other words, there occurred a "breakpoint" in patterns of human settlement and environmental degradation. As long as the lowlands were less than fully occupied, it made little difference to the uplands whether there was 50 percent or 10 percent space left. It was only when hardly any space at all was left that the situation altered radically. What had seemed acceptable became critical—and the profound shift occurred in a very short space of time.

The problem of land shortages is becoming widespread in many if not most developing countries, where land provides the livelihood for around three fifths of populations and where the great bulk of the most fertile and most accessible land has already been taken.

We encounter such non-linear relationships between resource exploitation and population growth with respect to many other resource stocks, notably soil cover, forests, fisheries, water supplies, and pollution-absorbing services of the atmosphere.[21] Whereas resource exploitation may have been expanding gradually for very long periods without undue harm, the switch in the scale of exploitation induced through a phase of rapid population growth can readily result in a slight initial exceeding of the sustainable yield, whereupon the debacle of resource depletion is precipitated with surprising rapidity.

Similarly, note that humans now engage in so much exploitation, diversion, and waste of plant growth that they are effectively appropriating 40 percent of all such growth on land each year, leaving 60 percent for the millions of other species.[22] What will happen when human numbers double, as is projected within another few decades? Even if this means that human impact on plant growth merely doubles (it is likely to be more as people demand more products from plants), the remainder of Earth's species could hardly make out with only 20 percent of plant growth per year. Species communities, being grossly reduced, would become ecologically unstable at best, and there could well emerge an entire series of environmental discontinuities. For instance, as ecosystems lose much of their biomass, they would lose much of their energy flow too, becoming less efficient at mobilizing the most basic natural resource of all, sunlight. They would be less able to maintain homeostasis. There would be a decline in communities' resilience to other forms of ecological disruption and environmental degradation.[23] Equally important, there would ensue an upsurge in the rate of species fallout from impoverished ecosystems, with cascades of extinctions leading to "shatter effects" throughout ecosystems.[24]

The biggest discontinuity in the foreseeable future will surely be global warming. The process is poised to trigger a pronounced shift in climate systems worldwide; and so far as we can discern, it will exert profoundly harmful impacts on the world's, and especially developing nations', capacity to grow food.[25] Even without climate change, increased droughts seem set to cause a 10 percent drop in grain harvests on average three times a decade, resulting in the malnutrition deaths of as many as 800 million people over twenty years.[26] In addition, global warming is projected to lead to a 10–15 percent decline in grain harvests, with substantial shortfalls for many other crops in large parts of the tropics, plus reduced yields in North America; and the consequences could include a rapid rise of 400 million in the number of people at risk from hunger, soaring to an eventual total of more than 1 billion.[27] Along the way there would be a steep upsurge in the number of environmental refugees, reaching as many as 150 million or even more within four or five decades, or ten times the total of all refugees today.[28] Note, moreover, that each of these analyses concludes that the most productive and readily available mode of adaptation to the greenhouse threat is to reduce population growth forthwith.

When we consider all environmental disruptions together, in conjunction with the compounding impacts of population growth, there is potentially a multitude of discontinuities, often with synergistic interactions, that will generate markedly adverse impacts.[29] As a result, there is good reason for us to expect a greater environmental debacle, arriving more rapidly, than is usually anticipated.

Policy Discontinuities

Fortunately, not all the news is downside. There is much scope for constructive discontinuities, notably in the policy sphere, to stave off environmental crisis. A sharply increased effort to tackle population growth can generate handsome payoffs: demographic momentum works both ways. Were Nigeria, for instance, to achieve the two-child family by 2010, its ultimate population size would be held to a projected 324 million people. Were the two-child family to be deferred by just twenty-five years, Nigeria's ultimate population size would soar to 622 million people, 92 percent larger. Were we to cater for developing world couples who possess the motivation to reduce their fertility but lack the birth-control facilities to do so,* the global population would eventually be around 2.2 billion smaller,[30] a reduction greater than the combined totals of China and India today.

Much the same applies on the environmental front. An expanded tree-planting campaign in developing countries—today's effort is only one fifth of what is needed to keep up

*See note on pages 86–87.

with tree cutting—would not only supply fuelwood and timber. It would yield additional benefits in the form of soil protection, windbreaks for field crops, restoration of watershed services, and carbon sinks to counter global warming, while also serving to relieve excessive exploitation pressure on remaining forests.[31]

No doubt about it, there is abundant scope for policy discontinuities of a positive type, provided we can identify those policy intervention points with highest leverage and most multiplier effects.

4

The Policy Prospect

On top of the two policy initiatives noted above, there is much we can do to avert the environmental debacle ahead. Let us look at three examples.

1. Perverse Policies

In many instances of environmental abuse, it turns out that a main motivating factor lies with "perverse" policies on the part of governments. That is to say, government subsidies, tax write-offs, fiscal incentives, and related measures serve to foster misuse and overuse of natural resources such as forests and water, as well as excessive applications of chemical fertilizers and pesticides.[1] Ivory Coast has promoted agricultural encroachment onto forests, leading to the unconsidered burning of commercial timber worth $5 billion. Brazil has encouraged cattle ranching in Amazonia, likewise resulting in the burning of timber worth $2.5 billion per year.[2] Note too that one of the rainforests undergoing most rapid depletion is not Amazonia or Borneo, but a temperate forest, the Tongass National Forest in Alaska, again thanks to government subsidies.

Many similar instances can be cited, especially with respect to the waste of scarce water supplies in, for example, the western United States, Mexico, and India.[3] Governments in North America, Europe, Japan, and Australia pay out $300 billion per year in agricultural subsidies, unwittingly sponsoring the overloading of croplands and promoting soil erosion as severe in Indiana as in India. The fault lies not with farmers, who are merely heeding the signals of a distorted market. It lies with governments and their counterproductive policies. While the end result is the same, it can be more easily remedied through "education" of policy makers who do not always heed the ecologist's dictum that you can never do only one thing. Moreover, the situation belies the cynic's assertion that we often have to choose between human well-being and environmental welfare. Properly understood, the two are increasingly the same—and everyday experience shows we cannot have one without the other.[4]

2. Natural Resource Accounting

Natural Resource Accounting (NRA) entails a radical revision of the way in which governments assess the state of their economies. To date, our economic accountancy procedures fail to reflect our abuse of environmental resources. While we hear abundant detail about rates of economic growth, we hear little in comparable fine-grain analysis about rates of environmental resource depletion in terms of their impacts on Gross National Product (GNP). This discrepancy between the way we appraise our economic activities and the way we evaluate the state of the environmental resource base that ultimately sustains economic activity leads to a grossly distorted view of our economic health.[5]

When we make use of human-made assets such as equipment and buildings, we write off our use as depreciation. We do not view our environmental resources as productive capital, even though we utilize them as such. When we excessively exploit forests, overwork croplands until the soil erodes, and use our skies as a free garbage can and our rivers as costless sewers, our welfare as revealed via GNP actually registers an increase. When we engage in efforts to reduce or repair the damage, those economic activities are also registered as additions to GNP.

In the United States, GNP has shown an almost continuous rise for many decades. But Natural Resource Accounting (NRA) reveals that according to the alternative measure of "net sustainable economic welfare," the rise of Americans' true long-term prosperity flattened out in the late 1960s and switched to a slight decline from the early 1980s.[6] If Americans continue to underestimate the goods and services of their environmental resources, they may drive the sustainable economy down even while GNP rises—a consequence of treating the environment and economics as not only separate sectors but polar opposites.

Similarly, environmental decline of various sorts is estimated to have been penalizing several other rich-world economies to the tune of 3 to 4 percent of GNP per year; in the case of Hungary and other East European nations, 5 to 8 percent; of Brazil, 10 percent; of Mexico, 12 percent; and of Indonesia and Nigeria, 17 percent.[7] In many instances, it has amounted to half or more of GDP growth.[8] A detailed evaluation of environmental costs in Costa Rica shows that depletion of soils, forests, and fisheries has been costing the country an annual average of 5 percent of GNP over a period of twenty years, reducing the potential GNP growth rate by 1.5 to 2 percent per year, worth a full 25 to 30 percent of economic advance.[9]

So NRA would correct the partial accounting system employed at present, with its misleading signals for use of the environmental resources that ultimately underpin all economies. Being a policy intervention of comprehensive scope, it would quickly generate a host of concise messages as concerns legitimate use of our environmental resource base. In turn, policy makers would soon find they would have to engage in a whole series of adjustments when evaluating their policies, programs, projects, and other activities. The immediate knock-on effects would be significant and widespread, and would speedily generate their own multiplier effects.

3. Pricing Systems

A policy measure parallel to NRA lies with adjustment of those pricing policies that likewise send out inaccurate messages about sustainable use of environmental resources insofar as the messages do not reflect all costs of production and consumption.* This adjustment strategy is sometimes known as "full

*In 1980, Simon issued a $1,000 bet to Paul Ehrlich, together with two of Ehrlich's colleagues, John Holdren and John Harte, that the prices of five metals—copper, chrome, nickel, tin, and tungsten—would not show an overall rise during the 1980s. The Ehrlich group lost the bet, but through unusual circumstances of the 1980s that prompted Simon himself to write on October 17, 1989, in a letter to Ehrlich, "I have been lucky that this particular period has coincided so nicely with my argument." Much of the period was marked by a pronounced downturn in industrial growth worldwide and hence in the demand for metals, due to the fourfold increase in the price of oil during the 1970s, which unduly affected those energy-intensive sectors that are also metals-intensive sectors. That this generated an anomolous impact on the prices of the five metals is shown by the record of the pre-costly-oil era 1950–75, when the prices rose by anywhere between 1.3 and 2 times. Peterson, U., and R. S. Maxwell. "Historical Mineral Production and Price Trends." *Mining Engineers* (January 1979), 25–34; see also Abernethy, V. "How Julian Simon Could Win the Bet and Still Be Wrong." *Population and Environment* 13 (1991): 3–7.

There were other factors at work too. For instance, there was the basic economics tenet that prices do not always tell the whole story of resource scarcities, due to policy distortions such as subsidies leading to artificially cheap prices. Inaccurate prices are due too to the incapacity of the marketplace to reflect "true social costs," including environmental pollution

social cost pricing." Suppose, for instance, we were to internalize the many externalities of fossil-fuel burning, perhaps through a carbon tax to reflect urban smog, acid rain, carbon dioxide emissions, and other forms of pollution. We would then be obliged to pay a price for fossil fuels that reflected all the pollution costs entailed. The price of a gallon of gasoline might well double in European countries and would increase much more in the United States, where the social and unpaid costs (pollution, etc.) of car driving amount to as much as $300 billion per year (more than 5 percent of GDP, and almost $1,200 per American), equivalent to a $2 tax per gallon of gasoline.[10]

A hefty price hike for gasoline would induce massive shifts in our perception of the role of (formerly cheap) gasoline in our economies, and bring an end to the semi-free ride we currently enjoy. Car transportation would swiftly decline, with a concomitant shift to public mass transport systems that, reflecting suddenly increased demand, would be expanded by both official and private bodies. The ramifications would ripple throughout our economies, our societies, and our understanding of our status *vis-à-vis* our environmental-support base. In short, we

---

among other forms of eventually disposing of metals-based products. Nor do prices reflect the fact that one fifth of humanity lives off less than one dollar a day, hence it exists almost entirely outside the marketplace economy: these people have next to no way to register their dollar votes as concerns the relative worth of goods and services—even though they are the ones in most need of opportunity to demonstrate their views on prices.

In this connection, note that in his desire to show that we need never run short of resources, Simon has even asserted that copper can "be made from other metals." The most technologically feasible way to do this would be by reacting helium with iron leading to copper. To produce as much copper as the United States now utilizes would require ten times as much energy as the entire American energy economy today. D. B. Luten. "Energy and Material Resources." In P. R. Ehrlich and J. P. Holdren, eds., *The Cassandra Conference* (Texas A&M University Press, College Station, TX, 1988). Nonetheless Simon persists with his idea that "In the end, copper and oil come out of our minds. That's really where they are." (Simon, *The Ultimate Resource*, 1981).

would find ourselves obliged to think again not only when we visit the gas station but when we visit the supermarket with its increased prices for foods transported over long distances (the average item on an American meal table has traveled over 1,500 kilometers). We would encounter the impact of full social cost pricing at dozens of points in our daily lives.

This policy initiative, like that of NRA, should be supported with a number of related measures to foster sustainable use of our environments. They include fiscal incentives and disincentives to modify people's behavior; amendment of discount rates (when the rate is 10 percent, it implies there is no future beyond seven years); establishment of across-the-board environmental indicators; and implementation of additional policy guidelines such as the polluter pays principle and the precautionary principle (the latter proposing that in instances of scientific uncertainty and possibly major environmental injury stemming from resource exploitation, the prudent path lies with an exceptionally cautious approach).[11]

These various interventions would entrain a radical reorientation in the outlook of policy makers, producers, and consumers, indeed, every last member of society. Our present attitudes and perceptions are deeply entrenched in myriad ways, inducing an institutional inertia throughout virtually all spheres of human activity. This inertia factor is a superpowerful force—though a new form of inertia can work to our benefit when once the corrective measures are in place, generating a constructive form of momentum.

5

Our Changing Relationship to Nature

All this points up the ostensible dichotomy between conventional economists and environmental biologists. Fortunately, a growing number of economists recognize there need be no essential dichotomy.[1] But there remain a few economists such as Julian Simon who see humankind as a species so different from all the rest that it can somehow operate independently of the planetary ecosystem. Other economists see us as heavily and increasingly dependent upon natural resources, environmental processes, and vital ecosystems: our own future is intricately intertwined with their future.

None of this has mattered much as long as humans remained a part of nature. Today, we try to be apart from nature. This is the first time in humankind's existence that we have been able to indulge hubris of this extreme sort. In fact, we have achieved the technological muscle to undertake an experiment with the entire planetary ecosystem, no less, through our massive depletion of topsoil, vegetation, water supplies, species stocks, and the ozone layer. The experiment is completely unplanned. We have little idea of its outcome, except that evidence to date suggests it will be largely harmful to human welfare for untold generations into the future. Our experiment has become so far reaching that we are actually disrupting Earth's climate.

This last factor troubles me greatly in a personal sense. On top of the severe economic dislocations that global warming will cause,[2] I feel it is simply "over the top" for us to intervene in the planet's workings to this grotesque extent. We have so thoroughly dominated the Earth that everything bears the imprint of human hand. Wherever we look, we see our own image reflected back in some form or other—the apotheosis of hubris-ridden humanity. It is not so much a case of DDT in Antarctic penguins; rather, it is the outdoors that is no longer an outdoors, that no longer lies significantly beyond our control. The world beyond the window has now been altered by us until the very climate is no longer "natural"; it is becoming human-determined.

In Britain, we have had virtually no winter for the past four years. No more sharp frosty days, no more crisp snow, and, for that matter, no more dreary drizzle with its soggy chill. I miss it all, the bad winter as well as the good winter, because I miss winter. I miss it not so much because I enjoy the turn of the seasons, but insofar as global warming will mean no more winters at all in Britain, I bitterly regret that something that seemed to lie forever beyond human reach has now been forever eliminated by human agency. My grandchildren and all their descendants will never know what I and all my forebears have known, and will not feel part of a greater order of things. We are unwittingly destroying something so precious that we shall not realize its ultimate value until it comes to its end.

Much the same applies to the millions of species that share the planet with us. Even if we were to expand several times over the amount of conservation effort we are putting into save-species campaigns, it would still be far from enough to assist all species in trouble. We have tried playing Noah and we have found our Ark is not nearly big enough. When we choose to spend scarce conservation funds on one species, we automatically deny those same funds to other species. The California

...n example: We have allocated $15 million to the ...m sufficient to save hundreds of endangered freshwa- ...molluscs in the United States and thousands of invertebrates in Amazonia. We have decided we prefer the first, so willy-nilly we have "decided" the others are not worthy of our support.[3] Reluctant as we may be to recognize it, it is an implicitly built-in factor of the situation that we choose in favor of some species and thereby give thumbs down to others. Having goofed at playing Noah, we find ourselves playing God. Yet we are only dimly aware of our new role as lords of creation. We have sought to elevate ourselves above the natural world, and too often we do it with the selective discretion of Neanderthals.

All this boils down to a critical question as concerns our changing relationship to nature. It is not: "How much do we want to save biodiversity, tropical forests, and the rest—and hence how much are we prepared to pay for it?" Rather, it is: "What sort of world do we want—for ourselves and for the trillions of people who come after us?" And that implies a further clincher question: "What sort of people do we want to be today?"

The Ethical Dimension

It is fitting to conclude this section with what could eventually turn out to be the biggest imperative of all. It reflects the long-term repercussions of our environmental assaults on the biosphere. As my numerous scientific citations indicate, we are polluting our ecosystems on a scale that, if the pollution were to be suddenly terminated in the year 2010, the time needed for natural processes and human efforts to make good the damage would be several decades. If we were to stop the spread of deserts in the same year, it would take at least a century to push them back again; and the same to enable the ozone layer to recover. Soil erosion is becoming so severe that it would require several centuries to replenish soil stocks; and much the same would apply to tropical deforestation and global warming. All these restorative efforts would be needed to compensate for environmental injuries imposed mainly within half a century. The most enduring biospheric impoverishment lies with mass extinction of species. Recall that the recovery period needed for evolution to come up with a replacement stock of species would certainly extend for 5 million years.

In effect, leaders and citizens of the present generation are taking decisions that will profoundly affect dozens of generations into the future—and in the case of mass extinction, at least 200,000 generations. This latter case means that we today are casually dismissing the massive uncertainty about what species can do for us; we are saying we have complete certainty that people in the future will be able to manage without them. Suppose that for the next 5 million years, the average sustainable world population is roughly half the current total, 2.5 billion, and that a new generation comes along every twenty-five years. This means that people alive today are taking a decision on the unconsulted behalf of 500 trillion people to come. To grasp the scale of 1 trillion, reckon that if we look back 1 trillion seconds, we are gazing into the cave of 32,000 years ago.

No human community in the past has ever wielded such capacity to impoverish communities that come after. But let us remember too that no community of the past has ever possessed such capacity to safeguard the planet at a time of unprecedented threat. It is a prospect that demands an unprecedented response from all of us alive today.

6

A Great Creative Challenge

Fortunately there is no doubt that people are up to the challenge if they are enabled to understand what the challenge amounts to in its full scope. Give people a challenge big enough to test their mettle, and they show they can come through time and again. Remember what they have achieved in the past few years. They have torn down the Berlin Wall. They have put an end to communism and they have dismembered the Soviet Union. They have started talking to each other in South Africa, even in the Middle East. It is astonishing what people accomplish when once they set their minds to it. In all these instances, what has counted is that people have looked not only at the costs of action (fearsome as they have often been), but at the concealed costs of inaction—whereupon the arithmetic becomes all too clear. With regard to environmental protection, the true question is not: "How can we afford to do the job sometime?" It is: "How can we afford not to do it right away?"

What is needed is to eliminate the Berlin walls of ignorance and indifference in people's minds. Show them what is what, tell 'em like it is, and they'll respond all right. There are signs on every side—recycling efforts, the readiness to do more with less, and the emphasis on quality of life as well as quantity of livelihood—that people now understand the environment/economics debate is no longer about the limits to growth. It is about the growth of limits.[1] These latter limits include the limits of our natural resource stocks, the limits to population growth, the limits to excessive consumption, and the limits to living as if the future can be left to take care of itself. Above all, it is about the limits of our "only one Earth." These ultimate limits have arisen in part because of the limits to our thinking in the past: they have stemmed both from the limits of the world outside the window and of the world inside our heads.

But when once we cast off these ultimate limits—the self-imposed restrictions on the way we view our Earth, together with our fellow passengers—we shall enter a world of limitless scope and aspirations. While it need *not* be a world of zero economic advancement, it will be far different from what we have known to date. A growth economy is one that becomes bigger in physical senses; an advancing economy is one that becomes better in human senses. The global economy cannot grow indefinitely, but it can certainly develop indefinitely—just as we don't need to expand the Earth in order to develop it.[2]

More important still, our new world will be one where we achieve a first and final accord with nature. We shall achieve that only by achieving an accord with one another; and the more we do that, the more we shall achieve our accord with nature—with our own nature, too. We shall find ourselves borne along by a virtuous cycle of enhanced living, where humankind functions as a single community, even as "human kind." We have the chance to live a little rather than merely exist. In fact, to live a lot—and then some.

No doubt about it, the challenge is superscale. We are talking about an entirely new mode of Earthling existence. It will amount to the most seismic shift in outlook since we came out of our cave—a shift in our attitudes, our goals, our values, everything that makes us what we are and enables us to preserve our Earth for what it can still be. The challenge is nothing less than a basic redesigning of our societies, culminating in the emergence of a truly global society. It is a challenge far greater and immensely more exhilarating than whatever faced the founders of the American nation in the halcyon days of the early Republic, when the talk from Washington and Jefferson and other luminaries was of how to turn profound problems into glorious opportunities.

What an adventure! We have the chance to take part in a pioneering enterprise to surpass the greatest explorations of the past. We can all play our part, each and every one of us; indeed we all must, or our enterprise will fail—and we cannot dare to envisage the alternative. It will be a collaborative endeavor to far outstrip the building of the Pyramids, the mapping of our round Earth, even our voyages to other planets. After all, we shall be building that shining citadel on the hilltop that has been a beacon for visionaries over the centuries. This time we can not merely dream, we can get on and do it forthwith. And it must no longer remain a dream deferred because there will be no second chance. The challenge is right now, and it is in our hands. We can do it for both posterity and prosperity. Remember that we live in a time when, thanks to modern telecommunications and other forms of "networking," everybody can be somebody and nobody need be nobody. Consider, too, that however "far out" this may sound, we live in an age when it is increasingly the same to be idealist and realist.

For those who feel daunted by the prospect, let us remind ourselves that no other human community has ever enjoyed a challenge so expansive. The problems of our Earth facing extreme threat have never arisen on a fraction of the scale we witness today. Nor will any human community of the future have our opportunity; if we do not get on with the job, our descendants will be left with nothing to do but pick up the pieces. It is up to us alone. Shall we not delight that we are alive at a time of unrivaled challenge? As we grasp the full nature of what we are to do, who would want to be a problem that gets in our way? Given our professional talents and our personal commitment, shall we not feel we face a prospect of insurmountable opportunities?

Look out, embattled Earth, here we come.

The Debate

Each debater made a fifteen-minute opening statement, followed by a five-minute response by his opponent. The moderator then made a couple of remarks and posed a question to each debater in turn. At that point the floor was opened for questions from the audience, which appear here in sharply edited form. At the end of the event, each debater delivered a five-minute closing statement. The order of presentation was determined by a toss of the coin at the beginning of the debate.

The words of the two authors, lightly revised and edited by them, appear in their entirety.

Opening Statement by Julian Simon

Please ask yourself: Is the trend of black infant mortality good or bad? Almost everyone's reaction is that black infant mortality is a bad situation. But look at a graph of black and white infant mortality in the United States since 1915. White infant mortality in 1915 was almost 100 deaths per 1,000 births, and black infant mortality was fully 180 deaths per 1,000 births. Both are horrifying. And the rates were even more horrifying in earlier years in some places—up to 300 or 400 deaths per 1,000 births.

Nowadays white infant mortality is about 9 per 1,000, and black infant mortality is about 18 per 1,000. Of course it is bad that black mortality is higher than for whites. But should we not be impressed by the tremendous improvement for both races—both falling to about 10 percent of what they were—with the black rate coming ever closer to the white rate? Is not this extraordinary improvement for the entire population the most important story—and a most happy story? Yet the press gives us the impression that we should be mainly distressed about the state of black infant mortality.

Figure 1. Infant Mortality Rate (per 1,000 live births)

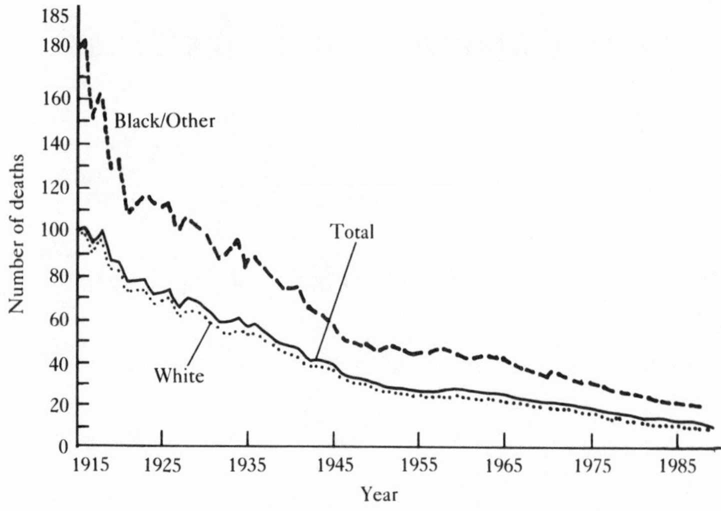

Source: U.S. Dept. of Commerce Bureau of the Census, *Historical Statistics of the United States: Colonial Times to 1970* (GPO, Washington, D.C., 1976); U.S. Dept. of Commerce Bureau of the Census, *Statistical Abstract of the United States* (GPO, Washington, D.C., various years).

The gloom-and-doom about a "crisis" of our environment is all wrong on the scientific facts. Even the Environmental Protection Agency acknowledges that U.S. air and our water have been getting cleaner rather than dirtier in the past few decades. Every agricultural economist knows that the world's population has been eating ever better since World War II. Every resource economist knows that all natural resources have been getting more available rather than more scarce, as shown by their falling prices over the decades and centuries. And every demographer knows that the death rate has been falling all over the world—life expectancy almost tripling in the rich countries in the past two centuries, and almost doubling in the poor countries in just the past four decades.

The picture also is now clear that population growth does

not hinder economic development. In the 1980s there was a complete reversal in the consensus of thinking of population economists about the effects of more people. In 1986, the National Research Council and the National Academy of Sciences completely overturned their "official" view away from the earlier worried view expressed in 1971. They noted the absence of any statistical evidence of a negative connection between population increase and economic growth. And they said that "The scarcity of exhaustible resources is at most a minor restraint on economic growth."

This U-turn by the scientific consensus of experts on the subject has gone unacknowledged by the press, the anti-natalist environmental organizations, and the agencies that foster population control abroad.

Here is my central assertion: Almost every economic and social change or trend points in a positive direction, as long as we view the matter over a reasonably long period of time.

For proper understanding of the important aspects of an economy, we should look at the long-run trends. But the short-run comparisons—between the sexes, age groups, races, political groups, which are usually purely relative—make more news. To repeat, just about every important long-run measure of human welfare shows improvement over the decades and centuries, in the United States as well as in the rest of the world. And there is no persuasive reason to believe that these trends will not continue indefinitely.

Would I bet on it? For sure. I'll bet a week's or month's pay—anything I win goes to pay for more research—that just about any trend pertaining to material human welfare will improve rather than get worse. You pick the comparison and the year. First come, first served. Material welfare, not emotional or spiritual or sexual or social. Not ozone but cancers. Not greenhouse warming but agriculture and standard of living. And I'll be happy to bet with Norman Myers about many of the trends that he thinks are going to be bad in the future.

Take a look at Figure 2. What do you think it portrays? It is a graph of human life expectancy at birth, which slowly crept

Figure 2. Life Expectancy Rates

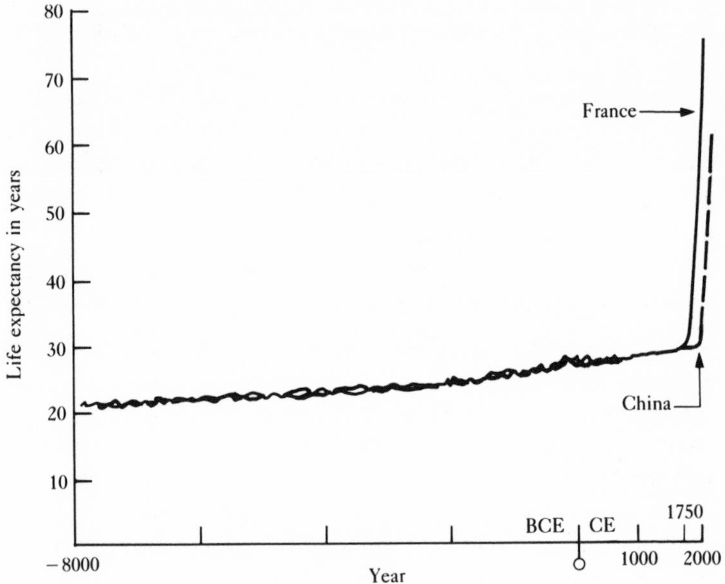

Source: Stylized and drawn by the author.

up from the low 20s thousands of years ago to the high 20s about 1750. Then in about 1750, life expectancy in the richest countries suddenly took off and tripled in about two centuries. In just the past two centuries, the length of life you could expect for your baby or yourself in the advanced countries jumped from less than thirty years to perhaps seventy-five years. What greater event has humanity witnessed?

Then starting well after World War II, the length of life you could expect in the poor countries has leaped upward by perhaps fifteen or even twenty years since the 1950s, caused by advances in agriculture, sanitation, and medicine. (See Figure 3.)

It is this decrease in the death rate that is the cause of there being a larger world population nowadays than in former times.

The most important and amazing demographic fact—the

greatest human achievement in history, in my view—is this decrease in the world's death rate.

The point of showing you the figure this way is that this shape of figure is used to scare people about population growth simply from the shape alone, and the argument that "This obvi-

Figure 3. Female Expectation of Life at Birth

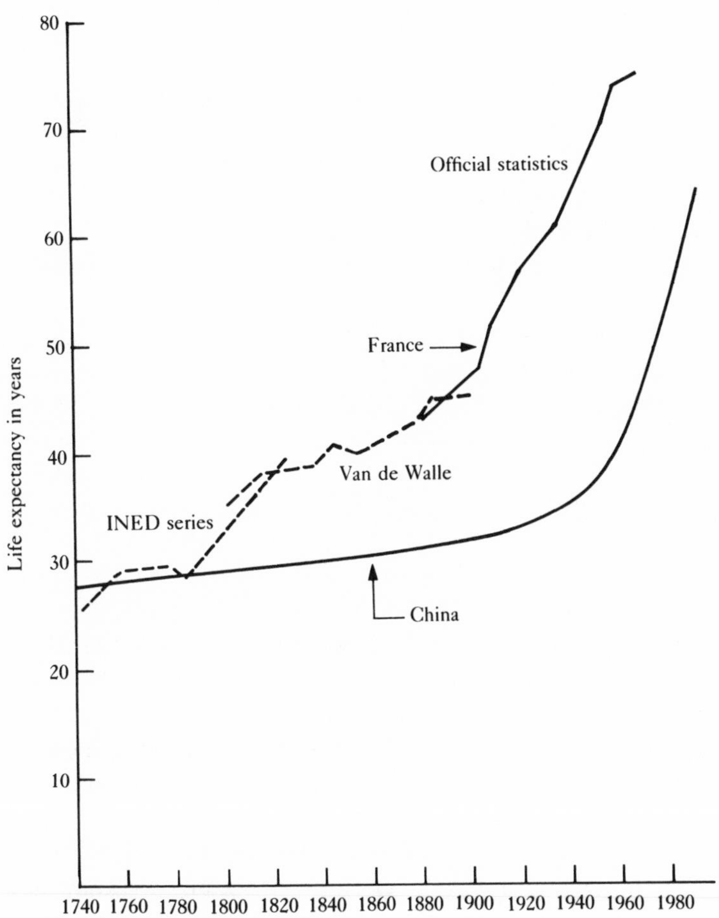

Source: Compiled by the author.

ously can't continue." Indeed, it was a figure like this one but of population growth that got me to enlist in the great war against population growth. Yet as is obvious from the fact that the upward zoom of the curve of life expectancy proves nothing, so the same shape for other variables proves nothing.

Let's put it differently. In the nineteenth century, the planet Earth could sustain only 1 billion people. Ten thousand years ago, only 4 million could keep themselves alive. Now, more than 5 billion people are living longer and more healthily than ever before, on average. The increase in the world's population represents our victory over death.

I would expect lovers of humanity to jump with joy at this triumph of human mind and organization over the raw killing forces of nature. Instead, many lament that there are so many people alive to enjoy the gift of life. Some even express regret over the fall in the death rate.

Throughout history, the supply of natural resources always has worried people. Yet the data clearly show that natural resource scarcity—as measured by the economically meaningful indicator of cost or price—has been decreasing rather than increasing in the long run for all raw materials, with only temporary exceptions from time to time. That is, resource availability has been increasing. Consider copper, which is representative of all the metals. In Figure 4a, we see the price relative to wages since 1801. The cost of a ton is only about a tenth now of what it was 200 years ago.

This trend of falling prices of copper has been going on for a very long time. In the eighteenth century BCE in Babylonia under Hammurabi—almost 4,000 years ago—the price of copper was about 1,000 times its price in the United States now relative to wages. At the time of the Roman Empire, the price was about 100 times the present price.

In Figure 4b, we see the price of copper relative to the consumer price index. Everything that we buy—pens, shirts, tires—has been getting cheaper over the years because we know how to make them cheaper. But, extraordinarily, natural resources

Figure 4a. Copper Prices Indexed by Wages

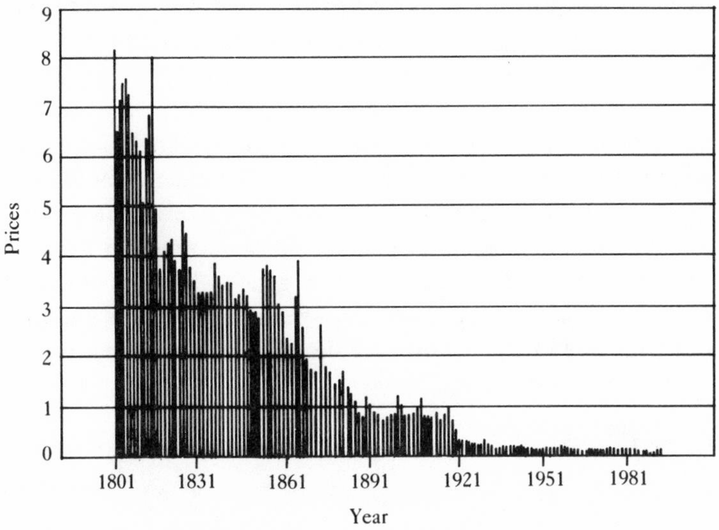

Source: U.S. Dept. of Commerce Bureau of the Census, *Historical Statistics of the United States: Colonial Times to 1970;* U.S. Dept. of Commerce Bureau of the Census, *Statistical Abstract of the United States* (various years).

have been getting cheaper even faster than consumer goods.

So by any measure, natural resources have been getting more available rather than more scarce.

Regarding oil, the price rise since the 1970s does not stem from an increase in the cost of world supply. The production cost per barrel in the Persian Gulf still is perhaps 50 cents per barrel. Concerning energy in general, there is no reason to believe that the supply of energy is finite, or that the price of energy will not continue its long-run decrease forever. I realize that it sounds weird to say that the supply of energy is not finite or limited, but I'll be delighted to give you a whole routine on this in the question period if you ask.

Food is an especially important resource. The evidence is

particularly strong for food that we are on a benign trend, despite rising population. The long-run price of food relative to wages is now only perhaps a tenth of what it was two centuries ago. Even relative to consumer products the price of grain is down, due to increased productivity.

There is only one important resource which has shown a trend of increasing scarcity rather than increasing abundance. That resource is the most important of all—human beings. Yes, there are more people on Earth now than ever before. But if we measure the scarcity of people the same way that we measure the scarcity of other economic goods—by how much we must pay to obtain their services—we see that wages and salaries have been going up all over the world, in poor countries as

Figure 4b. Copper Prices Indexed by CPI

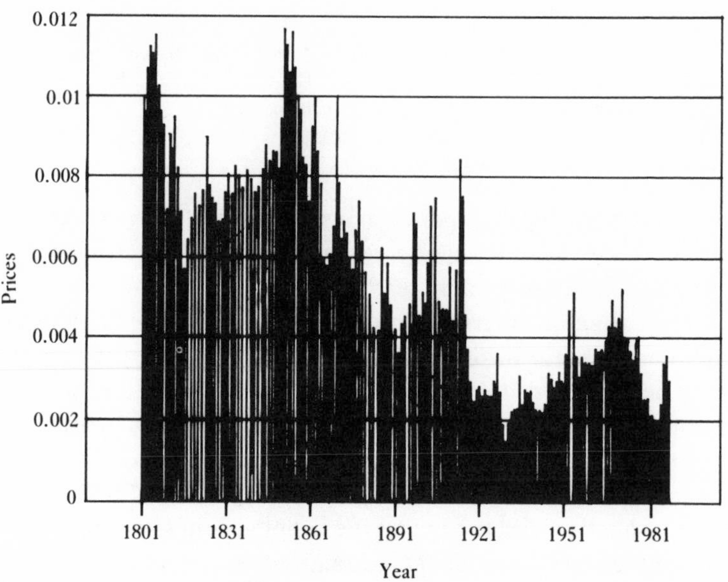

Source: U.S. Dept. of Commerce Bureau of the Census, *Historical Statistics of the United States: Colonial Times to 1970;* U.S. Dept. of Commerce Bureau of the Census, *Statistical Abstract of the United States* (various years).

well as in rich countries. The amount that you must pay to obtain the services of a barber or a cook has risen in India, just as the price of a barber or cook—or economist—has risen in the United States over the decades. This increase in the price of people's services is a clear indication that people are becoming more scarce even though there are more of us.

About pollution now: The evidence with respect to air indicates that pollutants have been declining, especially the main pollutant, particulates. With respect to water, the proportion of monitoring sites in the United States with water of good drinkability has increased since the data began in 1961.

Species extinction is a key issue for the environmental movement. It is the subject of magazine stories with titles like "Playing Dice with Megadeath," whose subtitle is: "The odds are good that we will exterminate half the world's species within the next century."

The issue came to scientific prominence in 1979 with my debate opponent Norman Myers's book *The Sinking Ark*. It then was brought to an international public and onto the U.S. policy agenda by the 1980 *Global 2000 Report to the President*. "Hundreds of thousands of species—perhaps as many as 20 percent of all species on earth—will be irretrievably lost as their habitats vanish, especially in tropical forests," the report said.

The actual data on the observed rates of species extinction are wildly at variance with Myers's and following statements, and do not provide support for the various policies suggested to deal with the purported dangers. Here's what we know from his book (summarized in Figure 5):

1. The estimated extinction rate of known species is about *one every four years* between the years from 1600 to 1900.

2. The estimated rate is about *one a year* from 1900 to the present.

3. Some scientists (in Myers's words) have "hazarded a guess" that the extinction rate "could now have reached" 100 species per year. That is, the estimate is simply conjecture; it is not even a point estimate but rather an upper bound. The source given for the "some scientists" statement is a staffwrit-

Figure 5. Myers-Lovejoy Estimates of Species Extinction and Their Extrapolations to the Year 2000

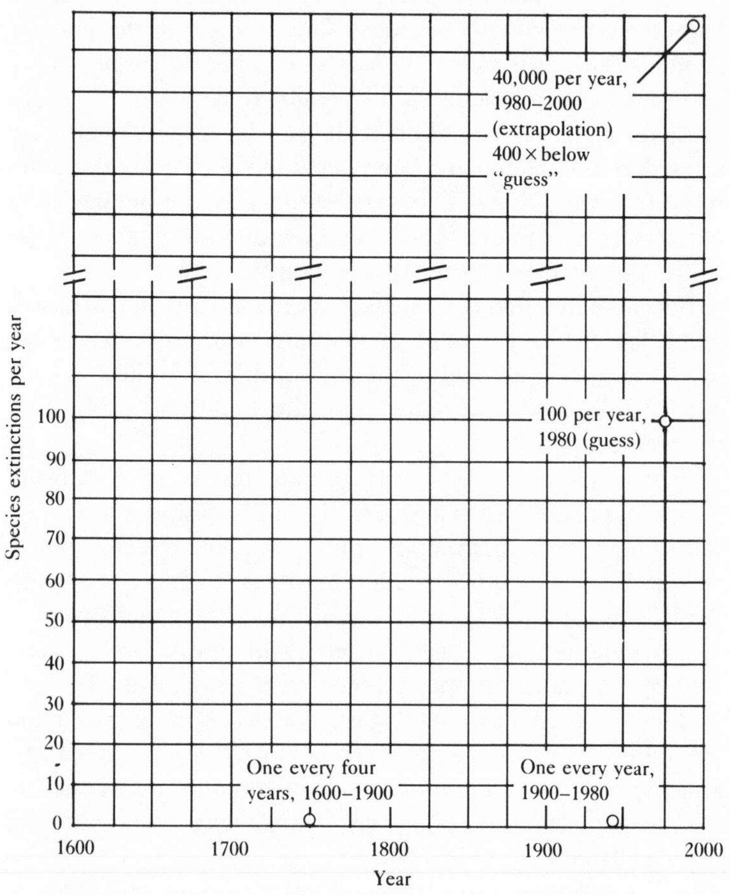

Source: See text.

ten news report. It should be noted, however, that the subject of this guess is different than the subject of the estimates in (1) and (2), because the former includes mainly or exclusively birds or mammals, whereas the latter includes all species. While this difference implies that (1) and (2) may be too low a basis for estimating the present extinction rate of all species, it also implies that there is even less statistical basis for estimating the extinction rate for species other than birds and mammals than it might otherwise seem.

4. This guessed upper limit in (3) is then increased and used by Myers in his 1979 book, and then by Lovejoy in *Global 2000* (1981), as the basis for the "projections" quoted above. In *Report to the President,* the language has become "are likely to lead" to the extinction of between 14 and 20 percent of all species before the year 2000. So an upper limit for the present that is pure guesswork has become the basis of a forecast for the future which has been published in newspapers to be read by tens or hundreds of millions of people and understood as a scientific statement.

With respect to population growth: A dozen competent statistical studies, starting in 1967 with an analysis by Nobel Prize winner Simon Kuznets, agree that there is no negative statistical relationship between economic growth and population growth. There is strong reason to believe that more people have a positive effect in the long run.

Population growth does not lower the standard of living—all the evidence agrees. And the evidence supports the view that population growth raises it in the long run.

Now we need some theory to explain how it can be that economic welfare grows along with population, rather than humanity being reduced to misery and poverty as population grows.

The Malthusian theory of increasing scarcity, based on supposedly fixed resources—the theory that the doomsayers rely upon—runs exactly contrary to the data over the long sweep of history. Therefore it makes sense to prefer another theory.

The theory that fits the facts very well is this: More people, and increased income, cause problems in the short run. Short-run scarcity raises prices. This presents opportunity, and prompts the search for solutions. In a free society, solutions are eventually found. And in the long run the new developments leave us better off than if the problems had not arisen.

When we take a long-run view, the picture is different, and

considerably more complex, from the simple short-run view of more people implying lower average income. In the very long run, more people almost surely imply more available resources and a higher income for everyone.

I suggest you test this proposition as follows: Do you think that our standard of living would be as high as it is now if the population had never grown from about 4 million human beings perhaps 10,000 years ago? I don't think we'd now have electric light or gas heat or autos or penicillin or travel to the Moon or our present life expectancy of over seventy years at birth in rich countries—in comparison to the life expectancy of twenty to twenty-five years at birth in earlier eras—if population had not grown to its present numbers. If population had never grown, instead of the pleasant lunch you had, you would have been out chasing rabbits and digging roots.

Opening Statement by Norman Myers

Good evening, ladies and gentlemen. I believe that, by contrast with Julian Simon, we are at a watershed in human history because of the grand-scale environmental degradation that is overtaking our planet in conjunction with excessive population growth and consumerism. Unless we change these trends and patterns, we are going to have a tough time of it. And not only us, but dozens and hundreds of human generations into the future. In fact, in the case of mass extinction of species, as many as 200,000 generations to come will be impoverished because of what we are doing during the present few decades.

That's the bad news. The better news is that we still have time to ward off the final catastrophe insofar as it has not yet arrived with complete clout. And the best news is that if we recognize the full nature and scope of the threats from environmental problems and population growth, and if we mobilize our talents incisively and urgently enough, we can still cut off many of those problems at the pass. I wouldn't say entirely, but largely: we can get on top of many of our problems before they get on top of us. There is no doubt in my mind that we can still do it if we set ourselves to the task.

Ladies and gentlemen, I want to emphasize that I am not a doomster-and-gloomster. Sure, I will give you an awful lot of gloom and doom this evening. But I firmly believe we are at a point of environmental breakdown *or* breakthrough.

What do I mean when I speak of prospective environmental ruin worldwide? Let me give you a few quick statistics, all of them supported by reports from the World Bank, United Nations agencies, the Rockefeller Foundation, and organizations of similar reputable sort. Soil erosion: during the past year we have lost 25 billion tons of topsoil around the world—and it's as severe in parts of Indiana as in India. This lost topsoil has cost us 9 million tons of grain, enough to make up the diets of well over 200 million people who are "undernourished" (the jargon term for people who are semi-starving). Also during the past year we have lost 150,000 square kilometers of tropical forest, taking with them a host of watershed services. The economic costs are sizable: in the Ganges Valley alone in India, deforestation in the Himalayan foothills causes downstream flooding that imposes costs that, according to the Government of India, amount to well over $1 billion per year. During the past year, too, desertification has totaled 60,000 square kilometers, taking out agricultural lands with potential food output worth $42 billion.

Also during the past year, we have lost tens of thousands of species, again with an economic cost. When you visit your neighborhood pharmacy, there is one chance in two that the product on the counter before you would not be there if it were not for startpoint materials from wild plants and animals. The commercial value of these products is more than $40 billion a year. Think, then, of what we are losing when we hear of tens of thousands of species disappearing every year.

In the past year too, we have depleted the ozone layer still further. We have taken a solid step toward a greenhouse-affected world. And at the same time our Earth has taken on board another 93 million people, equivalent to more than a "new Mexico"—and this at a time when our Earth is straining under the burden of its present population of 5.5 billion people.

Ladies and gentlemen, you have heard from Professor Simon that he believes there is no environmental crisis whatever. He has emphasized (to remind you, I will quote from one of his writings): "It is an indubitable economic fact that natural resources are increasingly less important with each passing decade." Contrast this statement with my documented evidence of the past year.

Professor Simon has made much play with a statement by the National Academy of Sciences in 1986, proposing that population growth and environmental degradation were not really problems at all. Let me tell you of another statement issued by the National Academy of Sciences in May 1992, in conjunction with the British Royal Society in London (I will not hazard a guess as to which one of these scientific bodies is the more prestigious). The statement goes like this—and note the wording, ladies and gentlemen, since you know that National Academy scientists tend to be sober-sided characters who do not engage in way-out statements:

> If current predictions of population growth prove accurate and patterns of human activity on the planet remain unchanged, science and technology may not be able to prevent either irreversible degradation of the environment or continued poverty for much of the world. . . . Unrestrained resource consumption for energy production and other uses . . . could lead to catastrophic outcomes for the global environment. Some of the environmental changes may produce irreversible damage to the Earth's capacity to sustain life. The overall pace of environmental change has unquestionably been accelerated by the recent expansion of the human population. . . . The future of our planet is in the balance.

Let's move on to consider biodiversity and mass extinction of species. The issue is on this evening's agenda as one of the critical points for our debate. It is all the more important, I suggest, because mass extinction is a unique environmental problem: it is irreversible. All our other environmental problems can be turned around if we want to spend enough time and money. We can push back the deserts. We can replant tropical forests. We can wait until topsoil is restored, the ozone layer is replenished, and global climate is stabilized. True, these recoveries will take a few centuries. But no doubt about it, all these problems can be fixed up. Mass extinction of species is different. When a species is gone, it's gone for good.

You might say, of course, that evolution will generate replacement species in fullness of time. So it will. But if we allow the present species extinction spasm to continue unchecked as we have done for the last several decades, the length of time it will take for evolution to make good the damage will be, according to what we can discern from mass extinction episodes in the prehistoric past, at least 5 million years and possibly as many as 25 million years. This is an impoverishment we are imposing on hundreds of thousands of human generations to come, all as a result of what we are doing in just a few decades.

What is the evidence for the mass extinction under way? Consider a 1992 book by Professor Edward O. Wilson of Harvard University, *The Diversity of Life.* Wilson has calculated, using analytic models which are thoroughly established in the biological field, that we are now losing, very roughly reckoned, at least 30,000 species every year. That is 120,000 times the natural background rate of the prehistoric past. Professor Wilson's estimate is paralleled by those of a dozen other eminent scientists in this country, and by my own estimate as well. We all come up with very similar figures. Fifteen leading scientists in the United States have banded together into what they call the Club of Earth. It is a group open only to biologists who are members of both the National Academy and the American Academy, meaning they are scientists whose professional credentials are beyond question. They have all come up with the same basic conclusion as concerns the figure of 30,000 species becoming extinct per year.

This contrasts with Professor Simon's statement which you

have just heard. He has taken me to task for my 1979 book, saying, "There is no documentation or further data produced by biologists since 1979 to demonstrate what Norman Myers was saying." During those thirteen years, the number of papers published on the mass extinction crisis is over three hundred, many of them by the fifteen scientists in the Club of Earth. No documentation, no data, Professor Simon?

Let's move on to the population factor, and the question of how far we may have too many people on Earth already. Consider this from one of the most basic standpoints, our capacity to feed people. Technologists will say, with justification, that from 1950 right through 1984, we did a marvelous job. Thanks to the Green Revolution, each year we produced more food at a rate of increase that was greater than the rate of population growth. For all of those three and half decades, we had more food per person worldwide, on average. But since 1985, there has been a leveling off in grain production. The increase per year has averaged only 0.7 percent, by contrast with those thirty-five years when it was around 3 percent. Meantime population growth remains almost 2 percent. So the upshot is that food availability per person worldwide has been declining for eight long, lean years.

Fortunately, there's some better news on the population front. It concerns family planning. Some people, and you have put yourself among them, Julian, have referred to family planning as an imperialist imposition on people in the developing world. Today, 90 percent of all people in the developing world live in countries that have declared their population growth rates are too high—and they want to bring them down as quickly as they can. They are clamoring for family planning support from whatever nations in the world will supply it. This applies especially to the 300 million couples who have decided they want no more children, but lack access to birth-control facilities.

There's a further consequence to this sad situation, specifically the lack of family planning support. The abortion rate has been soaring in developing countries. It used to be roughly 25 million per year in the late 1970s; today it is more like twice as many. This is a fearful consequence of denying birth-control facilities to all those who are clamoring for them.

A final point: our changing relationship to nature. We are now in control of the Earth. We are no longer a part of nature, we are apart from nature. Or so we like to think—even though we still have to breathe and eat and perform all kinds of other biological functions. With regard to our fellow species, we have reached the point where we have tried to play Noah, and we are finding that our Arks have been far too small (otherwise we would be saving those 30,000 species disappearing every year). Each time we assign a pile of dollars to save one species, we are automatically denying those same dollars to other species. There simply are not enough funds to go around, not by a long way. We don't make this dreadful choice deliberately. But the choice is built into a situation where we have insufficient funds to save all species. Essentially, then, we are deciding which species we shall save and which species we shall put over the side of the boat. Having goofed at playing Noah, we are now playing God. This is a fundamental change in our entire relationship to nature.

A final key question arises from my remarks, ladies and gentlemen. I believe we have to ask ourselves not only how much do we want to spend to save tropical forests or to save species or to grow more food, and so on. The basic question at a crisis stage in human history is this: What sort of a world do we want to live in? What sort of a world do we want to pass on to future generations—not just our children and grandchildren, but hundreds and thousands of generations? In other words, What kind of people do we want to be? That is a question that is not answered by citing reams of statistics from the marketplace.

Thank you, ladies and gentlemen.

Response by Julian Simon

Before I start, a point of personal privilege: I want to correct something Norman said I said but I did not say—that family planning is an imposition on people. I have never said this. I've said for twenty-some years that to have the family size that you want is one of the great human rights and privileges. And if there is anything that I could ever do to help people get the size of family they would want—the number of children they want—I'd do my very best to help them. I have never ever said anything different.

Norman Myers does not show us any trend data. Consider a book of his (Myers, 1991), which came out last year. There are only two data series in it—the growth of population, and life expectancy. If there's anything to be learned from these data, he shows it's that more people are living longer.

There are no other trend data. He presents no historical data to support his assertions.

With respect to species extinction: Norman Myers says that I cannot challenge the credentials of the many writers he cites.

True, I cannot challenge their credentials. But I can and I will challenge their assertions.

Professor Wilson himself has said that though there are hundreds of anecdotal reports, there are no aggregate data on numbers of species beyond what was earlier cited by Mr. Myers. Garrett Hardin, another biologist, has retreated to the point of saying that it is unknowable how many species are being extinguished. There are no additional data beyond what Mr. Myers cited earlier.

There are many things Mr. Myers and I can bet on, one of them being soil erosion. For example, there are data going back to the 1930s in the United States—surveys done by U.S. Department of Agriculture—showing that the soil on our farms is becoming less eroded rather than more eroded. I'd be prepared to bet with you that surveys in the future will show that the quality of our farmland in the United States is even better than now—for any year Mr. Myers picks.

With respect to the rest of the world, it's a little more complicated because in many parts of the world land is not individually owned, and one crucial point about the economics of population resources is the extent to which the political-economic-social system provides people personal freedom to take care of their assets as well as to create new knowledge. Skilled people require an appropriate economic and social framework. If people are to guard such assets as their farms, and take care of their land, they require the proper framework. This means, in the case of farmers, private ownership.

With respect to the world as a whole, the data for the last thirty years show less rather than more desertification, as measured by the only available measure—the amount of arable land in the world. This quantity has been going up rather than going down, so I'm prepared to bet with Norman Myers: Pick any year in the future, and I'll bet you that there's more arable land in the world then than now. So that's a second thing that we can bet on.

A third bet: Mr. Myers said that resources are becoming more important. A reasonable measure of the importance of natural resources is how big a part of our national economy they account for. It used to be that agriculture and mining accounted for 80 percent. Now, agriculture and mining are down to about 3 percent in the United States. And I'm prepared to bet that the proportion of our economy that natural resources accounts for is even less than now in any year that you pick in the future, showing that resources are becoming less rather than more important.

With respect to food, you say that the situation has turned around as of 1985. Again, pick any year in the future and I'll bet you that food prices are lower than they are now. And I'll also bet that the nutrition that people get—as measured by the standard measures of nutrition, calories per person—is better throughout the world in any future year than now. Pick a year, Norman. Pick even an individual country, if you like.

This is the overarching theory that I offer to explain why it is that all of these things can be happening in exactly the opposite way than Malthus and the contemporary Malthusians predict. This is also why I can offer to bet that any measure of human welfare will show improvement rather than deterioration.

In 1951, Theodore Schultz, the only Nobel Prize winner in agricultural economics, published an article in the *Economic Journal* called "The Declining Economic Importance of Land." It showed that food production per person was going up because of technological change, and the need for agricultural land was going down—just the opposite of what everybody thought.

Then in 1963 Harold Barnett and Chandler Morse in their book *Scarcity and Growth* showed that despite the widespread worry about limited quantities of raw materials, all the raw materials they studied had over the years become less expensive rather than more expensive relative to consumer goods.

A general process underlies these specific findings. That general process is that, on average, human beings create more than they use in their lifetimes. It has to be so or we would be an extinct species. This process is, as the physicists say, an invariancy. It applies to all metals, all fuels, all food, all measures of human welfare. It applies in all countries. It applies in all times. In other words, this is a theory of all of economic history. This is the theory which I believe explains how these good things can all be happening at once.

A word about appreciation of the environment: some say that people like me don't appreciate nature. Well, I spend more hours outside every year than almost any environmentalist you could name. I'm outdoors nine hours a day, 150 days a year, because I so much appreciate being outside. Two pairs of binoculars are within my reach at all times to look at the birds; I can check on the tens of species that come to the mulberry and to the other trees in my backyard . . . The issue here is not caring about the environment. The issue is caring about human beings.

Response by Norman Myers

There is a lengthy list of points raised by Julian in his opening statement and in his retort just now. I will take them in random order.

First of all, his idea that human welfare has been steadily increasing and will continue to do so right into the future. I have adduced evidence that in many respects, Julian is way off target. I have documented my arguments with backup materials from the World Bank, the United Nations, the National Academy of Sciences, the Rockefeller Foundation, and so forth. Citing these sources (I will be very glad to give you reference details), I show that the number of absolutely impoverished people on Earth has been steadily increasing until they now total 1.2 billion. These are people trying to make out off a cash income of less than one dollar a day. Of these 1.2 billion, 800 million are chronically malnourished, and another 400 million are semi-starving. All these totals have been increasing since 1980.

Next, the question of mass extinction of species—and whether Professor Wilson's book and all the other papers I have mentioned contain evidence which constitutes scientific data or is made up of what Julian calls "anecdotes." In Professor Wilson's chapters on tropical deforestation, he offers data from the remote-sensing agency NASA—data that are as objective, comprehensive, and systematized as one could wish for, with millions of pixels (information points) indicating precisely what is happening on the ground. "Anecdotes"—or reputable data? It is up to you, ladies and gentlemen, to choose. Julian and I could bat the argument back and forth for a long time: you judge for yourselves where the real evidence lies.

Moreover, of the thirty-odd papers I have written on mass extinction of species, two deal with what I call "hot spot" areas, being localities where one fifth of all species are confined to 0.5 percent of the Earth's land surface, and in localities where they face imminent habitat destruction. The two papers' findings are supported by over 600 references in the professional literature, including papers in *Science, Nature, BioScience, American Scientist,* and *Scientific American*—all prominent journals whose editors don't allow scientists to get away with anecdotes.

Next, food intake: Julian has said that it is consistently increasing. But in 1985, the world's grain harvest "plateaued": there was hardly any increase that year. There has been the same unfortunate outcome in virtually every year since 1985. During that same period, the planet has taken on board more than 626 million extra people. The consequence is that food availability per person worldwide has declined by nearly 9 percent. Of course, a lot of people in your country and my country are still getting their calories. But a lot more people around the world are getting fewer and fewer calories. In sub-Saharan Africa, as documented widely by governments and UN agencies, average per capita food production for half a billion people has declined by a whopping one fifth since 1960. Worse, because of environmental degradation such as soil erosion, agricultural experts anticipate that food production in the region will decline by a further one fifth during the next thirty years—a period when the population is projected to double. This hardly accords with the superpositive picture that Julian has been painting for both the past and the future.

Julian says that the price of oil is growing cheaper and

cheaper. Sure it is at the pump. In real terms, Americans are paying less for their gasoline today than sixty years ago (it is even cheaper than bottled water in the supermarket). According to analyses undertaken by professional economists at the World Resources Institute in Washington, D.C., the unpaid costs of burning gasoline, especially pollution costs, total $300 billion a year. That's over $1,000 per American, or more than 5 percent of Gross Domestic Product (GDP). If those externalities were to be internalized—that is, if you paid the real costs of what you are doing when you burn gasoline—you would be forking out not $1.35 per gallon but at least $3.00 per gallon. That real price is going to have to be paid someday. Either you pay it now, or you continue to take a semi-free ride and the price will be paid in the future—but a far greater price, and paid by your children.

In short, the signals we get from the marketplace are indicative. But they are very far from telling us the true price of what we are up to.

Julian has been talking about the price of copper, and how it has been constantly declining. He wrote in 1981 in his book *The Ultimate Resource* that we need never run out of copper because if natural copper were to be used up, we could always make copper from other minerals. Various analyses have been conducted with respect to the engineering and production processes involved. The cheapest one would involve the use of energy (to convert one metal into another) that would amount to ten times the entire energy budget of the United States today, and the price of copper would zoom to 1500 times as much as it is now.

John Ruggie:

Well, ladies and gentlemen, I had hoped for a livelier debate with more disagreement between our speakers about the issues before us.

In a more serious vein, I would like to begin the questioning by probing some of the bases of the differences between our two speakers.

To Julian Simon: Does the difference in scale of humanity's impact on the environment make any difference to your scheme of things? Is it significant, in terms of your mode of analysis, that what we do in terms of our patterns of industrialization, for example, may now affect the global climate as opposed merely to our local environment, as in the past?

Julian Simon:

How does that change enter into my way of thinking? There are two sides to this matter. There's the side about how far away from us we can do damage and there's also the side about how far away we can reap benefits. Yes, the further away we can throw our garbage, the more we've got to be concerned about it—no doubt about that. But, similarly, our capacities to create and to reap benefits at a distance have grown—to an even greater extent.

Consider an example of that creative capacity: 200 years ago in the richest country in the world, France, there frequently were localized famines when people were starving 20 miles away from where there was plenty of food. That's a real environmental problem. We don't have those famines any longer because we now have roads, vehicles, and communications to handle those famines. So yes, we can create problems at a greater distance. But on balance our new planetary capacities leave us better off than if we didn't have this increase in our capacities to affect conditions at a distance.

John Ruggie:

To Norman Myers: Does the fact that various "limits to growth" scenarios that have come out since the early 1970s have been proved wrong empirically make any difference to your scheme of things, to how you view the world?

Norman Myers:

The *Limits to Growth* published by The Club of Rome in 1972 had a number of conceptual errors. It did not allow for feedbacks, whether negative or positive, and to this extent it was a flawed analysis. I still think it served a valuable purpose in opening up a public debate and alerting us to the prospect that there could be all kinds of environmental limits to the way we live on Earth. Whatever its deficiencies, the book was certainly worthwhile.

Today we are learning that our predicament is not so much a case of limits to growth, but of growth of limits. Here are one or two quick examples. I have mentioned that since 1985, our capacity to keep on increasing grain harvests by 3 percent per year has plateaued. Since that time, we have thrown hundreds of billions of dollars at the problem, in the form of more fertilizer, new technologies, and better grain types, yet for some reason we seem to have bumped our heads against the ceiling on that one. We are not able to work the technological trick as we did before. We don't really know why. The problem baffles scientists and technologists. It could well be that our crops are reaching some kind of photosynthetic limit. You put 1 ton of fertilizer per acre on a crop and it flourishes; 2 tons and it flourishes still more; 5 tons, it flourishes yet again; 10 tons, no change because there is a limit to the amount of fertilizer that a crop can absorb.

Another example of limits lies with land availability. Costa Ricans have been accustomed to land abundance for 400 years. But in just the last decade, farmers have expanded their croplands until they have reached both seas and both frontiers. In every corner of the country, they have suddenly run out of new land to open up for agriculture. So land abundance has suddenly switched to land shortage. Farmers have encountered a critical limit, and they are finding it very hard to cope with.

Still another limit, this time in the social field and related to population growth. Because of extended population growth in the past, the developing world is going to have to generate nearly 40 million jobs every single year for the next several decades just to keep up with population growth, let alone to relieve the roughly 30 percent unemployment and underemployment. The developing world as a whole has an economy only three fifths the size of the United States'. Your country often finds it tough to produce another 2 million jobs each year, yet the developing world is going to have to try to produce nearly 20 times as many. So here is another critical limit.

Questions from the Audience

Q: I've listened very carefully to both of you and in your arguments I think you make very different assumptions about both geography and time scale. By geography, I mean the difference between the developing South and the developed North. In the South, a population explosion is cutting caloric consumption. The European Community, on the other hand, has a problem with the overproduction of European and to some extent U.S. farmers. The question seems to be one of time scale: Is there enough time for humans to solve their environmental problems, or will we reach a critical period before the problems can be solved?

Julian Simon:

You say that in the developing world the story of nutrition, life expectancy, and standard of living is different than in the developed world—and getting worse. All I can do is offer to bet. Pick any part of the world you want. Pick any country you want. Pick nutrition. Pick life expectancy. Pick the standard of living. Pick any measure of human welfare you want. Pick any year in the future. I will bet with you a substantial amount (to go to charity if I win) that the condition will be better rather than worse than now, because the trend in the past until now shows conditions getting better rather than worse.

Q: In what time span?

Julian Simon:

Not in every single place, not in every single time span, but on the average. That's why I can afford to bet. Pick any time span you want—ten years, twenty years, five years. Obviously for one year you can't see much happening. But in five or ten years one can observe change. My children will be empowered to pay off if I lose. Pick any time span you want. Pick any place you want. Pick any resource. What more can I say?

Norman Myers:

In response to the question about global generalizations and predictions versus the tremendous diversity in the world (geographically, culturally, economically), I think we have to be more specific in our assumptions. For instance, there is a great deal of difference between your country and mine even though we speak the same language. The Atlantic is a very wide place—socially, economically, and politically. I would still say, however, that we can make some big generalizations. China and India between them comprise two fifths of humankind, and they are both afflicted by grand-scale poverty. At the same time, let's note that southeastern China is booming, following in the track of Hong Kong. So there can be differences within a generalization.

When it comes to generalized extrapolations, I feel we should be extra careful. We need to be wary of saying that because things have constantly improved in the past (as Julian sees it), they will continue that way in the future. Unless we take clear account of covert costs of apparent economic progress in the past, we can hardly say that things will continue to improve in the future. It is like jumping out of a fifteenth-floor window, and saying as you pass the tenth floor, "Everything's fine so far."

To reiterate, I believe there is much evidence we are at a breakpoint in the human enterprise. We are no longer producing enough additional food each year. We are running short of more arable land, we are desertifying existing farmlands, and so on. When we generalize about the world in big-picture terms, we can simplify to some extent—but we must be very careful not to oversimplify.

Q: I'd like to address a question to Mr. Simon. You used what I thought was a form of logic which bordered on the wildly perverse when you said we needn't really worry about our environment because all the problems of the past have caused us to find solutions that have made us better. You used the example of penicillin. As a student here who is striving to become an effective public manager, I wonder whether you think we should then let things like racial hatred and disease and other problems that are plaguing us just continue to escalate as a quicker way for us to find an eventual solution to them?

Julian Simon:

Let me correct a misapprehension. I have never said that we don't need to worry about anything. We need to worry about everything, in the same sense that you had to worry whether you'd get here on time, whether there'll be enough food in your kitchen for next week, and so on. The world needs the best efforts of us all.

I'm saying that the result of all of this worry—and of your constructive work, of your throwing your life into trying to do good things for the world and for other people—is that on balance you will create more than you will use in your lifetime, and you will leave the world a little better place than before, on average. So, while we all need to worry, we can forecast that the result of all the worries will be that we will wind up better off than we are now.

I don't preach complacency. And certainly in my own life I don't think you'll find complacency. We have to struggle like the dickens. But we'll win, we'll overcome.

Can I take a minute to tell a joke, as Norman Myers told a joke about jumping out the window? I think the better story, Norman, is about somebody who has a rope lifeline and falls off the fifteenth floor. Somewhere about thirty feet above the ground, she lets go of the rope. You ask her, "Why did you let go of the rope?" And she answers, "It was going to break anyway." That's how many activists would like us to behave.

Norman Myers:

As I have said, I believe we are at a watershed in human affairs. We need to make unprecedented efforts to address unprecedented threats in terms of the environmental destruction that undercuts our economic resource base—a process aggravated by excessive population growth. At the same time, I firmly believe (or I wouldn't stay in the environmental business, I'd go and sell second-hand cars) that we can get on top of many of our problems before they get on top of us. People sometimes ask me, "How can you remain hopeful when the situation keeps on deteriorating?" That reminds me of the person who defined an optimist and a pessimist. The optimist proclaims, "This is the best of all possible worlds," to which the pessimist responds, "I suspect you're right." But then, I also think of what we have achieved in the past few years—and here is a bet I am totally glad I did not take on. If somebody had said to me in 1989 that by the year 2000 we would get rid of the Berlin Wall, communism, the Soviet Union, and the Cold War, that in the Middle East and South Africa people would really be talking turkey to each other, I'd have said we'd be doing very well to achieve even half of those advances within ten years. When the human mind really addresses itself to problems and looks them right in the eye, and determines just what they amount to through the best scientific evidence available, there's little limit to what we can achieve.

While this doesn't altogether answer the question, I am trying to respond to the questioner.

Q: I'd like to raise the case of California because it gets at Dr. Myers's key point about how quality of life suffers with population growth. California had about 7 million people living in the state in the 1930s, about 25 million in 1980, and today its population is about 31 million people. This incredible growth has had a strong negative effect on the quality of life in California: farmland loss, air pollution, traffic congestion, overwhelmed public schools and hospitals, species extinction, etc. In response, California residents are fleeing the state in record numbers, to Oregon, Colorado, and Utah, for example. As many people are leaving the state each year as are immigrating, which is unprecedented. My question for Dr. Simon is: What is your response to the fact that residents of California, whatever the economic benefits they may have had, are deciding on their own that their quality of life has declined and are voting with their feet by leaving?

Julian Simon:

My first reaction is to ask to see the data. Exactly what numbers are you referring to? The mere fact that people go from one state to another does not mean that something has declined in the state they're leaving. It only means that relative to one place, they preferred someplace else. Preferences differ, and change. Some move out, while others move in. Some people leaving is not by itself an indicator of decline.

What are the indicators you're looking at? You mentioned education, housing, traffic congestion, and so on. Now, we can either make judgments looking backwards or bets toward the future. And I'm prepared to bet you that the years of education per student in California will be higher five or ten years from now, as has been the trend in the past. I'm prepared to bet you that the pupil / teacher ratio will be better—that is, more teachers per student—five or ten years from now, because it is better now than ten years ago or thirty years ago; the pupil / teacher ratio has been falling through the decades. The number of years of education per student has been going up. Even traffic congestion has improved, I'd guess—I'll even bet you that people spend fewer minutes getting to work ten years from now in California on average than they do now.

I don't hear anybody taking me up on the offered bets yet. Not Norman Myers, not anybody. I make this offer in the newspapers and on television, but I don't get any takers. How come?

Norman Myers:

The question is about the quality of life versus quantity of livelihood. Conceivably we could, one distant day, support 10 billion people on this planet if we really stretched things. But why turn the Earth into one giant human feedlot? There's more to the good life than more and more goodies.

Fortunately, a number of economists are addressing this issue. They've recognized that GNP is only a very crude and blunt instrument for measuring human material wealth, let alone human happiness. They have looked at what happens to GNP when you introduce an environmental dimension. When we run down our environment, we build in a number of covert costs. Let me give you an example: Suppose a farmer in Iowa overloads his croplands because he foresees exceptional wheat profits for the year. The resulting profits are registered as an increase in GNP. The next year, in order to compensate for the overloading, he has to apply additional fertilizer and engage in other corrective activities. These are compensatory measures that should be deducted from GNP, but because they are registered as an economic activity, they're actually added to GNP. Economists have found that if we take away those losses rather than adding them to GNP, environmental factors are eliminating as much as 4 percent of GNP in the United States each year. In Germany, it is 4 percent as well; in Mexico, 12 percent; and in Nigeria, 17 percent. Costa Rica has been losing at least one third of its annual economic advance over the last ten years because of environmental problems—a proportion that is rising. By the year 2000, Costa Rica may well be achieving no economic advance—in the sense of real sustainable advance—because of environmental problems. So we need much more refined indicators of what is going on in our economies, rather than just talking about GNP and signals from the marketplace. Marketplace signals are helpful and illuminating, and they tell much truth—but far from the whole truth and nothing but the truth.

Julian Simon:

Norman has gone a long way from the California question and addressed many aspects of the rest of the world. May I say a couple of words about those far-reaching issues; and especially about a matter that he has brought up three or four times? He mentions phenomena that we don't see and are not counting because we can't count them and don't know what they are. Yes, there are hidden phenomena that we know must be there, even though we can't see them. But some can be counted.

Let's take the specific issue of farmland. We know we go on year after year using the same farmland. Yet the farmland becomes ever richer, produces ever more; the state of the environment in those farms, by every measure we have, gets better and better and better. So the notion that there must be some bad things going on there—well, maybe there must be, but we never seem to be able to see them. This has the status of a metaphysical proposition—something we know must be there but we cannot put our hands on—these Iowa farms you're talking about. And with respect to Costa Rica and the bad things happening there: again, let's bet on life expectancy in Costa Rica five or ten years from now, on the nutrition, the standard of living, whatever. You keep coming back to these things that we can't see and we can't measure but we know must be there. *But sometimes we can see them and it's not them, and then we see they are not the way you fear them to be.*

John Ruggie:

I'd like to follow up on this issue because I think it touches something very deep. There may be a fundamental difference of view between the two debaters that one might almost call spiritual. If I may say so, your perspective, Julian, is a sort of utilitarian one. The measures you describe are measures of material improvement. You view the world as an economist, and I don't mean this in a derogatory sense at all—some of my best friends indeed are economists. Now, in Norman's perspective, there is a very different, spiritual world view that we hear as well. It is much more aesthetic and seems to me to be drawing on a biological ethic: The things you can't measure, the things you can't see, but the things you suspect that we ought to be taking into account. Would either of you like to comment on that?

Julian Simon:

I don't think I am as you describe me. I don't like to swat flies and squash spiders, I'd much rather shoo them out of the house. The notion that one of us has more of a feeling for some aspects of nature or the environment, which explains what we say . . . I don't think that explains our differences at all. Yes, if the fly or the mosquito is about to bite me, I'd prefer to hit it first. But I don't think that Mr. Myers and I stand in different relation ships spiritually to nature or to anything else that accounts for our views. I think that what does account for our views is this: I consistently look at the evidence of the past and I look at the longest possible data series, and I examine what has happened and I extrapolate that into the future. In contrast, instead of looking at the historical evidence of the past, Norman (in common with most biologists and many people on his side of the fence) looks at a set of theoretical propositions about phenomena that "must" be happening based on supposed physical, chemical, or biological principles. That I believe is the difference. His is a speculative analysis of what *must* happen versus my empirical analysis of what *has* happened over the long sweep of history. That I believe is the fundamental difference between us.

Norman Myers:

In the early 1970s there was a little talk about what acid rain from our factories and automobiles might eventually do to fisheries, lakes, and forests. The talk was almost entirely dismissed. Skeptics said, "Where is the evidence? How is it precisely going to work out? Show us the mechanism." Then by 1975 we found a whole lot of acid rain damage emerging in North America and Western Europe. Around the same time, Dr. Joe Farmer, a meteorologist at the University of Cambridge in my country, said that if we kept emitting CFCs into the atmosphere, they would eat up ozone to the extent that the ozone layer would be seriously depleted. People said to him, "Joe, what is the exact mechanism? How is it precisely going to work out?" And he said, "I can't tell you exactly, but I do anticipate it." Many critics responded, "Rubbish, nonsense"—until the mid-1980s, when the evidence became all too plain.

Today, we should be asking ourselves what new acid rains, what new ozone-layer depletion, and what other new problems of similar sort are building up because of the way we are pummeling our planet as if with impunity—waiting to jump out of the woodwork to levy their emphatic price at some stage down the road.

There's no doubt that we operate in a situation of very great uncertainty. We are conducting a global-scale experiment with our planet. We know very little about the outcome. The experiment is entirely unplanned. Indeed, we operate in a situation of immense uncertainty. Julian has *some* justification in saying to me, "Why don't you demonstrate your doubts concisely, with a hundred percent certainty? Why aren't you completely specific and definite in your assertions?" I respond again, we operate in a situation of deepseated uncertainty. Many factors can't be quantified, not every last parameter. But let us not get so hung up with what can be counted if that is to the detriment of what also counts. Would it not be better for us to find down the road, ten years or fifty years hence, that we have been roughly right rather than exactly wrong?

Q: I'm from New Jersey, and would like to ask the debaters about a problem in my state. We've had a lot of development and according to the state Department of Environmental Protection, fresh water is being drawn from the underground water table faster than it's being replenished by natural means. The implication is that there will be less drinking water available to New Jersey residents. How should I look at this phenomenon in terms of your world views?

Norman Myers:

Being from England, I am not much acquainted with the water situation in New Jersey. I offer a parallel analysis. Consider what is happening to freshwater stocks in many parts of the world. In your Great Plains, the Ogallala aquifer, which supplies irrigation water to a large part of your great grain belt, is becoming overexploited at a rate which is, I believe, forty times greater than the rate of natural replenishment. So your farmers are going through a one-time and short-lived bonanza. Some people might say, "Well, technology always comes up with a substitute." We haven't found a substitute for water yet. It will not be long before those farmers find themselves short of a vital resource.

Water shortages in many other parts of the world are becoming acute. In the Indian subcontinent, northern China, much of sub-Saharan Africa, northeastern Brazil, and many other places, people are having to make out with less water, in fact with half of what hydrologists and public health officials consider is a minimum to maintain basic human decency standards. We hear a lot about energy shortages and food shortages. We don't hear very much about water shortages, even though it's becoming a pervasive phenomenon, including parts of your own country, along with Egypt, Israel, Jordan, India, Pakistan, and dozens of other countries.

Julian Simon:

Being originally from New Jersey myself, I share your concern about the state. If the water level is sinking, there is a problem. (Indeed, the world is full of problems. And it's going to be full of problems in the future, local problems and temporary problems.) If the water level is low in New Jersey, people are going to worry about the problem. And chances are that because of their worry, the drinking water situation in New Jersey will be better five years from now and ten years from now than it is now. Why do I think so? Because the water supplies of the United States, decade after decade, have been getting better rather than worse.

Here is some evidence that unfortunately runs only up to 1974—Environmental Protection Agency data on the conditions at all the monitoring stations in the United States. In 1961, 42 percent of the monitoring stations in the United States had water which was good, measured good by EPA criteria. By 1974 the proportion good was up to 61 percent. So chances are, based on all the evidence of history, that the drinking water in New Jersey will be better ten years from now than now. And I'm prepared to bet that it will be so, of course.

Norman Myers:

And what's the quality of the water when the well runs dry?

Julian Simon:

Well, you see, again here we have the difference in our basic views. Norman's view is "It cannot go on like this, it's impossible, the well must eventually run dry." In contrast, I say that all throughout human history people have thought they have been at the breaking point that Norman Myers think we're at now. Again and again you read in history: We're at the switching point at this moment. But it has never been so.

Norman Myers says that we cannot go on this way forever. Nevertheless, the evidence of history is that these positive trends have indeed gone on forever all throughout our history. And there's no reason that I know of why this cannot continue to go on forever.

Here are some data from Mr. Myers's own country. One hundred fifty years ago, 300 years ago, people used to worry terribly in England about smoke in the air. And for good reason: it was awful in London, as you can see in Figure 6. Now look at the average smoke levels at Kew Gardens observatory near London during October to March from 1922 to 1970–71 in Figure 7. The smoke levels have been going down, down, down. The air was awful early on, but became less and less awful.

Here's another measurement from Kew in Figure 7: the average hours of winter sunshine. Decade after decade, from 1946 to 1985, there was more and more sunshine each day, not

Figure 6. Estimated Decadal Mean Smoke and Sulphur Dioxide Concentrations in London, 1585–1940

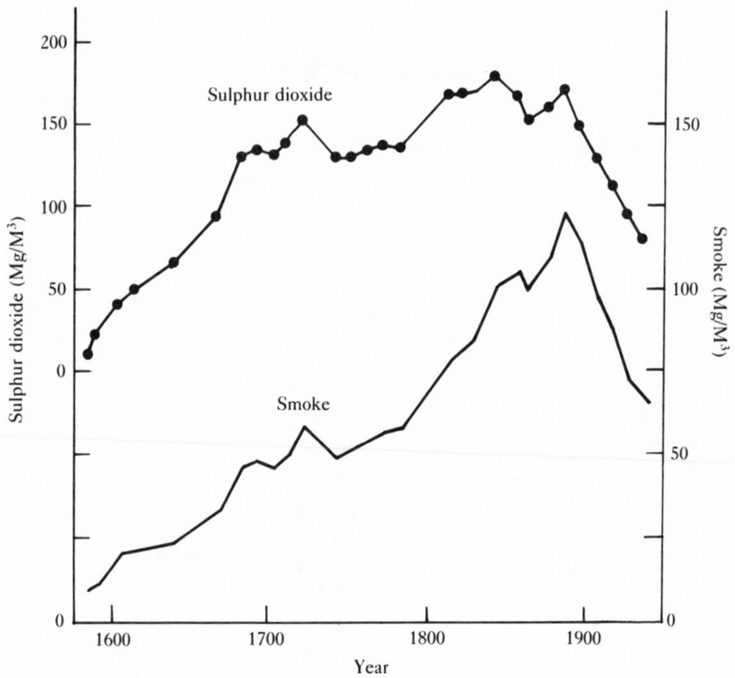

Source: Derek Elsom, "Atmospheric Pollution Trends in the United Kingdom," in Simon, ed., *The State of Humanity* (forthcoming).

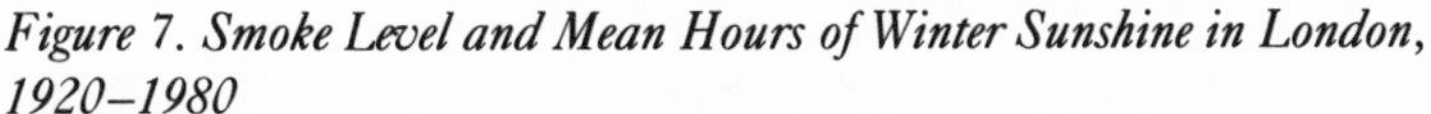

Figure 7. Smoke Level and Mean Hours of Winter Sunshine in London, 1920–1980

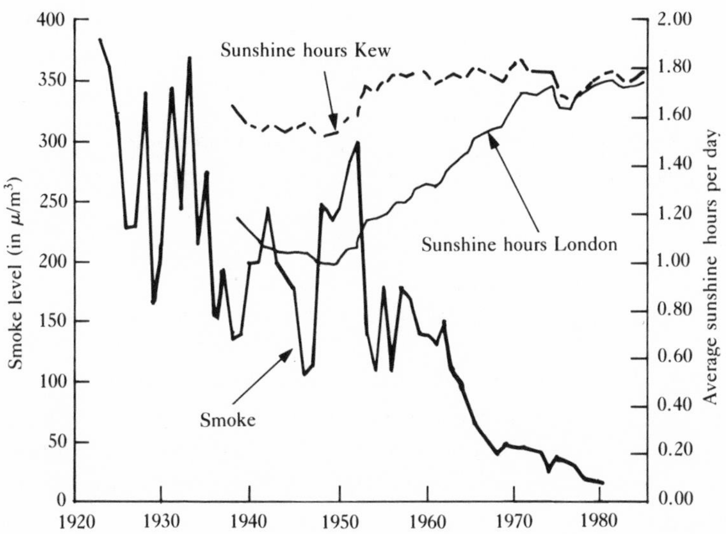

Source: Derek M. Elsom, *Atmospheric Pollution Trends in the United Kingdom;* Peter Brimblecombe and Rohde Henning, *Air Pollution—Historical Trends, Durability of Building Materials.* 5 (1988), pp. 291–308.

because the sun was shining more brightly but because the smog was going down and you could get more sunshine. So despite the fact that people were wringing their hands then just like they are wringing their hands now, things have been getting better and better. That's why I say it will be better in the future—I can't be one hundred percent sure, but sure enough for me to bet on.

Q: Dr. Simon, you claim that population growth is not a problem because increasing population will lead to an increase in genius which will solve our problems. But in heavily populated developing countries like India or China, which have such basic infrastructure problems, wouldn't it be better for them to maintain a steady population, and borrow the technology from the West to solve their problems, rather than attempt to create their own solutions?

Julian Simon:

It seems as if a small country could simply do no research and development, and simply hang onto the coattails of other countries. But like so many logical-seeming propositions, life doesn't turn out that way. It would seem, for example, that all you have to do to increase your agriculture in India is bring in soybeans from the United States and plant them in India. It does not work out that way because the angle of the sun is different in India than where they grow soybeans in the United States. So there must be research-and-development agricultural teams in India to adopt the technology from abroad. Hanging onto the coattails of other countries is not as easy as it might seem.

India's fundamental problem is its economic and political framework. It has failed to give sufficient economic freedom to agriculturalists and to business people to free up their creative energies. With economic freedom, India might take off like a rocket. That's why India is as poor as it is now. Nevertheless, India is much better off than it was in the past—life expectancy is greater, purchasing power is greater, the middle class is much larger . . . but with economic freedom, improvement would happen a lot faster.

Q: What is the model of change that each of you is promoting? I think we're under the illusion that Mr. Simon is promoting no change and Mr. Myers is promoting some kind of change. Both of you seem to be saying that the answer lies in working harder at our scientific, political, and economic problems, and coming up with answers. But neither of you has addressed a cultural change that many would say is the reason we're in a mess today; that is, that we are working so much harder and consuming so much more than we have in the past.

Norman Myers:

I do believe that change is coming. It will be change because we choose to change, or because change is imposed upon us by force of circumstances. This contrasts with what you are saying, Julian. If I understand you rightly, you are saying that in every respect the future will always be the same as before, only more so and better so. I believe that the future will be fundamentally different from what we've ever known. It *doesn't* have to be a lot worse. But I suspect that if we don't change very quickly, especially in terms of public policy, it will become a great deal worse.

Many people have difficulty in registering rapid change—change that builds up momentum covertly and then suddenly erupts. They say, "I can smoke cigarettes with impunity. I have been all right for ten or twenty years, so why should I get lung cancer?" And then a few years down the road, they're in deep trouble.

A lot of our environmental problems are like cancer. If they were akin to heart attacks, we'd rush our environments off to the intensive-care unit at the hospital and get them fixed up. Environmental problems also remind me of the experiment the schoolchildren conducted with a frog. They took the frog and dropped it into a saucepanful of boiling water. The frog reacted to this instantly hostile environment by skipping out. It was a bit scalded, but it was okay, it survived. The children then took the same frog and dropped it into another saucepan, this time full of cold water. They placed the saucepan on the stove and turned the heat up. The frog swam around and around, thinking, "This is a fine environment, this is what I am accustomed to." The water grew a little warmer, and the frog thought, "Better still, what an improvement." The water got warmer still: "Things are getting better and better minute by minute."

The water got hotter again, and the frog grew drowsy until it fell into a coma—and boiled to death. The world outside our window is our saucepan heating up. Do we have the capacity to recognize what is going on?

We live in 1992 with the evolutionary equipment between our ears that sufficed us while the human species was spending 2 million years with a hunter-gatherer lifestyle. Humans had to think in terms of a hunting band of fifty people and to sharpen their spears for tomorrow's hunt. Those people who could do that were the ones who survived through natural selection. Today, by contrast, we have to think in terms of a hunting band of 5 billion people and an endless long line of tomorrows. We might find our prey has suddenly become much scarcer than we have been accustomed to in the past. We might also find that the surrounding hunting areas are turning into desert and can't support much prey at all. These and many other changes add up to one very big change overtaking us. I do wonder whether we have the capacity, the instant responses, to respond to this entirely new situation.

At the same time, I remain hopeful that if we recognize the nature of the challenge in its full scope, then there is scant limit to what humankind can accomplish when it sets itself to a task. What we need to do is to eliminate the Berlin walls of ignorance, indifference, and incapacity, so that we can respond fast enough to the challenges of those walls that we've built into our minds for a long time. A very big challenge indeed. I believe we can still take it on—and that it will all turn out to be a tremendous adventure for us in the world outside the window, for the societies in which we live as well as for each of us individually. It's going to be an experience like humans have never encountered in the whole of human history.

Julian Simon:

Now comes a switch in tunes: Norman Myers has just spoken to you in a hopeful fashion, and I'm going to speak to you in a pessimistic fashion. I believe the future will be better materially. But I do not believe the future will necessarily be better in other ways. In fact, I'm pessimistic for the intermediate run with respect to many aspects of our lives. The questioner referred to the mess that we supposedly are in, despite the fact the world is in better shape in all measurable material ways than ever before. And I believe that that very mood—the pessimism that accompanies the belief that things are bad—is going to increase as we focus more and more away from problems of how we can beat away the wild beasts and keep ourselves alive, and how we can grow enough and keep ourselves alive. Instead, we increasingly focus on one group versus another group, struggles where there has to be a loser. One gender, one race must lose as another wins. I am very pessimistic about this unless we can find some radically different arena for our energies in the future than these intergroup struggles.

That brings me to the matter of change. I don't think you'll find many people who are more radically in favor of change than I am. I've been struggling to change things small and large all my life. In fact, pick up the *Wall Street Journal* today [October 14, 1992], look at the Op-Ed page, and you'll see a change I struggled for for twelve years and managed to get done despite the advice, "You can't change this, your idea is ridiculous." A lot of you have been on airlines when they ask for volunteers because the plane was oversold. I invented that system in the 1960s. Because I believe in change, I wanted to radically change the airline industry. I wrote that, instead of arbitrarily telling people to get off because the plane was overbooked, there should be a market system—a radical change. And eventually it got done. I'm for such radical changes. I'm for radical changes in the education market in the United States—vouchers and the like. I'm for radical change in China, allowing people to have economic freedom so that they can put their energies to work and bring their talents to fruition. That's big change, and I'm for that. I'm for even bigger change in the sense that instead of fighting against each other politically, we should put our energies to work terra-forming Mars, making it possible for human beings to live there. (There, by the way, is a real environmentalist's nightmare. Plans for terra-forming Mars include using mirrors to etch canals on Mars, and the like. Poor unsuspecting Mars. That's something to start environmentalists screaming.) Those are the kinds of radical changes I'm for. We need such big goals psychologically. In their absence, I'm pessimistic.

Closing Statement by Julian Simon

In the short run, all resources are limited. An example of such a finite resource is the amount of time allotted to me to speak. The longer run, however, is a different story. The standard of living has risen along with the size of the world's population since the beginning of recorded time. There is no convincing economic reason why these trends toward a better life should not continue indefinitely.

The key theoretical idea is this: The growth of population and of income create actual and expected shortages, and hence lead to price run-ups. A price increase represents an opportunity that attracts profit-minded entrepreneurs to seek new ways to satisfy the shortages. Some fail, at cost to themselves. A few succeed, and the final result is that we end up better off than if the original shortage problems had never arisen. That is, we need our problems, though this does not imply that we should purposely create additional problems for ourselves.

I hope that you will now agree that the long-run outlook is for a more abundant material life rather than for increased scarcity, in the United States and in the world as a whole. Of course such progress does not come about automatically. And my message certainly is not one of complacency. In this I agree with the doomsayers—that our world needs the best efforts of all humanity to improve our lot. I part company with them in that they expect us to come to a bad end despite the efforts we make, whereas I expect a continuation of humanity's history of successful efforts. And I believe that their message is self-fulfilling, because if you expect your efforts to fail as a result of inexorable natural limits, then you are likely to feel resigned; and therefore to literally resign. But if you recognize the possibility—in fact the probability—of success, you can tap large reservoirs of energy and enthusiasm.

Adding more people causes problems, but people are also the means to solve these problems. The main fuel to speed the world's progress is our stock of knowledge, and the brakes are (a) our lack of imagination, and (b) unsound social regulations of these activities. The ultimate resource is people—especially skilled, spirited, and hopeful young people endowed with liberty—who will exert their wills and imaginations for their own benefit, and so inevitably will benefit not only themselves but the rest of us as well. Thank you.

Closing Statement by Norman Myers

Ladies and gentlemen, I do hope that during the course of this evening we have found that some of the issues have been clarified. I say this because there is a lot of misunderstanding around, like some of the statements about population. Recall that frequently quoted verse in Genesis, "Go forth and multiply"—an injunction issued when the population of the world was two.

I have learned a lot this evening. I have much to chew over, especially as concerns the questions that you yourselves have raised from the floor. You have suggested to me, if I am hearing you right, that you believe there is more to our situation than just measurement of human material welfare via indices of the marketplace with its limited capacity to tell the entire truth today. More important still, I believe that our future is going to be fundamentally different from anything we have known in the past. In this respect, I contrast basically and profoundly with you, Julian. I go along with the 1992 statement of the National Academy of Sciences in Washington and the British Royal Society in London, to the effect that due to grand-scale environmental problems and excessive population growth, the future of our planet is in the balance and we are running the risk of undermining the very capacity of Earth to support life itself. To repeat, this was a statement produced by a very sober-sided group of scientists.

We are going to have to change. We shall either change voluntarily because we choose to do so, or change because change will be imposed upon us—a rather unhappy sort of change. At the same time, I feel that we still have time to transform profound problems into magnificant opportunities. To do that, we shall have to recognize the full scale and scope of our problems; and we shall not only have to bring to bear what we have between our ears (which Julian has rightly described as a remarkable resource), but to mobilize something else in our beings which I have heard some of you raising in your comments and questions. There's something here that appeals not just to our brains, but—I make no bones about this, let's use the big word—to our hearts as well. We are trying to make a judgment tonight on what our future is going to be. By next week, let alone next month or next year, the mountains of statistics and pieces of data you have heard tonight will have faded off your mental radar screens. You will be left with an impression—an impression that will reflect the whole of what you are, the whole of what makes you human.

We have to make a judgment about how far we are to take responsibility for future generations extending for millions of years. We have the capacity right now to impoverish the Earth to a degree that has not been available to any other human community in the whole course of human history. But we also have the capacity to save the Earth at a time of unprecedented risk—no less. Just as we can eliminate species in a way no other individual species has ever accomplished, we can also save species, save them in their millions if we so wish. We can not only devastate the planetary ecosystem, as we seem bent on doing in many respects. We can save the planetary ecosystem at a time of possibly terminal threat as concerns the future of human life.

This is a challenge, I suggest, that will eventually leave us feeling we are standing ten feet tall as we match up to the glorious challenge. We have the capacity to become giants of the human condition as we stand at a breakpoint in the whole course of human history.

If it's difficult to recognize a breakpoint like this (remember the frog), recall the 1992 statement from the National Academy of Sciences. No scientific community has ever used language and propositions of that sort since science started up 5,000 years ago. We are actually putting the future of our planet in the balance.

At the same time, I believe that if we recognize the prospect for what it truly is, then we shall find ourselves ready to get to grips with it. We shall eliminate the Berlin walls of indifference and ignorance and incapacity to respond. We shall do the job—and while doing it, we shall have a great time.

Frankly—and this is the bottom-line message that I want to leave with you—I thank my lucky stars that I am alive right now. I'd much rather be around today than in the Golden Age of Greece, or Elizabethan England, or Pioneer America. This is because the scale of the issues we have to deal with is far greater than any other human community has ever confronted in the past.

People in the past have not faced what we face because the problems were just not there. No human community in the future will ever have our chance to save the planetary ecosystem because if we don't master the problems, they'll have nothing left to do but to pick up the pieces we pass on to them. Shall we not count ourselves, then, a privileged generation?

As I say, I feel fortunate beyond dreams to be living right now. Just as, ladies and gentlemen, I count myself delighted to have had this opportunity to cross the ocean, to participate in this debate, and to share with you my thoughts and feelings and to hear your views. I have thoroughly enjoyed the evening, and I hope you have enjoyed it too. I trust you have learned much along the way, as I have—and that you will go out of the door feeling that, after hearing what we have both said, there's still realistic hope out there. Thank you.

Post-Debate Statement

Norman Myers

Rebuttals to Julian Simon

In his pre-debate statement, Simon opposes the overwhelming consensus of leading experts in the fields of population, environment, and development.

1. Population

Simon makes great play with the 1986 statement of the National Academy of Sciences, to the effect that population growth has little if any adverse impact on economic growth. He does not mention the Academy's 1992 statement with its assertion that population growth, in conjunction with environmental ruin (to which it "unquestionably" contributes), puts "the future of our planet in the balance." Fortunately at least 90 percent of developing world citizens live in countries that have long decided their population growth rates should be brought down forthwith. During the decade 1983–92, however, the United States government, strongly prompted by Simon, offered less support for family planning in developing countries than during previous times—to the keen frustration of more than 100 countries clamoring for expanded support. In fact, the United States spent less on family planning than on Halloween costumes. Partly as a result of the fall-off in U.S. support, more developing world women died of pregnancy-related problems than women and men combined died of AIDS.[1] This has been all the more regrettable in that we are now headed toward the high rather than the medium population projection of the United Nations (Table 1, and Figures 1a and 1b).

Further, Simon states that "The economics profession has turned almost completely away from the previous judgment that population growth is a crucial negative factor in economic development." Check leading economists with a contrary position, e.g., Kenneth Boulding, former president of the American Economics Association, Tom Schelling, outgoing president of the association, and Trygve Haavelmo, Nobel Prize winner in Economics, among many others.[2] Instead of references to support his position, Simon merely speaks of "two dozen competent statistical studies": readers need details of these studies if they are to evaluate them.

"On average, countries whose populations grew faster did not grow slower economically": might they not have grown faster economically if they had not been burdened with population growth that often wiped out half their per capita economic growth? Per capita growth of the world economy has not kept up with population growth for well over two decades (Table 2).

"People create more resources of all kinds. . . . When schoolhouses become crowded, we build new schools—more modern than the old ones." In countries with a population growth rate of 2.5 percent, as is the average for parts of the developing world containing well over 1 billion people, governments must double their schools—also houses, food, water and energy supplies, jobs, health facilities, etc.—every twenty-eight years just to stay even. The record shows they simply have not been keeping up.[3]

Simon likewise asserts that "The most important benefit of population size and growth is the increase it brings to the stock

Table 1. World Population Projections, 1990–2100
(billions)

	Impact of varying fertility assumptions on population growth				
Year	*Low* 1.8 children per woman by 2025; 1.7 by 2100	*Medium* 2.3 children per women by 2025; 2.1 by 2100	*High* 2.8 children per woman by 2025; 2.5 by 2100	*Instant Replacement-Level Fertility* Were fertility to have dropped in 1990 to 2.1 children per woman	*Constant Fertility* Fertility stays at 1990 level of 4.3 children per woman until 2025
1990	5.3	5.3	5.3	5.3	5.3
2000	6.1	6.3	6.4	5.8	6.5
2025	7.6	8.5	9.4	7.1	11.0
2050	7.8	10.0	12.5	7.7	21.2
2075	7.1	10.8	15.7	7.9	46.3
2100	6.0	11.2	19.2	8.1	109.4

Source: Long-Range World Populations: Two Centuries of Population Growth, 1959–2150 (United Nations, New York, 1992), Sales No. E.92.XIII.3.

Figure 1a. Momentum of Population Growth

Ultimate Stable World Population Size Depending on When the Two-Child Family Becomes the Norm

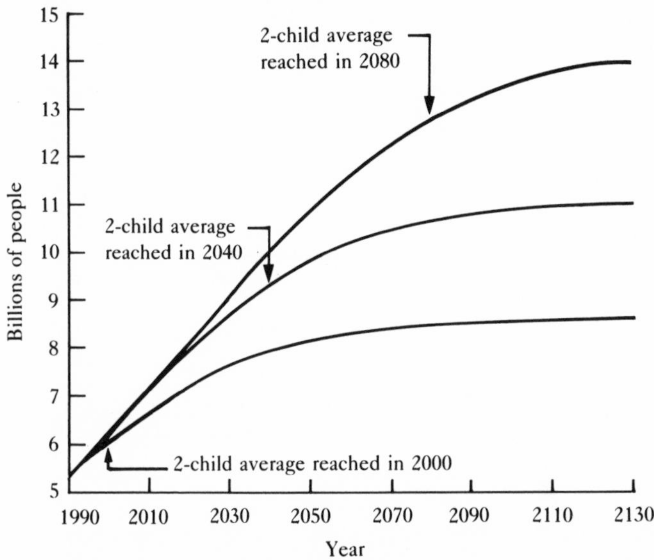

The crucial factor is the pace of fertility decline in the near future. Each 20-year delay in establishing replacement-level fertility, i.e., an average of 2.1 children per woman, will add at least 1 billion to the world's population size when it ultimately stabilizes at zero growth.

Note: Two-child average family size = replacement-level fertility, or an average of 2.1 children per woman with low mortality.

Source: C. Haub, M. M. Kent, and M. Yanagishita. *World Population Data Sheet 1990* (Population Reference Bureau, Washington, D.C., 1990).

of useful knowledge." If that were true, we would see a paragon of economic advancement in India with its 900 million people, yet a per capita GNP of only $350; during the past quarter century, India's citizens have grown richer by an average of $6 per year. The region with the highest population growth rates, Sub-Saharan Africa, has lost one fifth of its per capita GNP

Figure 1b. Slowing Population Growth by Meeting Family Planning Needs, 1950–2100

Effect of Family Planning Programs and of Avoiding All Unwanted Births on Developing Country Population Growth

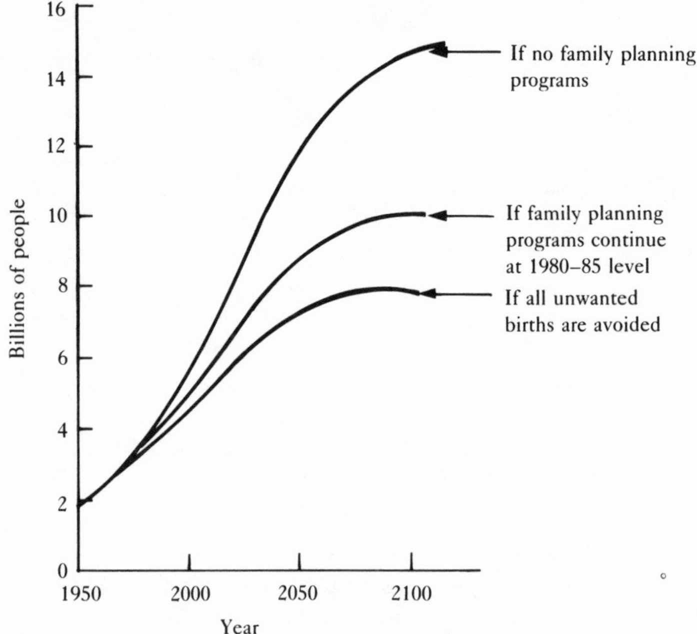

If family planning programs continue at their level of impact in 1980–85, they will reduce population growth by more than 4 billion by the year 2100. Expanded programs, which help couples to make sure that all births are wanted births, will reduce population growth by more than another 2 billion, assuming that women's desired fertility stays at current levels.

Source: J. Bongaarts, W. P. Mauldin, and J. F. Phillips. "The Demographic Impact of Family Planning Programs." *Studies in Family Planning* 21(6) (1990): 299–310.

Table 2. World Population and Economic Growth by Decade, 1950–1992

Decade	*Annual Growth of World Economy (%)*	*Annual Growth per Person (%)*	*Annual Growth of World Population (%)*
1950–60	4.9	3.1	2.0
1960–70	5.2	3.2	2.2
1970–80	3.4	1.6	2.0
1980–90	2.9	1.1	1.8
1990–92	0.6	−1.1	1.7

Sources: World Economic Outlook October 1992 (International Monetary Fund, Washington, D.C., 1992); and L. R. Brown, and eleven others. *State of the World 1993* (W. W. Norton, New York, 1992).

since 1980.[4] Contrast countries with small populations and virtually zero population growth, e.g., the Netherlands, Switzerland, and Sweden, which are among the most prosperous in the world.

Simon speaks of "our newfound capacity to support human life—healthily, and with fast-increasing access to opportunity all over the world." The number of people in absolute poverty is now 1.2 billion; of people chronically malnourished, 800 million; and of semi-starving, 400 million—all totals that have been increasing steadily for more than a decade, with no improvement in sight.[5]

2. Raw Materials

Simon states that "Raw materials—all of them—are becoming more available rather than more scarce . . . as measured by the economically meaningful indicator of cost or price of copper, which is representative of all raw materials." Yet at least one person in five of today's global community lives off a cash income of a dollar at most per day, so they are effectively shut

Table 3. People in Absolute Poverty, 1990

Region	*Number (millions)*	*% of Regional Population*	*% of All People in Absolute Poverty*
Middle East and North Africa	75	28	6
Sub-Saharan Africa	325	62	27
Latin America	150	35	12
Asia	675	25	55
Total	1225	23*	100

*Percent of world population.

Note: The 1990 total of 1.2 billion has increased from 944 million in 1970 and is projected to reach, without massive corrective measures, 1.3 billion by the year 2000 and 1.5 billion by 2025.

Sources: A. B. Durning. *Poverty and the Environment: Reversing the Downward Spiral* (Worldwatch Institute, Washington, D.C. 1989); R. W. Kates and V. Haarmann. *Poor People and Threatened Environments: Global Overviews, Country Comparisons and Local Studies*. (The Alan Shawn Feinstein World Hunger Program, Brown University, Providence, RI, 1991); and *Long-Range Population Projections: Two Centuries of Population Growth, 1959–2150* (United Nations, New York, 1992), Sales No. E.92.XIII.3.

out of the marketplace; and another one person in five manages only about twice as much of a cash income, hence they are able to register only a minuscule vote in the marketplace (Table 3 and Figure 2).[6] A long-run decrease in the price of wheat and other grains is of scant interest to those who cannot buy them, even though they are the ones most in need of affordable food. As for copper, the world price (as opposed to the price just in the United States) has risen in constant 1980 dollars from $1,970 per ton in 1975 to $2,166 in 1989.[7]

Many other raw materials are becoming scarcer per person; for instance, food and arable / irrigated land (see my pre-debate statement), and household water and fuelwood, among other

Figure 2. Global Economic Disparities, 1989

Distribution of economic activity: percentages of world total (quintiles of population ranked by income)

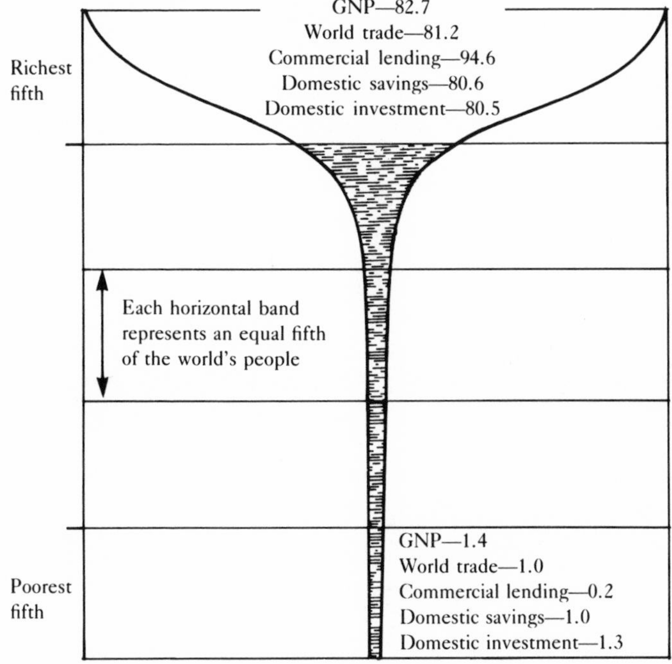

Source: United Nations Development Programme (UNDP). *Human Development Report 1992* (Oxford University Press, New York, 1992).

essentials of daily life. In many developing countries, the per capita daily water consumption for household needs averages half of what an American uses each time he or she flushes the toilet. The problem is projected to grow worse for several more decades if only because of population growth (Figure 3 and Table 4).[8] Water shortages cause major diseases, including 150 million cases of schistosomiasis, 200 million cases of diarrhea, and 300 million cases of roundworm.[9] The economic cost just

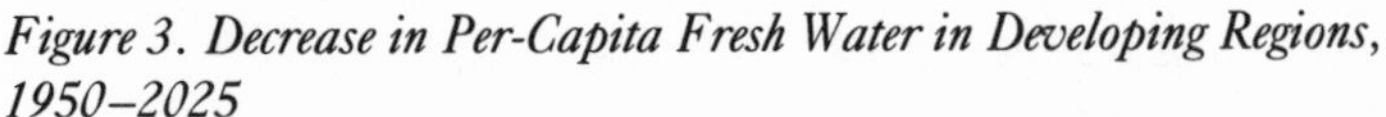

Figure 3. Decrease in Per-Capita Fresh Water in Developing Regions, 1950–2025

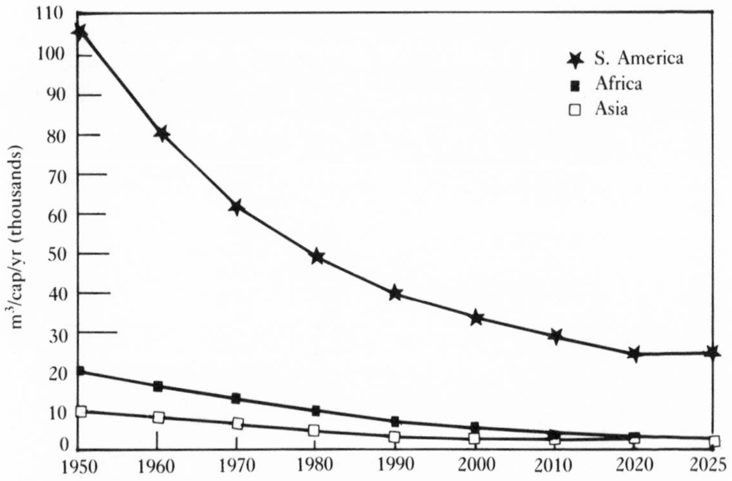

Source: A. Ayibotele and M. Falkenmark. "Fresh Water Recources." In J. C. I. Dooge, *et al. An Agenda of Science for Environment and Development into the 21st Century* (Cambridge University Press, New York, 1992).

through workdays lost to sickness is $125 billion a year, or roughly 10 percent of the Gross Collective Product of the regions in question.[10]

Similarly, fuelwood deficits (Table 4) carry economic costs of at least $50 billion a year, or one third of the collective GNP of the region with the worst fuelwood shortages, Sub-Saharan Africa.[11]

Simon even asserts, "We now have . . . the technology to feed, clothe, and supply energy to an ever-growing population for the next 7 billion years." This would be 1.4 million times longer than since the start of civilization. In support of this remarkable assertion, the amount of evidence and analysis offered by Simon is zero. If we have 1 million years' stock of a resource with fixed supply, and we keep on consuming it at the present rate plus 2 percent to reflect today's population growth

Figure 4. Water Supplies: 1990 and 2025

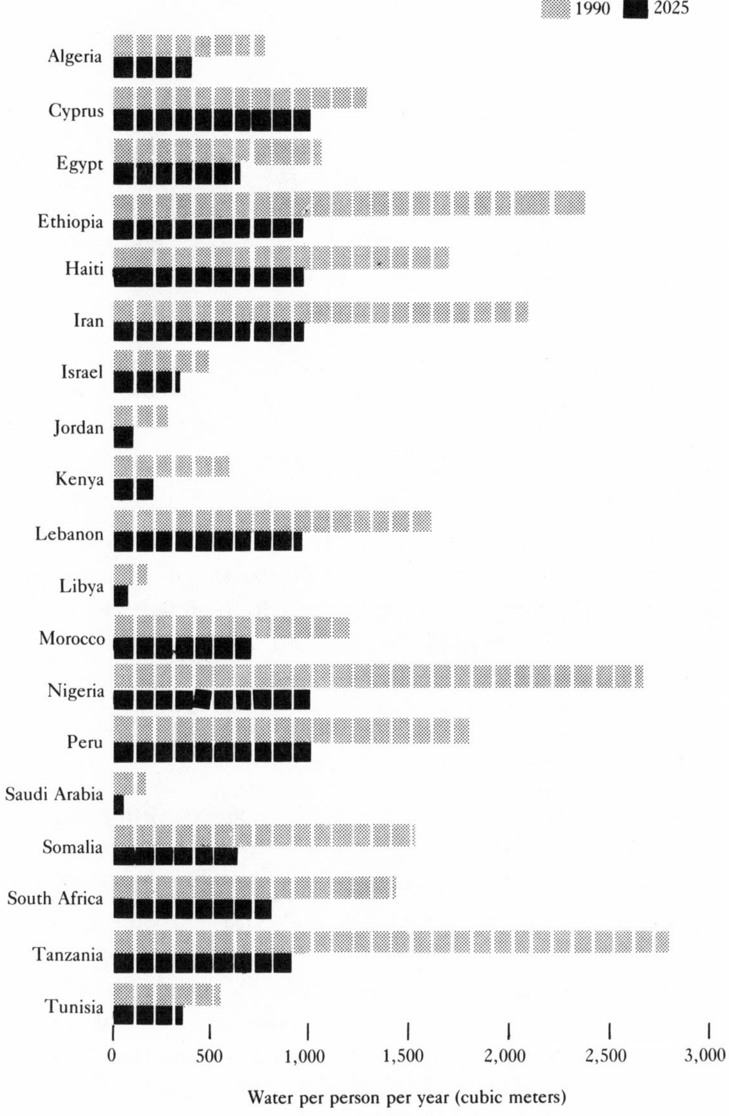

Source: T. F. Homer-Dixon, J. H. Boutwell, and G. W. Rathjens. "Environmental Change and Violent Conflict." *Scientific American* 268(2) (1993): 38–45.

Table 4. Fuelwood Shortages, 1980–2000 (millions of people suffering deficits)

Region	*1980*	*2000 (projected; and % increase)*
Sub-Saharan Africa	146	535 (266)
North Africa and Near East	104	268 (158)
Asia	832	1671 (101)
Latin America	201	512 (155)
Total	1283	2986 (133)

Source: M. K. Tolba, et al., eds. *The World Environment 1972–1992* (Chapman and Hall, London, 1992).

rate and a little expansion of per capita consumption to reflect growing affluence, the length of time the supply would last is 501 years. Moreover, the current population growth rate means we would reach a situation of 1 square meter of ice-free land per person within 600 years.[12]

3. Food Consumption

Contrary to Simon's statement that "Food consumption per person is up over the last thirty years," it is a fact of daily life for billions of developing world people that for almost a whole decade, the increase in grain harvests has consistently fallen behind the increase in human numbers—and grain accounts for roughly 70 percent of people's calories. The result: the amount of grain per person since 1985 has declined by nearly 9 percent worldwide, and by much more for those who most need extra food.[13] (For details, see Table 5.)

More important still is the future outlook, which Simon assures us can only grow better in every respect. Because of ever-worsening population pressures, the amount of cropland

Table 5. World Grain Availability, 1950–1992

Year	Production (mill. tons) & % increase		Per Capita (kgs.) & % change		World Population (millions) & % increase	
1950	631		246		2565	
1960	847	+34.2	278	+13.0	3050	+18.9
1970	1,096	+29.4	295	+6.1	3721	+22.0
1980	1,447	+32.0	323	+9.5	4476	+20.2
1984	1,649	+13.9	344	+6.5	4794	+7.1
1985	1,664	+0.9	341	−0.9	4876	+1.7
1986	1,683	+1.1	339	−0.6	4959	+1.7
1987	1,612	−4.2	319	−5.9	5047	+1.8
1988	1,564	−2.9	304	−4.7	5136	+1.8
1989	1,685	+7.7	322	+5.9	5226	+1.8
1990	1,780	+5.6	335	+4.0	5317	+1.7
1991	1,696	−4.7	314	−6.3	5409	+1.7
1992	1,711	+0.9	312	−0.6	5502	+1.7

In summary, between 1985 and 1992 grain production has increased by only 2.8 percent, population has increased by 12.8 percent, and per capita grain availability has declined by 8.5 percent.

Sources: L. R. Brown, C. Flavin, and H. Kane. *Vital Signs 1992: The Trends That Are Shaping Our Future* (W. W. Norton, New York, 1992); and *World Grain Database* (U.S. Department of Agriculture. Washington, D.C., 1991).

per person is projected to plunge for several decades (Figure 5). Moreover, a "continuing trends" scenario reveals that per capita grain production will decline worldwide from 345 kilograms in 1991 to 280 kilograms in 2050, with marked slumps in all regions of the developing world except China. Even an optimistic scenario foresees a fall-off for the hungriest region today, Africa, from 146 to 131 kilograms per person; the amount needed to maintain normal physical well-being is 170 kilograms.[14] In Sub-Saharan Africa, the food gap is expected to grow from 12 million metric tons today to 50 million tons by the year 2000 and to 250 million tons as early as 2020.[15] (The scope

Figure 5. Cropland Supplies, 1989 and 2025

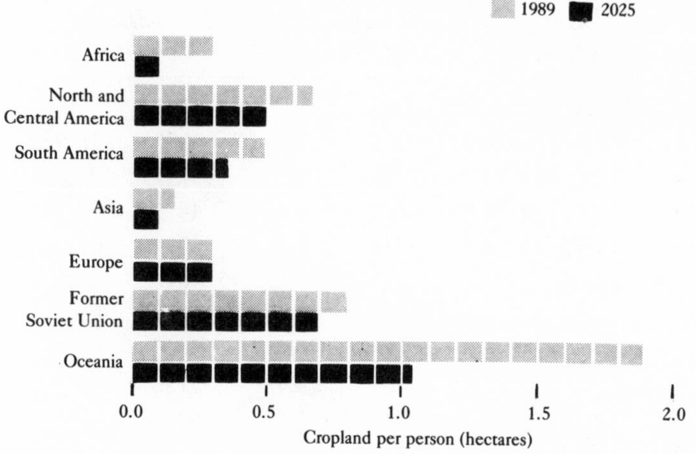

Source: T. F. Homer-Dixon, J. H. Boutwell and G. W. Rathjens. "Environmental Change and Violent Conflict." *Scientific American* 268(2) (1993): 38–45.

for African countries to buy food elsewhere is limited when debt repayments consume half of foreign exchange earnings.) Worse, the amount of food aid available worldwide today is only 12 million tons.

4. Cleanliness of the Environment

Simon claims, "The irrefutable facts are that air in the United States (and in other rich countries) is safer to breathe now than in decades past." Still, 150 million Americans live in areas with air unhealthy due to ozone, carbon monoxide, and lead, among other pollutants[16]—a situation that leads to 120,000 deaths each year, plus costs through health care and lost worker productivity worth $40 billion.[17]

Nor does Simon mention the developing countries with over three quarters of humanity. In Mexico City, Bombay, and dozens of other megacities, the air is so polluted that breathing it is equivalent to smoking two packs of cigarettes a day.[18] Households often feature so much woodsmoke from open cooking stoves that their air is several times more polluted than the danger level established by the World Health Organization.[19] As many as 700 million women and children are affected, and respiratory infections cause the deaths of 4 million children each year.[20]

5. Species Extinctions

Simon bases his argument on what he says "are still the canonical texts," being my 1979 book and Lovejoy's 1980 paper. How about the dozens of books and hundreds of papers published since then, and to which I have repeatedly drawn Simon's attention, notably through two face-to-face debates? He claims that "the observed rates of species extinction are wildly at variance" with my own and others' findings, but he cites no broad-ranging support for his assertion. In fact, "the only available evidence" he invokes is a Lugo paper in a 1988 book;[21] yet he omits reference to the couple of dozen papers in the same book with a unanimous stance directly opposed to Lugo's. Lugo deals only with species in Puerto Rico's tropical rainforests, which comprise 0.04 percent of all such forests.

Simon characterizes island biogeography theory as "mere speculation," despite the hundreds of papers supplying empirical evidence. Nor does he adduce any alternative analysis to help us determine the true species extinction rate. This notwithstanding, he calls for "as clear and unbiased an understanding as possible" of the species extinction question, "stating the facts as best we know them, especially in a scientific context." Yet after more than a decade we are still waiting for evidence from Simon to match even one hundredth of what we hear from biologists.

On the economic value of species, Simon protests that "it seems hard to even *imagine* that we would be enormously better off with the persistence of any such imagined species" (i.e., extinct species that could have offered economic benefits).

How about the wild relative of corn, discovered in the late 1970s with just a few thousand individual stalks in a Mexican forest patch totaling 4 hectares?[22] Resistant to no fewer than seven diseases of commercial corn, and capable of growing in cool and moist environments outside the usual range of commercial corn, this wild corn offers benefits estimated at $4.4 billion per year.[23] Similarly, germplasm from a wild rice in India's forests rescued the Asian rice crop, main source of sustenance for over 2 billion people, from a devastating blight; it was discovered shortly after its forest habitat was saved from obliteration.[24] There are many other such cases.[25]

So too with species' contributions to medicine: startpoint materials from plants alone will generate prescription drugs, with their many health benefits both direct and indirect, with a commercial value of $500 billion for all rich nations during the 1990s.[26] The economic value, counting in the many health benefits, both direct and indirect, will be several times larger.

In this, as in many other instances, I wish Simon would cite more findings and analyses, and from a broader range of experts, including economists—then we could engage in a solid exchange of views. As it is, I am left with the feeling that if his arguments are the best the optimists have to offer, our environmental predicament could be even worse than the experts indicate.

6. Urban Sprawl and Soil Erosion

Simon speaks of opposing opinions on these issues as a "scam," "smoke screen," "foofarah," and "hokum," and a "phony scare campaign [that] steals taxpayers' money"—just as, on other issues, he talks of "fraud," "bogey," "flummery," "widespread hysteria," "false alarms," and "purposeful mis-statements." Hardly the language of professional debate.

Simon asserts that in the United States, "[soil] erosion has been lessening rather than worsening since the 1930s." Yet in 1977 the nation's soil loss was found to match the Dust Bowl's peak.[27] While there has been some improvement since the mid-1980s,[28] one quarter of croplands are still eroding faster than acceptable.[29] Total on-farm costs of soil erosion are $18 billion per year,[30] plus off-farm costs (through, e.g., damaged watershed functions) of $10 billion.[31] Compare the annual value of the U.S. grain harvest: $42 billion.

Moreover, Simon limits his remarks to the United States once again. The three other leading food producers—India, China, and the former Soviet Union, which together with the United States grow half the world's food—continue to experience severe and worsening soil losses.[32] Recall that worldwide losses are around 25 billion tons per year, causing a shortfall of 9 million tons of grain, or enough to make up the diets of more than 200 million undernourished people.[33]

As for urban sprawl, suffice it to say that each year the United States loses a widely documented total of 35,000 square kilometers of land to houses, offices, roads, and other forms of urban expansion.[34] This is equivalent to over 600 Manhattans. How long do Americans want to continue down that track?

7. Global Warming

While admitting he is not an "atmospheric scientist," Simon urges the "concerned" reader "to examine the state of your own knowledge on the subject—what you know about technical facts, and the sources of the supposed information." Yet he feels qualified to offer the "guess" that "global warming will simply be another transient concern, barely worthy of consideration ten years from now." The two multi-volume reports by the Intergovernmental Panel on Climate Change represent the expertise of several hundred leading atmospheric scientists,[35] yet Simon does not even mention these books, let alone critique them.

The scientists' conclusion is that we can be all but certain that global warming is on its way in the wake of our century-long emissions of greenhouse gases—and that its consequences will be adverse if not critical for humanity. The only uncertainty accepted by the experts concerns the speed with which global warming will arrive and its specific impacts in various parts of the world. In the face of uncertainty, the prudent response is to do all we can to hedge our bets by reducing greenhouse gas emissions forthwith. When confronting undetermined risk in other walks of life, especially if the downside outcome could be severe, it makes sense to adopt an "insurance premium" approach. (Which reader does not pay for insurance to counter all manner of daily risks with their abundant uncertainties?) On the global-warming front, as with many other environmental threats, we shall never know with complete assurance how far we can press against Earth's limits before we find we have exceeded them. Final knowledge comes only with a postmortem. The adverse effects of global warming could be singularly severe in the food sector alone.[36]

Fortunately, we can readily cut back on the greenhouse gas that accounts for half of global warming, carbon dioxide, and do our economies a power of good at the same time. The U.S. economy could be run with half as much fossil-fuel energy as today, possibly less, simply through energy efficiency and conservation.[37] To cite an energy aficionado, Amory Lovins, whose expertise is in demand by hundreds of corporations worldwide (that is, he is as "real world" as they come), there will be economic gains rather than lifestyle losses: "Our industrial performance will leap ahead, our pollution flows will decline (so will our monthly bills), and our showers will still be hot and our beer cold."[38]

The United States has already saved itself $150 billion per year through these measures, worth almost $600 per American.[39] Between 1980 and 1992, Americans derived four and a half times as much new energy from savings as from net increases in energy supply.[40] If Americans were to match Western Europeans' efforts, they would save twice as much energy; and if they were to match the Japanese, three times as much. Along the way, the United States would free itself from growing dependence upon oil imports from the Middle East and other OPEC nations. Whereas in 1990 the nation imported 42 percent of its oil supplies, the amount is projected, in light of recent trends, to reach 70 percent in the year 2010.[41] Oil imports between 1970 and 1990 accounted for nearly three quarters of the U.S. trade deficit, with $1 trillion transferred to OPEC nations.[42] If the United States had kept on saving oil as fast as it did from the mid-1970s, then by 1985 it would have needed to import no more oil from the Persian Gulf. Instead, as has been pointed out by Amory Lovins, American soldiers drove 0.56-mile-per-gallon tanks because American citizens did not drive 32-mile-per-gallon cars—a car efficiency eminently attainable if Detroit had not been let off the hook of producing ever better cars.[43] Moreover, energy conservation could generate almost 300,000 new jobs by 1995.[44] In short, Americans face a win-win prospect all round.

Simon proposes that we pursue an alternative source of energy in the form of nuclear fission. But nuclear energy has simply not proven competitive in the U.S. marketplace, despite his unvarying insistence upon marketplace signals as supreme indicators. Not a single nuclear plant has been commissioned in the United States since 1978.

8. Acid Rain

Simon asserts that "the acid rain scare has now been exposed as one of the great false alarms of our time." Yet acid rain damage in eastern Canada costs $1 billion per year.[45] In Europe, Simon says that "the supposed effects of acid rain in reducing forests and tree growth have turned out to be without foundation." But as a result of damage to date and in the absence of stringent pollution controls, forestry losses will be $30 billion a year for many decades.[46]

9. Ozone-Layer Depletion

As a self-avowed "non-expert," Simon says, "The likelihood is very low that a scare that is only a few years old will turn out to be a truly difficult problem for society." In Montreal in 1987 and a series of follow-up meetings, a large body of front-rank atmospheric scientists has drawn on decade-long evidence to declare that there is hardly any other environmental problem on which such unanimity of opinion exists.[47] The only point over which they differ is the amount and rate of ozone loss—and time and again it has turned out they have underestimated the amount of damage both today and over the next century (remember, the uncertainty factor can cut both ways).[48] Governments were sufficiently persuaded of the case at Montreal that within just a few months (lightning speed for governments) they launched an action program accepted by well over seventy nations. They have subsequently beefed up their efforts in order to reflect the growing urgency and gravity of the threat.

Simon goes on to propose that "Even if the ozone layer should be thinning right now, it need not be a permanent thinning. If human intervention is causing the change, human intervention can reverse it." He knows something nobody else knows; details, please (not a single backup reference cited). The chief ozone-destroying chemicals continue to eliminate ozone molecules for sixty years or more.

Without the planned phase-out of the offending chemicals, Americans would suffer an additional 350 million cases of skin cancer and tens of millions of additional cases of eye cataracts.[49] It is estimated, albeit in preliminary and exploratory terms, that preventive action will yield cumulative health benefits over the next one and three-quarter centuries worth $40 trillion against phase-out costs of $36 billion, a ratio of well over 1000:1.[50] Ozone-layer damage already done will also cause suppression of immune systems, with marked increase of infectious diseases. On top of these health damages, there will be ecological injury to major crop plants; of 200 plant species tested, most of them crops, two thirds prove to be adversely affected by increased ultraviolet radiation through ozone-layer depletion.[51]

10. Debate Responses

(a) Simon states that our subject is "material welfare, not emotional or spiritual or sexual or social." Why not? Material welfare is not a value in itself, it is a means to an end. Should we not consider human development in its full scope, with every form of welfare?

In any case, marketplace indicators—the supreme measures of material welfare, according to Simon—are of limited relevance. First, they reflect the evaluation only of those people who can register their money votes in the marketplace—an option that, as we have seen, is almost entirely denied to two people out of five worldwide. What would be these people's reaction to Simon's assurances that spending power is steadily enhanced through declining prices—or that the Waldorf is increasingly open to all?

Second is the question of spillover effects, known to economists as "externalities." The goods we purchase have often been produced at a concealed cost of pollution during the production process, and when we consume them or throw them away after use, still more pollution ensues, for instance, acid rain, ozone-layer depletion, and global warming. This is pollution for everybody today and tomorrow, not just for the purchaser. Yet the social costs are far from reflected in the prices we pay: the economic externalities are rarely internalized, even though they should be if prices are to serve as realistic indicators. Externalities are nothing less than larcenous costs imposed on other people. For details of how environmental externalities affect the United States and other nations, see Table 6 and Figure 6.

Consider the "true social cost" of a gallon of gasoline in the United States. It is at least $3 in terms of just the most pressing of our environmental problems today (let alone global warming and other problems of the future), or two and a half times the price of gasoline as revealed through the marketplace.[52] The total externality costs of the auto culture in the United States, including congestion, noise, and other problems, total as much as $700 billion per year, worth an extra $6.30 per gallon.[53] The concealed costs of cheap gasoline are deferred, not forgotten. They will eventually be paid in the form of pollution damages, and by the time they are paid, they will often be larger precisely

Table 6. The Ecomomic Cost of Environmental Damage

Country	*Environmental Damage as % of GNP*	*GNP Lost ($ billion)*
Japan	2	66.7
Poland	3	2.1
Philippines	4	1.8
United States	4	227.4*
Germany (W)	4	46.8
Hungary	5	1.4
Czechoslovakia	7	2.7
Costa Rica	8	0.5
Brazil	10	44.7
Mexico	12	30.3
Indonesia	17	18.9
Nigeria	17	5.8

*Equivalent to two thirds of the federal deficit, and almost as large as the Pentagon budget.

Source: Based on D. W. Pearce and G. Atkinson. *Are National Economies Sustainable? Measuring Sustainable Development* (Centre for Social and Economic Research on the Global Environment, University College, London, 1992).

because they have been deferred and allowed to exert greater cumulative injury. What will people in the future say about Simon's assertion that "there is no reason to believe that . . . the price of energy will not continue its long-run decrease forever"?

In still other ways, the marketplace takes scant account of the future, even though many of our environmental problems' impacts will persist for centuries. A cost of $100,000 accruing in 100 years would, with the usual 10 percent discount rate, have a present value of only $7.25.[54] Again, what will people of the future say in response to Simon's reliance upon the supposedly absolute truth of the marketplace? Like the other

Figure 6. Per Capita GNP in Comparison with Per Capita Sustainable Economic Welfare in the United States, 1950–1986

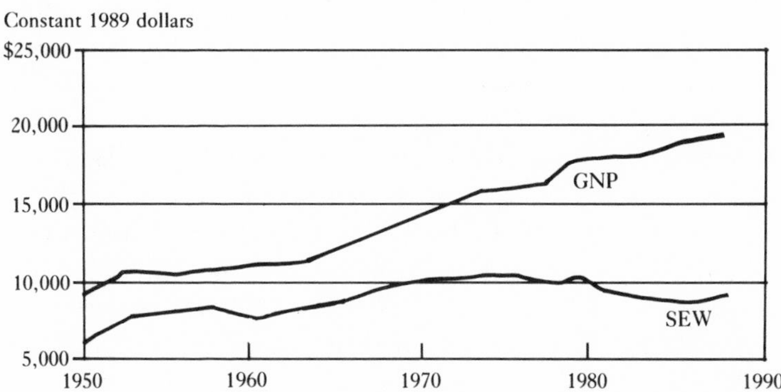

Source: H. E. Daly and J. B. Cobb, Jr. *For the Common Good: Redirecting the Economy Toward Community, the Environment and a Sustainable Future* (Beacon Press, Boston, 1990).

disenfranchised people mentioned above, they are denied a voice.

(b) "the death rate has been falling all over the world": Simon does not mention that the past two decades have witnessed the deaths of 200 million people from starvation and malnutrition-related diseases, being the greatest mass mortality this century. "Victory over death" in a full proper sense?

(c) ". . . wages and salaries have been going up all over the world, in poor countries as well as in rich countries." How about the unemployed in the United States, totaling 8 million in 1992, one of the highest totals ever? And another 20 million workless in the European Community, and at least 100 million in the developing world? Plus, the number of people living off a cash income of a dollar at most per day is 1.2 billion (more than one person in five worldwide), and rising.

(d) Simon protests that I do not use "any trend data," citing my 1991 book *Population, Resources and the Environment: The Critical Challenges*, in which he asserts there are only two data series. There are actually thirteen tables, graphs, and other figures with time-series data, obvious enough; not so obvious to the casual reader are the dozens of such instances in the text.

(e) ". . . the data for the last thirty years show less desertification rather than more as measured by the only available measure—the amount of arable land in the world. This quantity has been going up rather than going down" (no references cited in support). We lose 20,000 square kilometers of arable land each year to desertification even though we need an extra 50,000 square kilometers of farmland each year to feed additional people. Although Simon does not mention it, desertification also accounts for 40,000 square kilometers of stock-raising grasslands. All in all, desertification among other forms of land degradation threatens a whopping one quarter of Earth's lands outside natural deserts, and it is expected to reduce food production by at least 15 percent over the next twenty-five years.[55]

(f) Simon's enthusiasm for birdwatching: has he noticed that the numbers of songbirds returning to the United States from the tropics each year has fallen drastically in recent decades, due largely to habitat loss and other forms of environmental degradation? Simon might also express concern for the 1,000-plus bird species worldwide that are expected to disappear within the foreseeable future.[56]

(g) "Traffic congestion—I'll even bet you that people spend fewer minutes getting to work ten years from now in California on average than they do now." Because traffic congestion on the Los Angeles freeways is projected to quadruple during the next twenty years, average vehicle speed is anticipated to fall to 11 miles per hour.[57] Rush-hour congestion across the country already costs the economy $100 billion per year.[58]

11. Simon's Bet

Julian Simon frequently urges me and others to take on a bet with him about future prospects. I am not averse to betting; I occasionally punt on horse races or football games. And there is stacks of scope for sure-fire bets on environmental problems and other issues. Long-term trends indicate there will soon be hundreds of millions more people without adequate supplies of food, energy, and water, without work, and without housing except in shantytown slums. The number of environmental refugees is set to increase several times over.[59] Numerous agencies predict a horrific increase in AIDS worldwide. But I feel it is inappropriate to bet on matters that concern the bedrock welfare of human beings, especially when it is likely we shall witness human deprivation and suffering on unheard-of scale. It would be like watching a child play with a burning stick and wagering on whether it will hurt itself.

Conclusion

And so to an end—or rather, a beginning of a great new departure, providing we choose to choose.

Remember, it need not cost the Earth to save the Earth (Table 7). The Rio Earth Summit of June 1992 came up with a budget to address those developing world environmental problems that are so profound and widespread that it is in the interest of all humanity to fix them. (Thus it left out problems located in developed nations with little international import, such as waste dumps in the United States.) The total price tag: $625 billion a year. Subsidies that foster misuse and overuse of croplands, fossil fuels, fertilizers, pesticides, water supplies, forests, and fisheries now total at least as much. (The trouble is that too many governments are Marxist: not Karl but Groucho.) The poor nations' share of the Rio budget is $500 billion a year. If the rich nations were to give the poor nations a proper break on aid, trade, debt, investment, technology transfer, and a host of similar items, that would effectively release $500 billion per year.[60] Yet in the face of these magnificent opportunities for all, the rich nations protest they have never been poorer.

Nor have the rich nations figured that it would be in their own economic interest to pitch in their share to the global cause

Table 7. Selected Environmental Programs in Developing Countries: Estimated Costs and Long-Term Benefits

	Additional Investment in 2000			
Program	*Billions of $ per Year*	*% of GDP in 2000*	*% of GDP Growth, 1990–2000*	*Long-Term Benefits*
Controlling particulate matter (PM) emissions from coal-fired power stations	2.0	0.04	0.1	PM emissions virtually eliminated. Large reductions in respiratory illnesses and acid deposition, and improvements in amenity
Reducing acid deposition from new coal-fired stations	5.0	0.1	0.25	
Changing to unleaded fuels; controls of the main pollutants from vehicles	10.0	0.2	0.5	Elimination of pollution from lead; more than 90% reductions in other pollutants, with improvements in health and amenity
Reducing emissions, effluents, and wastes from industry	10.0–15.0	0.2–0.3	0.5–0.7	Appreciable reductions in levels of ambient pollution, and improvements in health and amenity, despite rapid industrial growth. Low-waste processes often a source of cost savings for industry.

Increased investment in water and sanitation	10.0	0.2	0.5	Over 2 billion more people provided with service. Major labor savings and health and productivity benefits. Child mortality reduced by more than 3 million a year
Soil conservation and afforestation	15.0–20.0	0.3–0.4	0.7–1.0	Improvements in yields and productivity of agriculture and forests.
Additional funding for agricultural and forestry research	5.0	0.1	0.2	Lower pressures on natural forests. All agricultural areas eventually brought under sustainable forms of cultivation and pasture
Family planning: incremental costs of an expanded program	7.0	0.1	0.3	Long-term world population stabilizes at 10 billion or less, instead of 12.5 billion or more
Increased education for girls, both primary and secondary	2.5	0.05	0.1	Primary education for girls extended to 25 million more girls, and secondary education to 21 million more
Total	66.5–76.5	1.29–1.49	3.15–3.65	

Source: World Development Report 1992 (World Bank, Washington, D.C., 1992).

(they have so far contributed only about one tenth of their Rio budget allocation). As long as environmental ruin helps to hold back economic advance in developing nations—which have mostly made next to no progress since 1980—developed nations can export fewer goods to them. Due to economic stagnation in developing nations, U.S. exports in 1990 were down by $60 billion, costing 1.8 million American jobs.[61] Developing world poverty is a luxury we can no longer afford.

We could also upgrade developing country agriculture enough to end malnutrition, at a cost of $40 billion a year. The amount spent by developed countries to counter their own form of malnutrition through slimming aids is likewise $40 billion a year.

Finally, note a statement in November 1992 by the Union of Concerned Scientists, signed by 1,680 scientific leaders in 70 countries, of which 104 are Nobel laureates (including laureates in economics):

> If not checked, many of our current practices . . . may so alter the living world that it will be unable to sustain life in the manner that we know. . . . Pressures resulting from unrestrained population growth put demands on the natural world that can overwhelm any efforts to achieve a sustainable future. If we are to halt the destruction of our environment, we must accept limits to that growth.

According to the chairman of the Union of Concerned Scientists, Dr. Henry Kendall of MIT, a Nobel Prize winner himself,

> This kind of consensus is truly unprecedented. There is an exceptional degree of agreement within the international scientific community that natural systems can no longer absorb the burden of current human practices. The depth and breadth of authoritative support for the warning should give great pause to those who question the validity of threats to our environment.

Remember, reader, that we can still turn this bad news into better news. Our window of opportunity is wider open than ever, even though it is closing faster than ever. Suppose we allow ourselves until, say, the year 2000 to take the vital decisions that will affect our planetary home for hundreds, thousands, and even millions of years. After the year 2000, the processes of environmental ruin and population growth will have worked up so much momentum that it will cost us far more to achieve far less. Until the decade's end there are around 2,000 days. We lose 1 percent of our maneuvering room every three weeks. Exciting times to be alive!

If we switch from breakdown to breakthrough, however, we shall be acclaimed way beyond the year 2000. Generations will look back and say, "Those people of the early 1990s, when they realized what was what, did they ever get to grips with the greatest challenge in history—and didn't they make themselves giants of the human condition!"

Take-home message: We live in much more than exciting times.

Post-Debate Statement

Julian Simon

These are some additional thoughts that I would have spoken during the debate if there had been the opportunity to do so:

1. Here is the overarching theory that I offer you to explain why things happen exactly the opposite of the way Malthus and the contemporary Malthusians predict—and why I offer to bet that any measure of human welfare that you choose will show improvement rather than deterioration.

In 1951, Theodore Schultz published an article called "The Declining Economic Importance of Land." He showed that because of technological change, two related things were happening: Food production per person was going up, and the need for agricultural land was going down—even as population was growing very fast. In 1963, Harold Barnett and Chandler Morse showed that despite all the theory about limited quantities of raw materials, and reducing richness of the lodes that are mined, all the raw materials they studied had become less expensive and more available for the decades since the 1870s.

A general process underlies these specific findings: Human beings create more than they use, on average. It had to be so, or we would be an extinct species. And this process is, as the physicists say, an invariancy. It applies to all metals, all fuels, all foods, and all other measures of human welfare, and it applies in all countries, and at all times. In other words, this is a theory of "everything economic," or really, a theory of economic history.

2. Consider this example of the process by which people wind up with increasing availability rather than decreasing availability of resources. England was full of alarm in the 1600s at an impending shortage of energy due to the deforestation of the country for firewood. People feared a scarcity of fuel for both heating and the iron industry. This impending scarcity led to the development of coal.

Then in the mid-1800s, the English came to worry about an impending coal crisis. The great English economist W. S. Jevons calculated that a shortage of coal would bring England's industry to a standstill by 1900; he carefully assessed that oil could never make a decisive difference. Triggered by the impending scarcity of coal (and of whale oil, whose story comes next), ingenious profit-minded people developed oil into a more desirable fuel than coal ever was. And in 1993 we find England exporting both coal and oil.

Another element in the story: Because of increased demand due to population growth and increased income, the price of whale oil for lamps jumped in the 1840s, and the U.S. Civil War pushed it even higher, leading to a whale oil "crisis." This provided incentive for enterprising people to discover and produce substitutes. First came oil from rapeseed, olives, linseed, and camphene oil from pine trees. Then inventors learned how to get coal oil from coal. Other ingenious persons produced kerosene from the rock oil that seeped to the surface, a product so desirable that its price then rose from $0:75 a gallon to $2:00. This high price stimulated enterprisers to focus on the supply of oil, and finally Edwin L. Drake brought in his famous well in Titusville, Pennsylvania. Learning how to refine the oil took a while. But in a few years there were hundreds of small refiners in the United States, and soon the bottom fell out of the whale oil market, the price falling from $2:50 or more at its peak around 1866 to well below $1:00.

We should note that it was not the English or American governments that developed coal or oil, because governments are not effective developers of new technology. Rather, it was individual entrepreneurs who sensed the need, saw opportunity, used all kinds of available information and ideas, made lots of false starts which were very costly to many of those individuals but not to others, and eventually arrived at coal as a viable fuel—because there were enough independent individuals investigating the matter for at least some of them to arrive at sound ideas and methods. And this happened in the context of a competitive enterprise system that worked to produce what was needed by the public. And the entire process of impending shortage and new solution left us better off than if the shortage problem had never arisen.

Here we must address *another crucial element in the economics of resources and population*—the extent to which the *political-social-economic system provides personal freedom* from government coercion. Skilled persons require an appropriate social and economic framework that provides incentives for working hard and taking risks, enabling their talents to flower and come to fruition. The key elements of such a framework are economic liberty, respect for property, and fair and sensible rules of the market that are enforced equally for all.

3. The world's problem is not too many people, but lack of political and economic freedom. Powerful evidence (see Table 2-1) comes from pairs of countries that have the same culture and history, and had much the same standard of living when they split apart after World War II—East and West Germany, North and South Korea, Taiwan and China. In each case the centrally planned communist country began with less population "pressure," as measured by density per square kilometer, than did the market-directed economy. And the communist and non-communist countries also started with much the same

birth rates. But the market-directed economies have performed much better economically than the centrally planned economies. This powerful explanation of economic development cuts the ground from under population growth as a likely explanation.

4. My talk discussed the factual evidence concerning population, resources, and the environment. But in 1993 there is an important new element not present twenty years ago. The scientific community now agrees with almost all of what you have just heard. My comments today do not represent a single lone voice, but rather the scientific consensus.

The earlier remarks about agriculture and resources have always represented the consensus of economists in those fields. And now the consensus of population economists also is not far from what I have said to you.

In 1986, the National Research Council and the National Academy of Sciences published a book on population growth and economic development prepared by a prestigious scholarly group. This "official" report reversed almost completely the frightening conclusions of the previous 1971 NAS report. "Population growth at *most* a minor factor. . . . The scarcity of exhaustible resources is at most a minor constraint on economic growth," it now says. It found benefits of additional people as well as costs.

A host of review articles by distinguished economic demographers in the last three or four years have confirmed that this "revisionist" view is indeed consistent with the scientific evidence, though not all the writers would go as far as I do in pointing out the positive long-run effects of population growth. The consensus is more toward a "neutral" judgment. But this is a huge change from the earlier judgment that population growth is economically detrimental.

By 1993, anyone who asserts that population growth damages the economy must either be unaware of the recent economic literature on the subject, or turn a blind eye to the scientific evidence.

5. There are many reasons why the public hears false bad

news about population, resources, and the environment. Many of these matters are discussed in my earlier books. But lately I have come to emphasize the role of unsound logic and scientific understanding.

These are some of the elements of bad thinking that predispose people to doomsday thinking: (a) Lack of understanding of statistical variability, and of the consequent need for looking at a large and representative sample and not just a few casual observations. (b) Lack of historical perspective, and the need for looking at long time series and not just a few recent observations. (c) Lack of proportion in judgments. (d) Lack of understanding of the Hume-Hayek idea of spontaneously evolving cooperative social systems—Adam Smith's "invisible hand." (e) Seduction by exponential growth and the rest of Malthusian thinking. (f) Lack of understanding of Frédéric Bastiat's and Henry Hazlitt's one key lesson of policy economics—that we must consider not just the short-run effects of an action that we might take but also the effects well into the future, and not just the local effect but also the effect on faraway communities. That is, we must take into account not just the immediate and obvious impacts, but also the slow-responding adjustments which diffuse far from the point of initial contact and which often have the opposite result from the short-run localized effects.

6. In response to questions about species extinction, the World Conservation Union (IUCN) commissioned a book edited by Whitmore and Sayer (1992) to inquire into the extent of extinctions that appeared after the first draft of this book. The results of that project must be considered amazing. All the authors are ecologists who express concern about the rate of extinction. Nevertheless, they all agree that the rate of *known* extinctions has been and continues to be very low. This is a sampling of quotations (with emphasis supplied), first on the subject of the estimated rates:

> . . . *60 birds and mammals are known to have become extinct between 1900 and 1950*. (Reid, 1992, p. 55)

[F]orests of the eastern United States were reduced over two centuries to fragments totalling 1–2% of their original extent . . . during this destruction, only three forest birds went extinct—the Carolina parakeet (Conuropsis carolinensis), the ivory-billed woodpecker (Campephilus principalis principalis), and the passenger pigeon (Ectopistes migratorius). Although deforestation certainly contributed to the decline of all three species, it was probably not critical for the pigeon or the parakeet (Greenway, 1967). *Why, then, would one predict massive extinction from similar destruction of tropical forest?* (Simberloff, 1992, p. 85)

IUCN, together with the World Conservation Monitoring Centre, has amassed large volumes of data from specialists around the world relating to species decline, and it would seem sensible to compare these more empirical data with the global extinction estimates. In fact, these and other data indicate that *the number of recorded extinctions for both plants and animals is very small.* . . . (Heywood and Stuart, 1992, p. 93)

Known extinction rates are very low. Reasonably good data exist only for mammals and birds, and the current rate of extinction is about one species per year (Reid and Miller, 1989). If other taxa were to exhibit the same liability to extinction as mammals and birds (as some authors suggest, although others would dispute this), then, if the total number of species in the world is, say, 30 million, the annual rate of extinction would be some 2300 species per year. This is a very significant and disturbing number, but it is much less than most estimates given over the last decade. (Heywood and Stuart, 1992, p. 94)

. . . if we assume that today's tropical forests occupy only about 80% of the area they did in the 1830s, *it must be assumed that during this contraction, very large numbers of species have been lost in some areas. Yet surprisingly there is no clear-cut evidence for this.* . . . Despite extensive enquiries we have been unable to obtain conclusive evidence to support the suggestion that massive extinctions have taken place in recent times as Myers and others have suggested. On the contrary, work on projects such as Flora Meso-Americana has, at least in some cases, revealed an increase in abundance in many species

(Blackmore, pers. comm. 1991). An exceptional and much quoted situation is described by Gentry (1986) who reports the quite dramatic level of evolution in situ in the Centinela ridge in the foothills of the Ecuadorian Andes where he found that at least 38 and probably as many as 90 species (10% of the total flora of the ridge) were endemic to the "unprepossessing ridge." However, the last patches of forest were cleared subsequent to his last visit and "its prospective 90 new species have already passed into botanical history," or so it was assumed. Subsequently, Dodson and Gentry (1991) modified this to say that an undetermined number of species at Centinela are apparently extinct, following brief visits to other areas such as Lita where *up to 11 of the species previously considered extinct were refound*, and at Poza Honda near La Mana where six were rediscovered. (Heywood and Stuart, 1992, p. 96)

. . . *actual extinctions remain low*. . . . As Greuter (1991) aptly comments, "*Many endangered species appear to have either an almost miraculous capacity for survival*, or a guardian angel is watching over their destiny! This means that it is not too late to attempt to protect the Mediterranean flora as a whole, while still identifying appropriate priorities with regard to the goals and means of conservation." (Heywood and Stuart, 1992, p. 102)

. . . *the group of zoologists could not find a single known animal species which could be properly declared as extinct*, in spite of the massive reduction in area and fragmentation of their habitats in the past decades and centuries of intensive human activity. A second list of over 120 lesser-known animal species, some of which may later be included as threatened, show no species considered extinct; and the older Brazilian list of threatened plants, presently under revision, also indicated no species as extinct. (Cavalcanti, 1981; Brown and Brown, 1992, p. 127)

Closer examination of the existing data on both well- and little-known groups, however, *supports the affirmation that little or no species extinction has yet occurred* (though some may be in very fragile persistence) in the Atlantic forests. Indeed, an appreciable number of species considered extinct 20 years ago, including several birds and six butterflies, have been

> rediscovered more recently. (Brown and Brown, 1992, p. 128)

And here are some comments from that volume on the lack of any solid basis for estimation:

> . . . How large is the loss of species likely to be? *Although the loss of species may rank among the most significant environmental problems of our time, relatively few attempts have been made to rigorously assess its likely magnitude.* (Reid, 1992, p. 55)
>
> *It is impossible to estimate even approximately how many unrecorded species may have become extinct* (Heywood and Stuart, 1992, p. 95)
>
> While better knowledge of extinction rates can clearly improve the design of public policies, it is equally apparent that *estimates of global extinction rates are fraught with imprecision. We do not yet know how many species exist, even to within an order of magnitude.* (Reid, 1992, p. 56)
>
> . . . the literature addressing this phenomenon is relatively small. . . . Efforts to clarify the magnitude of the extinction crisis and the steps that can be taken to defuse the crisis could considerably expand the financial and political support for actions to confront what is indisputably the most serious issue that the field of ecology faces, and arguably the most serious issue faced by humankind today. (Reid, 1992, p. 57)
>
> The best tool available to estimate species extinction rates is the use of species-area curves. . . . This approach has formed the basis for almost all current estimates of species extinction rates. (Reid, 1992, p. 57)
>
> *There are many reasons why recorded extinctions do not match the predictions and extrapolations that are frequently published. . . .* (Heywood and Stuart, 1992, p. 93)

7. People who call themselves "environmentalists" sometimes say to people like me: "You don't appreciate nature."

I'll bet I spend more hours of the year outdoors than Norman Myers or any staff member of an environmental organization whose job is not specifically outdoors. I'm outside about nine hours a day perhaps 150 days a year—every day that it is not too cold for me to work. On average, only about one afternoon a year is it too hot for me to be outside (none in 1992 or 1993); shirtless and in shorts, with a fan blowing and a sponge of water on top of my head, I am comfortable outside if the temperature is less than 95 or even 100 degrees F. Does this not show some appreciation of the out-of-doors?

Two pairs of binoculars are within reach to watch the birds. I love to check which of the tens of species of birds who come to sup from the mulberry tree behind our house will arrive this year, and I never tire of watching the hummingbirds at our feeder. I'll match my birdwatching time with just about any environmentalist, and I'll bet that I've seen more birds this spring than most of your environmentalist friends. And I can tell you that Jeremy Rifkin is spectacularly wrong when he writes that a child grows up in the Northeast without hearing birds sing nowadays. I see more different birds around now than there were forty-five years ago, when I first started watching them. (The mulberry tree is a great attraction, of course.)

As to my concern for other species: I don't like to kill even spiders and cockroaches, and I'd prefer to shoo flies outside of the house rather than swat them. But if it's them versus me, I have no compunction about killing them, even if it is with regret.

The best part of my years in the Navy were the sunsets and sunrises at sea, the flying fish in tropical waters, the driving rain and high waves, too, even at the cost of going without sitdown meals. And being aboard a small ship smack in the middle of a killer typhoon—the same spot where thirteen U.S. ships foundered and sank in World War II—was one of the great experiences of my life. There is no more compelling evidence of the awesome power of nature.

When I was a Boy Scout I delighted in the nature study merit-badge learning. I loved building bridges over streams using only vines and tree limbs, and I was proud of my skill at making fires with flint and steel or Indian-style with bow-and-drill and tinder.

The real issue is not whether one cares about nature, but whether one cares about people. Environmental sympathies are not in dispute; because one puts the interests of one's children before the interests of the people down the street does not imply that one hates the neighbors, or even is disinterested in them. The central matters in dispute here are truth, and liberty, and the desire to impose one's aesthetic and moral tastes on others.

8. Regrettably, many remarks by Mr. Myers make me seem a fool, a knave, and without compassion. Therefore, I shall respond to a few as examples.

a. Mr. Myers writes, "Nor does he [Simon] spare a thought for the 40–60 million women who undergo abortions each year." What is the relevance of such speculation to the arguments in this book? Can Mr. Myers have any knowledge of my thoughts and feelings on such matters? I have written no word about abortion in this book, and hardly any elsewhere.

b. "Simon constantly dismisses the idea that there has been any starvation crisis at all," Mr. Myers writes. Even one death is a tragedy. And I have never "dismissed" the fact that death by starvation has occurred in all eras. Rather I say that the data show the incidence of famine to be decreasing over the past century despite the larger world population, the opposite of what is often asserted.

Concerning paragraphs 1 and 2: On what grounds does Mr. Myers attribute to himself but not to others feelings of compassion for suffering persons? Why does he attribute hardheartedness to me?

c. Mr. Myers refers to a well-known bet on the future prices of raw materials that I made in 1980 with the Paul Ehrlich group, which I won decisively at its expiration in 1990. Mr. Myers attempts to explain away this outcome by saying: "The Ehrlich group lost the bet, but through unusual circumstances of the 1980s that prompted Simon himself to write . . . 'I have been lucky that this particular period coincided so nicely with my argument.' "

Myers's statement is false; I was *not* "prompted" by

"unusual circumstances" to say "I have been lucky." Rather, there always is a certain amount of uncertainty in any wager, and the soundest wager can lose if one has bad luck; that is all that I meant. In fact, I consider the circumstances in the 1980s not the slightest bit unusual.

If Mr. Myers himself believes that the circumstances were unusual, why will he not take me up on my offer to repeat the wager—for any period he picks, for any commodities? During our debate I repeatedly challenged him to wager on this and any other trend of material welfare. But he merely ignored my offer, just as Ehrlich and others have ignored the offer of another go-round—in the same breath as they try to explain away losing the first time. As I suggested to Ehrlich in 1980: Please put your money where your mouth is. Ehrlich at least had the courage (foolhardy as it was) to accept the offer. Mr. Myers does not.

d. It is entirely inaccurate to say, as Mr. Myers does, that I have made any estimates of extinction rates. I have never written or spoken such an estimate; the only evidence he points to is a sentence I wrote in a letter to the editor of a newspaper: "A fair reading of the available data [one vertebrate per year in the twentieth century] suggests a rate of extinction not even one-thousandth as great as the doomsayers scare us with." Given that some of the doomsayers have made some estimates that are thousands of times as great as other doomsayers' estimates, my statement can hardly be sensibly construed as estimating any rate at all. Everything that I have said over the years goes to the *absence of evidence* for such estimates.

Mr. Myers's rhetoric is all the more striking in view of his own behavior. The rules were that we were not allowed to change our original opening statements. Yet he shifts from saying that "five species per year" went extinct to "roughly one species every four years," and changing his calculations from 5,000 higher to 120,000 times higher. This is one more piece of evidence about the lack of solid data for rates of extinction—my central point in our exchange on the matter.

I hope the reader wonders why Mr. Myers spends his efforts on attempting to discredit me rather than providing the appropriate time-series evidence against my arguments.

A well-known lawyer's expression goes as follows: When you have the law on your side, pound the law. When you have the facts on your side, pound the facts. When you have neither the theory nor facts on your side, pound the table. Mr. Myers pounds me instead of pounding the long-term trends or the economic theory of the economic matters under discussion here.

9. The most important difference between my and Norman Myers's (and the doomsters') approach to environmental issues is that I base my conclusions on the historical record of the past rather than Malthusian speculation that is inconsistent with the historical statistical record. For that reason, I shall now present, with little or no commentary, some striking examples of data showing that human welfare has been improving rather than deteriorating, while (and because) population has been growing.

Figure 1. Respiratory Tuberculosis: Standardized Death Rates, 1861–1964

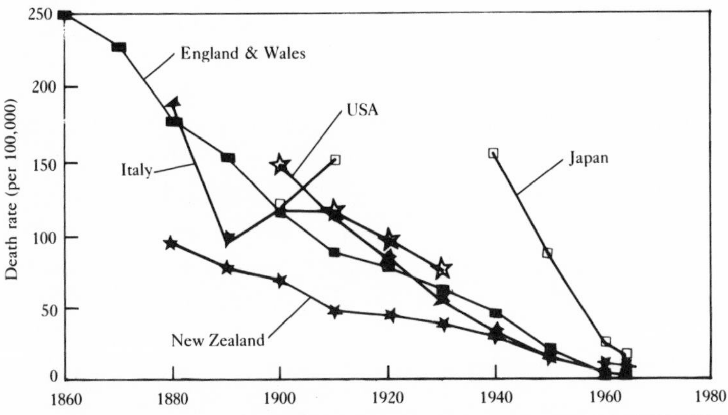

Source: Michael Haines, "Disease and Health Through the Ages," in Simon, ed., *The State of Humanity* (forthcoming).

Figure 2. Estimated Crude Oil Reserves

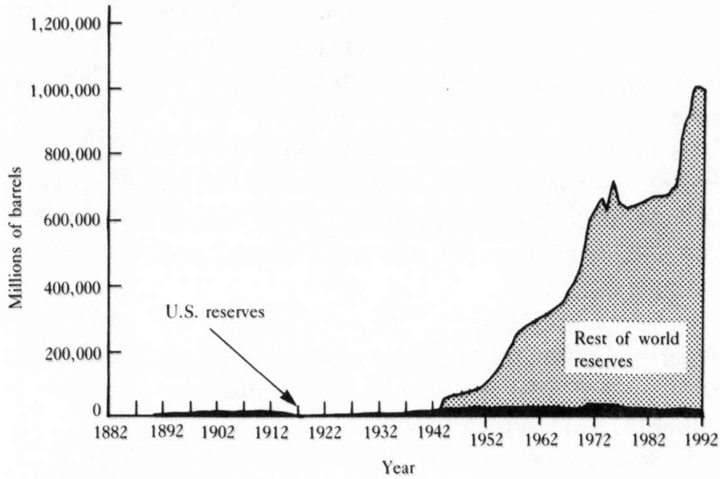

Source: See Figure 3.

Figure 3. Crude Oil: World Known Reserves / Annual World Production = Years of Reserves

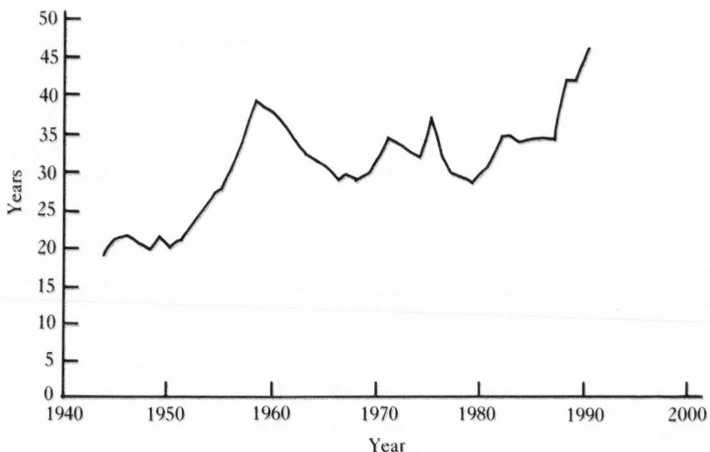

Source: DeGolyer and MacNaughton, *Twentieth Century Petroleum Statistics* (1990), p. 18; U.S. Energy Information Administration, *Crude Oil, Natural Gas and Natural Gas Liquids Reserves Report* (various years); American Petroleum Institute, *Petroleum Facts and Figures* (1959), p. 452; and *World Almanac & Book of Facts* (New York, various years).

Figure 4. Real Gasoline Prices, 1920–1989 (Index: 1982 = 100)

120
100
80
60
40
20
0
excluding taxes
including taxes
1920 1930 1940 1950 1960 1970 1980 1989

Source: Morris A. Adelman, "Trends in the Price and Supply of Oil," in Simon, ed., *The State of Humanity* (forthcoming).

Figure 5a. Female Age-Specific Death Rates for Sweden, 1751–1980

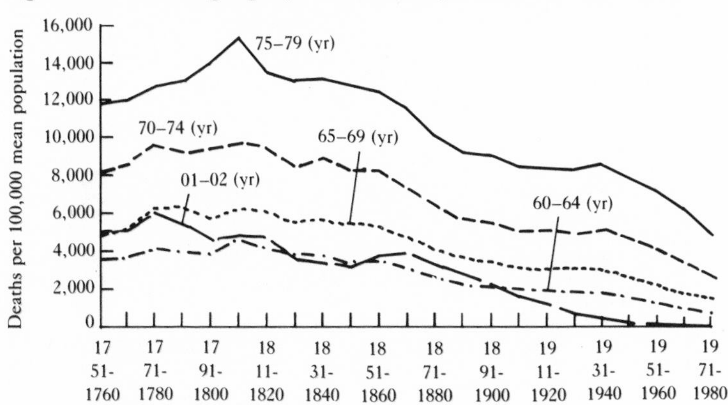

Note: 80+ has been omitted because including this data would reduce the scale of the graph, and the data are not very meaningful.

Source: H. O. Lancaster, *Expectations of Life* (Springer Verlag, New York, 1990), p. 403.

Figure 5b. Female Age-Specific Death Rates for Sweden, 1751–1980

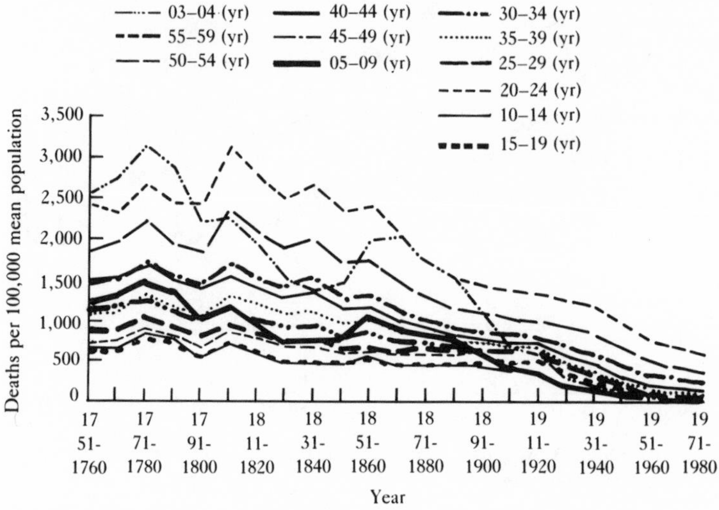

Note: 80+ has been omitted because including this data would reduce the scale of the graph, and the data are not very meaningful.

Source: H. O. Lancaster, *Expectations of Life* (Springer Verlag, New York, 1990), p. 403.

References

Julian Simon

Baden, John, ed., *The Vanishing Farmland Crisis*. Lawrence: University of Kansas, 1984.

Balling, Robert. C., Jr., *The Heated Debate*. San Francisco: Pacific Research Institute, 1992.

Bray, Anna J., "The Ice Age Cometh," *Policy Review* (Fall 1991), pp. 82–84.

Brookes, Warren T., "Acid Rain: The $140 Billion Fraud?", *Consumer Comments*, vol. 14, November 1990 (publication of Consumer Alert).

Brown, K. S., and G. G. Brown, "Habitat Alteration and Species Loss in Brazilian Forests," in T. C. Whitmore, and J. A. Sayer, eds., *Tropical Forest and Species Extinction*, pp. 119–142.

Colinvaux, Paul A., "The Past and Future Amazon," in *Scientific American* (May 1989), pp. 102–108.

Dunford, Richard W., "An Overview of the Farmland Retention Issue," Congressional Research Service, Dec. 9, 1983.

Easterbrook, Gregg, "Vanishing Farmland Reappears," *The New Republic* (July 1986), 17–20.

Elsaesser, Hugh, "The Holes in the 'Ozone Hole,' " *21st Century* (Summer 1990), pp. 8–11.

Frey, Thomas, "Land Use Trends in the United States," in Julian L. Simon, ed. *The State of Humanity*. Boston: Basil Blackwell (forthcoming).

Frieden, Bernard J., *The Environmental Protection Hustle* (Cambridge, Mass.: MIT Press, 1979).

Heywood, V. H., and S. N. Stuart, "Species Extinctions in Tropical Forests," in T. C. Whitmore and J. A. Sayer, eds., *Tropical Deforestation and Species Extinction*, pp. 91–118.

Idso, Sherwood B., *Carbon Dioxide and Global Change: Earth in Transition*. Tempe, AZ: IBR Press, 1989.

Landsberg, H. E., "Global Climatic Trends," in Julian L. Simon and Herman Kahn, eds., *The Resourceful Earth*, pp. 272–315.

Lugo, Ariel E., ed., "Diversity of Tropical Species," in *Biology International*, Special Issue, 1989.

Mayer, Leo V., "Farm Exports and Soil Conservations," *Proceedings of the Academy of Political Science*, vol. 34, 1982, pp. 99–111, quoted by Schultz, 1984.

Michaels, Patrick, *Sound and Fury: The Science and Politics of Global Warming*. Washington, D.C.: Cato Institute, 1992.

Myers, Norman, *The Sinking Ark*. New York: Pergamon Press, 1979.

———, "A Major Extinction Spasm: Predictable and Inevitable?", in David Western and Mary C. Pearl, eds., *Conservation for the Twenty-first Century*. New York and Oxford: Oxford University Press, 1989.

———, *Population, Resources and the Environment*. New York: UNFPA, 1991.

National Academy of Sciences, *Rapid Population Growth: Consequences and Policy Implications*. Baltimore: Johns Hopkins University Press, 1971.

———, *Rapid Population Growth: Consequences and Policy Implications*. Baltimore: Johns Hopkins University Press, 1971.

Penner, Joyce E., Robert E. Dickinson, and Christine A. O'Neill, "Effects of Aerosol from Biomass Burning on the Global Radiation Budget," in *Science*, vol. 256, June 5, 1992, pp. 1432–33.

Ray, Dixie Lee, with Lou Guzzo, *Trashing the Planet*. Chicago: Regnery Gateway, 1990.

Raymond, Robert, *Out of the Fiery Furnace*. Sydney, Australia: Macmillan, 1984.

Reid, W. V., "How Many Species Will There Be?", in T. C. Whitmore and J. A. Sayer, eds., *Tropical Deforestation and Species Extinction.*

Schultz, Theodore, "The Dynamics of Soil Erosion in the United States," in John Baden, ed., *The Vanishing Farmland Crisis,* pp. 45–57.

———, "The Declining Economic Importance of Land," *Economic Journal,* LXI (December 1951), pp. 725–740.

Sedjo, Roger A., and Marion Clawson, "Global Forests," in Julian L. Simon and Herman Kahn, eds., *The Resourceful Earth,* pp. 128–170.

Simberloff, D., "Do Species-Area Curves Predict Extinction in Fragmented Forest?", in Whitmore and Sayer, eds., *Tropical Deforestation and Species Extinction.*

Simon, Julian L., *Economics of Population Growth.* Princeton: Princeton University Press, 1977; translated into Chinese, Beijing: Peking University Press, 1984.

———, *The Ultimate Resource.* Princeton: Princeton University Press, 1981.

———, *Theory of Population and Economic Growth.* New York: Basil Blackwell, 1986.

———, *Effort, Opportunity, and Wealth.* New York: Basil Blackwell, 1987.

———, *Population Matters: People, Resources, Environment, and Immigration.* New Brunswick, NJ: Transactions Press, 1990.

———, *Population and Development in Poor Countries.* Princeton: Princeton University Press, 1992.

———, ed., *The State of Humanity.* Cambridge, MA: Basil Blackwell, forthcoming.

———, "Resources, Population, Environment: An Oversupply of False Bad News," *Science* 208, June 27, 1980, pp. 1431–1437.

———, "Disappearing Species, Deforestation, and Data," *New Scientist,* May 15, 1986, pp. 60–63.

———, "The Phony Farmland Scare," *Washington Journalism Review* (May 1990), pp. 27–33.

———, and Seymour Sudman, "How Much Farmland Is Being Converted to Urban Use? An Analysis of Soil Conservation Service Estimates," *International Regional Science Review,* vol. 7, no. 3 (1982), pp. 257–272.

———, and Herman Kahn, eds., *The Resourceful Earth: A Response to the Global 2000 Report.* New York: Basil Blackwell, 1984.

———, and Aaron Wildavsky, "On Species Loss, the Absence of Data, and Risks to Humanity," in Simon and Kahn, eds., *The Resourceful Earth*, pp. 171–183.

Singer, S. Fred, *Global Climate Change*. New York: Paragon House, 1989.

———, "My Adventures in the Ozone Layer," in Jay Lehr, ed., *Rational Readings on Environmental Concerns*. New York: Van Nostrand, 1992, pp. 535–545.

Swanson, Earl R., and Earl O. Heady, "Soil Erosion in the United States," in Simon and Kahn, eds., *The Resourceful Earth*, pp. 202–223.

U.S. CEQ and Department of State, *The Global 2000 Report to the President*, Vol. II. Washington, D.C.: Government Printing Office, 1980.

U.S. CEQ and Department of State, *Global Future: Time to Act*. Washington, D.C.: Government Printing Office, 1981.

Whitmore, T. C., and J. A. Sayer, eds., *Tropical Deforestation and Species Extinction*. New York: Chapman and Hall, 1992.

References

Norman Myers: Pre-Debate Statement

1. Introduction

1. World Commission on Environment and Development, 1987. *Our Common Future.* Oxford University Press, New York.

2. World Bank, 1991. *The Forest Sector.* World Bank, Washington, D.C.

3. High Level Committee on Floods, Government of India, 1983. *Report on the Emergent Crisis.* New Delhi, India.

4. Dregne, H., M. Cassas, and B. Rosanov, 1992. "A New Assessment of the World's Status of Desertification." *Desertification Control Bulletin* 20: 6–18; Grainger, A., 1990. *The Threatening Desert: Controlling Desertification.* Earthscan Publications, London; Mabbutt, J. A., 1984. "A New Global Assessment of the Status and Trends of Desertification." *Environmental Conservation* 11: 103–113; United Nations Environment Programme, 1991. *Status of Desertification and Implementation of the United Nations Plan of Action to Combat Desertification.* Nairobi, Kenya.

2. Biodiversity

1. Jablonski, D., 1991. "Extinctions: A Palaeontological Perspective." *Science* 253: 754–757; Myers, N., 1990. "Mass Extinctions: What Can the Past Tell Us About the Present and the Future?" *Global and Planetary Change* 82: 175–185; Raup, D. M., 1991. *Extinction: Bad Genes or Bad Luck?* W. W. Norton, New York.

2. Club of Earth, 1990. *Loss of Biodiversity Threatens Human Future* (a statement issued by twelve American biologists, all of them members of the National Academy and the American Academy), Department of Biological Sciences, Stanford University, Stanford, CA; Ehrlich, P. R., and A. H. Ehrlich, 1981. *Extinction.* Random House, New York; Myers, N., 1990, "Mass Extinctions"; Myers, N., 1990. "The Biodiversity Challenge: Expanded Hot-Spots Analysis." *The Environmentalist* 10(4): 243–256; Raven, P. R., 1990. "The Politics of Preserving Biodiversity." *BioScience* 40(10): 769–774; Soule, M. E., 1991. "Conservation: Tactics for a Constant Crisis." *Science* 253: 744–750; Western, D., and M. Pearl, eds., 1989. *Conserving Biology for the Next Century.* Oxford University Press, New York; Wilson, E. O., 1988. *Biodiversity.* National Academy Press, Washington, D.C.; Wilson, E. O., 1989. "Threats to Biodiversity." *Scientific American* 261: 108–117; Wilson, E. O., 1992. *The Diversity of Life.* Belknap Press, Cambridge, MA.

3. Press, F., and M. Atiyah, 1992. *Joint Statement on Biodiversity.* National Academy of Sciences, Washington, D.C., and British Royal Society, London.

4. See references in note 2 above; also Gaston, K. J., 1991. "The Magnitude of Global Insect Species Richness." *Conservation Biology* 5: 283–296; May, R. M., 1991. *Past Efforts and Future Prospects Towards Understanding How Many Species There Are.* Department of Zoology, University of Oxford, Oxford.

5. See, for instance, Erwin, T. L., 1991. "How Many Species Are There?: Revisited." *Conservation Biology* 5: 330–333. Note also P. R. Ehrlich and E. O. Wilson, 1991. "Biodiversity Studies: Science and Policy." *Science* 253: 758–762. See also Wilson, *The Diversity of Life.*

6. Myers, N., 1989. *Deforestation Rates in Tropical Forests and Their Climatic Implications.* Friends of the Earth, London; Myers, N., 1992. *The Primary Source* (revised and expanded). W. W. Norton, New York; Myers, N., 1992. *Future Operational Monitoring of Tropical Forests: An*

Alert Strategy. Joint Research Centre, Commission of the European Community, Ispra, Italy.

7. Gentry, A. H., 1992. "Tropical Forest Biodiversity: Distributional Patterns and Their Conservational Significance." *Oikos* 63: 19–28.

8. Ibid.

9. Bibby, C. J., and eight others, 1992. *Putting Biodiversity on the Map: Priority Areas for Global Conservation*. International Council for Bird Preservation, Cambridge, U.K.; Terborgh, J., and B. Winter, 1980. "Some Causes of Extinction." In M. E. Soule and B. A. Wilcox, eds., *Conservation Biology: An Evolutionary-Ecological Perspective*. Sinauer Associates, Sunderland, MA, 119–134.

10. Dodson, C. H., and A. H. Gentry, 1991. "Biological Extinction in Western Ecuador." *Annals of the Missouri Botanical Garden* 78: 273–295.

11. Case, T. J., and M. L. Cody, 1987. "Testing Theories of Island Biogeography." *American Scientist* 75: 402–411; MacArthur, R. H., and E. O. Wilson, 1967. *The Theory of Island Biogeography*. Princeton University Press, Princeton, NJ; see also Heaney, R., and B. D. Paterson, 1986. *Island Biogeography of Mammals*. Academic Press, New York; Shafer, C. L., 1991. *Nature Reserves: Island Theory and Conservation Practice*. Smithsonian Institution Press, Washington, D.C.; Wilcove, D. S., 1987. "From Fragmentation to Extinction." *Natural Areas Journal* 7: 23–29; Williamson, M., 1981. *Island Populations*. Oxford University Press, New York.

12. Wilson, 1989, "Threats to Biodiversity," and 1992, *The Diversity of Life*.

13. Raup, D. M., 1991. *Extinction: Bad Genes or Bad Luck?* W. W. Norton, New York; and 1991, "A Kill Curve for Phanerozoic Marine Species." *Palaeobiology* 17: 37–48.

14. Myers, N., 1988. "Threatened Biotas: 'Hot Spots' in Tropical Forests." *The Environmentalist* 8: 187–208; Myers, 1990, "The Biodiversity Challenge."

15. Myers, 1990, "The Biodiversity Challenge."

16. Mohsin, A. K. M., and M. A. Ambok, 1983. *Freshwater Fishes of Peninsular Malaysia*. University Pertanian Malaysia Press, Kuala Lumpur, Malaysia.

17. Baskin, Y., 1992. "Africa's Troubled Waters." *BioScience* 42: 476–481; Kauffman, L., 1992. "Catastrophic Change in Species-Rich Freshwater Ecosystems: The Lessons of Lake Victoria." *BioScience*

42: 846–858; Ogutu-Ohwayo, R., 1990. "The Decline of the Native Fishes of Lakes Victoria and Kyoga (East Africa) and the Impact of Introduced Species, Especially the Nile Perch, *Lates niloticus* and the Nile Tilapia *Oreochromis niloticus*." Environmental Biology of Fishes 27: 81–96; Witte, F., and six others, 1992. "The Destruction of an Endemic Species Flock: Quantitative Data on the Decline of the Haplochromine Species from the Mwanza Gulf of Lake Victoria." *Environmental Biology of Fishes* 34: 1–28.

18. Wilson, 1992, *The Diversity of Life.*

19. Ibid.

20. Raven, P. R., 1987. *The Global Ecosystem in Crisis.* The MacArthur Foundation, Chicago; Raven, 1990, "The Politics of Preserving Biodiversity."

21. Diamond, J. M., 1989. "The Present, Past and Future of Human-Caused Extinction." *Philosophical Transactions of the Royal Society of London B*325: 469–478; May, R. M., 1992. "How Many Species Inhabit the Earth?" *Scientific American* 267: 42–48; Myers, N., 1986. *Tackling Mass Extinction of Species: A Great Creative Challenge.* The Horace M. Albright Lecture in Conservation, University of California, Berkeley; Myers, 1990, "Mass Extinctions," and 1990, "The Biodiversity Challenge."

22. Ehrlich, P. R., and E. O. Wilson, 1991. "Biodiversity Studies: Science and Policy." *Science* 253: 758–762; Morowitz, H. J., 1991. "Balancing Species Preservation and Economic Considerations." *Science* 253: 752–754; Myers, 1986, *Tackling Mass Extinction of Species;* Nash, R. F., 1989. *The Rights of Nature.* University of Wisconsin Press, Madison, WI; Norton, B. G., 1987. *Why Preserve Natural Variety?* Princeton University Press, Princeton, NJ; Norton, B., 1992. *Toward Unity Among Environmentalists.* Oxford University Press, New York; Raven, 1990, "The Politics of Preserving Biodiversity"; Wilson, 1992, *The Diversity of Life.*

23. de Beer, J. H., and M. J. McDermott, 1989. *The Economic Value of Non-Timber Forest Products in Southeast Asia.* Netherlands Committee for IUCN, Amsterdam, Netherlands; Myers, N., 1983. *A Wealth of Wild Species.* Westview Press, Boulder, CO; Myers, N., 1984. *The Primary Source: Tropical Forests and Our Future.* W. W. Norton, New York; Nepstad, D. C., and S. Schwartzman, eds., 1992. "Non-Timber Products from Tropical Forests." *Advances in Economic Botany,* Vol. 9; Oldfield, M. L., 1989. *The Value of Conserving Genetic Resources.*

Sinauer Associates, Sunderland, MA; Plotkin, M., and L. Famolare, eds., 1992. *Sustainable Harvest and Marketing of Rain Forest Products.* Island Press, Washington, D.C.; Vaughan, D. A., and L. A. Sitch, 1991. "Gene Flow from the Jungle to Farmers." *BioScience* 41: 22–28; Waterman, P. G., 1986. "A Phytochemist in the African Rainforests." *Phytochemistry* 25: 3–17.

24. Duke, J., 1990. *News on Phytomedicinals.* Agricultural Research Service, U.S. Department of Agriculture, Beltsville, MD; Joyce, C., 1992. "Western Medicine Men Return to the Field." *BioScience* 42: 399–403; Oldfield, 1989, *The Value of Conserving Genetic Resources;* Rasoanaivo, P., 1990. "Rain Forests of Madagascar: Sources of Industrial and Medicinal Plants." *Ambio* 19: 421–424; Schultes, R. E., and R. F. Raffauf, 1990. *The Healing Forest: Medicinal and Toxic Plants of the Northwest Amazon.* Dioscorides Press, Portland, OR; Waterman, P. G., 1986. "A Phytochemist in the African Rainforests." *Phytochemistry* 25: 3–17.

25. Myers, 1992, *The Primary Source;* Principe, P. P., 1987. *The Economic Value of Biological Diversity Among Medicinal Plants.* Organization for Economic Cooperation and Development, Paris.

26. Cooper, D., R. Vellve, and H. Hobbelink, eds., 1992. *Growing Diversity, Genetic Resources and Local Food Security.* Intermediate Technology Publications, London; Meuninck, J., and J. Duke, 1988. *Edible Wild Plants.* Media Methods, Edwardsburg, MD; Myers, 1983, *A Wealth of Wild Species;* Myers, N., 1986. *The Wild Supermarket: The Importance of Biological Diversity to Food Security.* World Wildlife Fund, Gland, Switzerland; Oldfield, 1989, *The Value of Conserving Genetic Resources;* Pimentel, D., 1991. "Diversification of Biological Control Strategies in Agriculture." *Crop Protection* 10: 243–253.

27. Eisner, T., 1990. "Prospecting for Nature's Chemical Riches." *Issues in Science and Technology* 6(2): 31–34; Meinwald, J., 1986. "The Insect as Organic Chemist." *Bulletin of the American Academy of Arts and Sciences* 43: 27–34.

28. Farnsworth, N. R., and D. D. Soejarto, 1985. "Potential Consequences of Plant Extinction in the United States on the Current and Future Availability of Prescription Drugs." *Economic Botany* 39: 231–240; Soejarto, D. D., and N. R. Farnsworth, 1989. "Tropical Rain Forests: Potential Source of New Drugs?" *Perspectives in Biology and Medicine* 32: 244–256.

29. McNeely, J. A., ed., 1992. *Parks for Life: Proceedings of World*

Parks Congress, Caracas, Venezuela, February 1992. International Union for Conservation of Nature and Natural Resources, Gland, Switzerland.

30. Dixon, J. A., and P. B. Sherman, 1990. *Economics of Protected Areas: A New Look at Benefits and Costs.* Island Press, Covelo, CA; McNeely, J. A., 1988. *Economics and Biodiversity: Developing and Using Economic Incentives to Conserve Biological Resources.* International Union for Conservation of Nature and Natural Resources, Gland, Switzerland; Swanson, T., and E. B. Barbier, eds., 1992. *Economics for the Wilds: Wildlife, Wildlands, Diversity and Development.* Earthscan Publications, London.

3. The Population Factor

1. Sfeir-Younis, A., 1986. *Soil Conservation in Developing Countries—A Background Report.* World Bank, Washington, D.C. See also Lal, R., and B. A. Stewart, 1990. *Soil Degradation.* Springer-Verlag, New York; Pimentel, D., 1992. *World Soil Erosion and Conservation.* Cambridge University Press, New York.

2. Food and Agriculture Organization, 1990. *The State of Food and Agriculture, 1990.* Rome, Italy.

3. Brown, L. R., and nine others, 1990. *State of the World 1990.* W. W. Norton, New York; Brown, L. R., and eleven others, 1993. *State of the World 1993.* W. W. Norton, New York.

4. Ibid., 1990 and 1993. See also Conway, G. R., and J. M. Pretty, 1991. *Unwelcome Harvests: Agriculture and Pollution.* Earthscan Publications, London.

5. Potts, D., 1990. *A Penny a Day.* Family Health International, Research Triangle Park, NC.

6. Daily, G. C., and P. R. Ehrlich, 1992. "Population, Sustainability and Earth's Carrying Capacity." *BioScience* 42: 761–771; Ehrlich, P. R., and A. H. Ehrlich, 1990. *The Population Explosion.* Simon & Schuster, New York; see also Daly, H. E., and J. B. Cobb, 1989. *For the Common Good: Redirecting the Economy Toward Community, the Environment and a Sustainable Future.* Beacon Press, Boston; Grant, L., 1992. *Elephants in the Volkswagen.* W. H. Freeman, New York; Keyfitz, N., 1991. *The Impact of Population Growth on the Physical Envi-*

ronment. International Institute for Applied Systems Analysis, Laxemburg, Austria; Pimentel, D., and M. Pimentel, 1989. *Land, Energy and Water: The Constraints Governing Ideal U.S. Population Size*. Negative Population Growth, Teaneck, NJ; Ness, G. D., W. D. Drake, and S. R. Brechin, eds., 1993. *Population—Environment Dynamics, Ideas and Observations*. University of Michigan Press, Ann Arbor, MI. For a general review of responses to the pollyanna approach to population and carrying capacity, see Campbell, M., ed., 1992. "The Collected Responses to Simon and Other Population Revisionists." *Population Speakout*, Englewood, CO.

7. Chen, R. S., and four others, 1990. *The Hunger Report*. World Hunger Program, Brown University, Providence, RI; Millman, S. 1991. *The Hunger Report: Update 1991*. World Hunger Program, Brown University, Providence, RI.

8. For a detailed account of the analysis, see Brown, *et al.*, note 3 above.

9. Sadik, N., 1990. *The State of World Population 1990*. United Nations Population Fund, New York.

10. Sadik, N., 1992. *The State of World Population 1992*. United Nations Population Fund, New York.

11. Brown, L. R., and twelve others, 1992. *State of the World 1992*. W. W. Norton, New York; World Resources Institute, 1992. *World Resources 1992–93*. Washington, D.C.

12. Food and Agriculture Organization, 1984. *Potential Population Supporting Capacities of Lands in the Developing World*. Rome.

13. McNamara, R. S., 1991. *A Global Population Policy to Advance Human Development in the 21st Century*. United Nations Population Fund, New York; World Bank, 1992. *World Development Report 1992*. Washington, D.C.

14. International Labour Organization, 1992. *Annual Report, 1992*. Geneva.

15. Ehrlich and Ehrlich, 1990, *The Population Explosion;* Ehrlich, P. R., and A. H. Ehrlich, 1992. "The Most Overpopulated Nation." In Grant, ed., *Elephants in the Volkswagen;* Harrison, P., 1992. *The Third Revolution: Environment, Population and a Sustainable World*. I. B. Tauris and Co., London; Kessler, E., ed., 1992. "Population, Natural Resources and Development." *Ambio* 21(1) (special issue); Keyfitz, 1991, "Population Growth Can Prevent . . ."; Shaw, P. R., 1992. "The Impacts of Population Growth on Environment: The Debate Heats Up." *Environmental Impact Assessment Review* 12; Myers, N.,

1991. *Population, Resources and the Environment: The Critical Challenges.* United Nations Population Fund, New York; Myers, N., 1992. "Population / environment Linkages: Discontinuities Ahead." *Ambio* 21(1): 116–118.

16. Harrison, 1992, *The Third Revolution.*

17. Brown, *et al.*, 1992, *State of the World 1992;* Daly and Cobb, 1989, *For the Common Good;* Dregne and Tucker, 1988, "Desert Encroachment"; Ehrlich and Ehrlich, 1990, *The Population Explosion;* Ehrlich and Erlich, 1992, "The Most Overpopulated Nation"; Falkenmark, M., and R. A. Suprapto, 1992, "Population-Landscape Interactions in Development: A Water Perspective to Environmental Sustainability." *Ambio* 21(1): 31–36; Lal and Stewart, 1990, *Soil Degradation;* Myers, 1991, "Population Resources and the Environment: The Critical Challenges," and 1992, "Population / environment Linkages"; Myers, N., 1991. "The World's Forests and Human Populations: The Environmental Interconnections." In K. Davis and M. S. Bernstam, eds., *Resources Environment and Population: Present Knowledge, Future Options.* Oxford University Press, New York; Pimentel, 1992, *World Soil Erosion and Conservation;* Repetto, R., and T. Holmes, 1983. "The Role of Population in Resource Depletion." *Population and Development Review* 9: 609–632; World Bank, 1990. *World Development Review* 9: 609–632; World Bank, 1990. *World Development Report 1990.* Washington, D.C.; World Resources Institute, 1992. *World Resources 1992–93.* Washington, D.C.; see also Grainger, A., 1993. *Controlling Tropical Deforestation.* Earthscan Publications, London, and Ness, et al., 1993, *Population—Environment Dynamics.*

18. Simon, J. L., 1981. *The Ultimate Resource.* Princeton University Press, Princeton, NJ; Simon, J. L., 1990. *Population Matters: People, Resources, Environment, Immigration.* Transaction Press, New Brunswick, NJ; Simon, J. L., 1992. *Population and Development in Poor Countries.* Princeton University Press, Princeton, NJ; Simon, J. L., and Herman Kahn, eds., 1984. *The Resourceful Earth.* Basil Blackwell, New York.

19. Myers, 1992, "Population / environment Linkages."

20. Myers, N., 1988. "Environmental Degradation and Some Economic Consequences in the Philippines." *Environmental Conservation* 15: 205–214; World Bank, 1990. *Population Pressure: The Environment and Agricultural Intensification in the Philippines.* Washington, D.C.

21. Keyfitz, 1991, "Population Growth Can Prevent . . ."; Myers, 1992, "Population / environment Linkages."

22. Vitousek, P. M., P. R. Ehrlich, A. H. Ehrlich, and P. M. Matson, 1986. "Human Appropriation of the Products of Photosynthesis." *BioScience* 36: 368–373.

23. Ehrlich, P. R., and J. Roughgarden, 1987. *The Science of Ecology*. Macmillan, New York; Odum, E. P., 1989. *Ecology and Our Endangered Life-Support Systems*. Sinauer Associates, Sunderland, MA.

24. Gilbert, L. E., 1980. "Food Web Organization and the Conservation of Neotropical Diversity." In Soule and Wilcox, eds., *Conservation Biology;* Terborgh, J., 1992. *Diversity and the Tropical Rain Forest*. W. H. Freeman, New York.

25. Houghton, J. T., G. J. Jenkins, and J. J. Ephramus, eds., 1990. *Climate Change: The IPCC Scientific Assessment*. Cambridge University Press, New York; Houghton, J. T., B. A. Callander, and S. K. Barney, eds., 1992. *Climate Change 1992: The Supplementary Report to the IPCC Scientific Assessment*. Cambridge University Press, New York.

26. Daily, G. C., and P. R. Ehrlich, 1990. "An Exploratory Model on the Impact of Rapid Climate Change on the World Food Situation." *Proceedings of Royal Society of London B* 241: 232–244.

27. Rosenzweig, C., and M. L. Parry, 1992. *Implications of Climate Change for International Agriculture: Global Food Trade and Vulnerable Regions*. Environmental Protection Agency, Washington, D.C.

28. Myers, N., 1992. "Environmental Refugees: How Many Ahead?" *BioScience* (in press); Tickell, C., 1990. *Environmental Refugees: The Human Impact of Global Climate Change*. National Environment Research Council, Swindon, U.K.

29. Ehrlich and Ehrlich, 1990, *The Population Explosion;* Myers, 1990, *Population, Resources and the Environment;* Odum, 1989, *Ecology and Our Endangered Life-Support Systems*.

30. Bongaarts, J., 1990. "The Measurement of Wanted Fertility." *Population and Development Review* 16: 487–506.

31. World Bank, 1990, *World Development Report 1990*.

4. The Policy Prospect

1. Repetto, R., W. Magrath, M. Wells, C. Beer, and F. Rossini, 1989. *Wasting Assets: Natural Resources in the National Income Accounts*. World Resources Institute, Washington, D.C.

2. Repetto, R., and M. Gillis, eds., 1988. *Public Policies and the*

Misuse of Forest Resources. Cambridge University Press, New York. For a useful summary, see Repetto, R., 1990. "Deforestation in the Tropics." *Scientific American* 262: 36–42.

3. Repetto, *et al.*, 1989, *Wasting Assets*. With particular reference to the western United States, see M. Reisner, 1986, *Cadillac Desert: The American West and Its Disappearing Water*. Viking, New York.

4. Costanza, R., ed., 1991. *Ecological Economics: The Science and Management of Sustainability*. Columbia University Press, New York; Daly and Cobb, 1989, *For the Common Good;* Pearce, D. W., A. Markandya, and E. B. Barbier, 1989. *Blueprint for a Green Economy*. Earthscan Publications, London; Pearce, D. W., and five others, 1991. *Blueprint 2: Greening the World Economy*. Earthscan Publications, London; Repetto, R., 1992. "Accounting for Environmental Assets." *Scientific American* 266: 94–100. Pearce, D. W., and J. J. Warford, 1992. *World Without End: Environment, Economics and Sustainable Development*. Oxford University Press, New York.

5. Folke, C., and T. Kaberger, 1991. *Linking the Natural Environment and the Economy*. Kluwer Publishers, Dordrecht, Netherlands; Lutz, E., and S. El Serafy, 1988. *Environmental and Resource Accounting: An Overview*. World Bank, Washington, D.C.; Peskin, H. M., and E. Lutz, 1990. *A Survey of Resource and Environmental Accounting in Industrialized Countries*. World Bank, Washington, D.C.; Repetto, *et al.*, *Wasting Assets*. Pearce, D. W., 1993. *Economic Values and the Natural World*. Earthscan, London.

6. Daly and Cobb, 1989, *For the Common Good*.

7. Pearce, D. W., and G. Atkinson, 1992. *Are National Economies Sustainable? Measuring Sustainable Development*. Centre for Social and Economic Research on the Global Environment, London.

8. Repetto, *et al.*, notes 2 and 3 above.

9. Repetto, R., and nine others, 1991. *Accounts Overdue: Natural Resource Depreciation in Costa Rica*. World Resources Institute, Washington, D.C.

10. MacKenzie, J. J., and M. P. Walsh, 1990. *Driving Forces: Motor Vehicle Trends and Their Implications for Global Warming, Energy Strategies and Transportation Planning*. World Resources Institute, Washington, D.C.; MacKenzie, J. J., R. C. Dower, and D. D. T. Chen, 1992. *The Going Rate: What It Really Costs to Drive*. World Resources Institute, Washington, D.C. See also Office of Technology Assessment, 1991. *Improving Automobile Fuel Economy, New Standards, New Approaches*. U.S. Government Printing Office, Washington, D.C.; National Acad-

emy of Sciences, 1992. *Automotive Fuel Economy: How Far Should We Go?* National Academy Press, Washington, D.C.; Renner, M., 1988. *Rethinking the Role of the Automobile.* Worldwatch Institute, Washington, D.C.; and Romm, J. J., and A. B. Lovins, 1993. "Fueling a Competitive Economy." *Foreign Affairs* 72(5): 46–62; Nadis, S., and J. J. Mackenzie, 1993. *Car Trouble.* World Resources Institute, Washington, D.C.

11. For a detailed discussion of these policy measures, see Pearce, *et al.*, 1989 and 1991, note 4 above; see also Maler, K-G., 1989. *Risk and the Environment: An Attempt at a Theory.* Stockholm School of Economics, Stockholm; O'Riordan, T., 1992. "The Precaution Principle in Environmental Management." In U. E. Simonis and R. U. Ayres, eds., *Sustainable Development in Industrial Economies.* United Nations University Press, Tokyo; Perrings, C., 1991. "Reserved Rationality and the Precautionary Principle: Technological Change, Time and Uncertainty in Environmental Decision Making." In R. Costanza, ed., *Ecological Economics: The Science and Management of Sustainability.* Columbia University Press, New York.

5. Our Changing Relationship to Nature

1. Costanza, ed., 1991, *Ecological Economics;* Pearce, *et al.*, 1989, *Blueprint for a Green Economy,* and 1991, *Blueprint 2;* Daly and Cobb, 1989, *For the Common Good;* Repetto, R., 1987. "Population, Resources, Environment: An Uncertain Future." *Population Bulletin* 42(2): 1–44; Simonis, U. E., 1990. *Beyond Growth: Elements of Sustainable Development.* Wissenschaftszentrum, Berlin.

2. Cline, W. R., 1992. *The Economics of Global Warming.* Institute for International Economics, Washington, D.C.; Oppenheimer, M., and R. H. Boyle, 1990. *Dead Heat: The Race Against the Greenhouse Effect.* Basic Books, New York; Pearce, *et al.* 1991, *Blueprint 2;* Perdomo, M. and P. Vellinga, eds., 1992. *Global Climate Change and the Rising Challenge of the Sea.* Intergovernmental Panel on Climate Change, World Meteorological Organization, Geneva, Switzerland, and United Nations Environment Program, Nairobi, Kenya; Schneider, S. H., 1989. *Global Warming.* Sierra Club Books, San Francisco.

3. Myers, N., 1983. "A Priority Ranking Strategy for Threatened Species?" *The Environmentalist* 3: 97–120.

6. A Great Creative Challenge

1. Meadows, D. M., D. L. Meadows, and J. Randers, 1992. *Beyond the Limits*. Earthscan Publications, London.

2. Daly, H. E., 1992. "UN Conferences on Environment and Development: Retrospect on Stockholm and Prospects for Rio." *Ecological Economics* 5: 9–14; see also Strong, M. F." 1978. "Where Are We Growing?" In *The Frontiers of Human Knowledge:* Skrifter Rorande Uppsala Universitet, Acta Universitatis Uppsaliensis, Uppsala, Sweden.

References

Norman Myers: Post-Debate Statement

1. World Health Organization, 1992. *Our Planet, Our Health.* Geneva; World Health Organization, 1992. *Reproductive Health: A Key to a Brighter Future.* Geneva.

2. Bjo, J., K.-G. Mahler, and L. Unemo, 1990. *Environment and Development: An Economic Approach*, Kluwer, Dordrecht, Netherlands; Boulding, K. E., 1992. *Towards a New Economics: Critical Essays on Ecology, Distribution and Other Themes.* Edward Elgar, London; Dasgupta, P., 1993. *An Inquiry into Well-Being and Destitution.* Oxford University Press, Oxford; Haavelmo, T., and S. Hansen, 1992. "On the Strategy of Trying to Reduce Economic Inequality by Expanding the Scale of Human Activity." In R. Goodland, H. E. Daly, and S. El Serafy, eds., *Population, Technology, and Lifestyle.* Island Press, Washington, D.C.; Pearce, D. W., 1993. *Economics and Environment: Essays on Ecological Economics and Sustainable Development.* Edward Elgar, London; Repetto, R., 1987. "Population, Resources, Environment: An Uncertain Future." *Population Bulletin* 42(2). Population Reference Bureau, Washington, D.C.; Schelling, T. C., 1992. "Some Economics of Global Warming." *The American Economics Review* 82(1): 1–14.

3. United Nations Development Programme, 1993. *Human Development Report 1993.* Oxford University Press, New York; World Bank,

1990. *World Development Report 1990: Poverty*. Washington, D.C.; World Bank, 1992. *World Development Report 1992: Development and the Environment*. Oxford University Press, New York.

4. Myers, N. 1993. "Sub-Saharan Africa and Carrying Capacity." *Environmental Awareness* (in press); World Resources Institute. 1992, *World Resources Report 1992–93*. Washington, D.C.

5. Brown, L. R., and eleven others. 1993. *State of the World 1993*. W. W. Norton, New York; Food and Agriculture Organization, 1992. *World Food Supplies and Prevalence of Chronic Undernutrition in Developing Regions as Assessed in 1992*. Rome; World Bank, 1990, *World Development Report 1990;* World Bank, 1992, *World Development Report 1992;* World Resources Institute. 1992, *World Resources Report 1992–93*.

6. Haq, M., 1992. *Human Development in a Changing World*. United Nations Development Programme, New York.

7. World Resources Institute, 1992, *World Resources Report 1992–93*.

8. Falkenmark, M., and C. Widstrand, 1992. *Population and Water Resources: A Delicate Balance*. Population Reference Bureau, Washington, D.C.; Postel, S., 1992. *Last Oasis: Facing Water Scarcity*. W. W. Norton, New York.

9. Ibid.; World Health Organization, 1992, *Our Planet, Our Health*.

10. Pearce, 1993, *Economics and Environment;* see also Christmas, J., and C. de Rooy, 1991. "The Water Decade and Beyond." *Water International* 16: 127–134; World Health Organization, 1992, *Our Planet, Our Health*.

11. Author's own calculations; see also Tolba, M. K., *et al.*, eds., 1992. *The World Environment 1972–1992*. Chapman and Hall, London.

12. Grant, L., 1992. *Elephants in the Volkswagen*. W. H. Freeman, New York.

13. Brown, *et al.*, 1993, *State of the World 1993;* Food and Agriculture Organization, 1992, *World Food Supplies*, and 1992, *Food and Nutrition: Creating a Well-Fed World*, Rome; World Bank, 1992, *World Development Report, 1990;* World Resources Institute, 1992, *World Resources Report 1992–93;* see also Ehrlich, P. R., A. H. Ehrlich, and G. C. Daily, 1993. "Food Security, Population and Environment." *Population and Development Review* 19: . .

14. Kendall, H. W., and D. Pimentel, 1993. "Constraints on the Expansion of the Global Food Supply." *Ambio* (in press).

15. Pinstrup-Andersen, P., 1993. *Socioeconomic and Policy Considerations for Sustainable Agricultural Development.* International Food Policy Research Institute, Washington, D.C.

16. Environmental Protection Agency, 1989. *National Air Pollution Emission Estimates, 1949–1987.* Washington, D.C.

17. American Lung Association, 1989. *Health Effects of Air Pollution.* New York; see also Cannon, J. S., 1985. *The Health Costs of Air Pollution.* American Lung Association, New York; French, H. F., 1990. *Clearing the Air: Global Agenda.* Worldwatch Institute, Washington, D.C.; and World Health Organization, 1992, *Our Planet, Our Health.*

18. Schteingart, M., 1989. "The Environmental Problems Associated with Urban Development in Mexico City." *Environment and Urbanization* 1: 40–48; United Nations Environment Programme and World Health Organization, 1988. *Assessment of Urban Air Quality.* Global Environment Monitoring System, Nairobi and Geneva.

19. World Health Organization, 1992, *Our Planet, Our Health.*

20. World Bank, 1992, *World Development Report, 1992.*

21. Lugo, A. U., 1988. "Estimating Reductions in the Diversity of Tropical Forest Species." In E. O. Wilson, ed., *Biodiversity.* National Academy Press, Washington, D.C.

22. Iltis, H. H., J. F. Doebley, R. M. Guzman, and B. Pazy, 1979. "*Zea Diploperennis* (Graminaea), a New Teosinte from Mexico." *Science* 203: 186–188.

23. Fisher, A. C., 1982. *Economic Analysis and the Extinction of Species.* Department of Agriculture and Resource Economics, University of California, Berkeley; Witt, S. C. 1985. *Biotechnology and Genetic Diversity.* California Agricultural Lands Project, San Francisco.

24. Oldfield, M. L., 1989. *The Value of Conserving Genetic Resources.* Sinauer Associates, Sunderland, MA; see also Myers, N., 1983. *A Wealth of Wild Species.* Westview Press, Boulder, CO.

25. Ibid.

26. Principe, S., 1991. "Valuing Biodiversity in Medicinal Plants." In O. Akerle, V. Heywood, and V. Synge, eds., *The Conservation of Medicinal Plants.* Cambridge University Press, New York; and 1993, "Monetizing the Pharmacological Benefits of Plants." In M. J. Balick, *et al.*, eds., *Tropical Forest Medical Resources and the Conservation of Biodiversity.* Columbia University Press, New York (in press); see also H. Wagner, H. Hikino, and N. Farnsworth, 1989. *Economics and Medicinal Plant Research.* Academic Press, New York.

27. U.S. Department of Agriculture, 1980. *The Soil and Water*

Resources Conservation Act: 1980 Appraisal, Part II. Washington, D.C.

28. Brown, L. R., 1992. "U.S. Soil Erosion Cut." In L. R. Brown, C. Flavin, and H. Kane, eds., *Vital Signs: The Trends That Are Shaping Our Future*. W. W. Norton, New York.

29. World Resources Institute, 1992, *World Resources Report 1992–93;* see also U.S. Department of Agriculture, 1990. *Agricultural Resources: Cropland, Water and Conservation Situation Outlook Report*. Washington, D.C.

30. Pimentel, D., and thirteen others, 1993. "Soil Erosion and Agricultural Productivity." In D. Pimentel, ed., *World Soil Erosion and Conservation*. Cambridge University Press, New York.

31. Clarke, E. H., 1985. "The Off-Site Costs of Soil Erosion," *Journal of Soil and Water Conservation* 40: 19–22; World Resources Institute, 1991. *Paying the Farm Bill: U.S. Agricultural Policy and the Transition to Sustainable Agriculture*. Washington, D.C.

32. Brown, 1992, "U.S. Soil Erosion Cut"; see also Lal, R., and B. A. Stewart, 1990. *Soil Degradation*. Springer-Verlag, New York; Lal, R., 1990. *Soil Erosion in the Tropics*. McGraw-Hill, New York; Pimentel, D., ed., 1993, *World Soil Erosion and Conservation*. Cambridge University Press, New York.

33. Brown, L. R., *et al.*, 1991. *State of the World 1991*. W. W. Norton, New York.

34. U.S. Bureau of the Census. 1990. *U.S. Decennial Census*. U.S. Bureau of the Census, Washington, D.C.; see also National Growth Management Leadership Project, 1992. Washington, D.C.

35. Intergovernmental Panel on Climate Change (edited by J. T. Houghton, G. J. Jenkins, and J. J. Ephramus), 1990. *Climate Change: The IPCC Scientific Assessment*. Cambridge University Press, New York; Intergovernmental Panel on Climate Change (edited by J. T. Houghton, B. A. Callander, and S. K. Varney), 1992. *Climate Change 1992: The Supplementary Report to the IPCC Scientific Assessment*. Cambridge University Press, New York; see also Oppenheimer, M., and R. H. Boyle, 1990. *Dead Heat: The Race Against the Greenhouse Effect*. Basic Books, New York; Schneider, S. H., 1989. *Global Warming: Are We Entering the Greenhouse Century?* Sierra Club Books, San Francisco.

36. Daily, G., and P. Ehrlich, 1990. "An Exploratory Model of the Impact of Rapid Climatic Change on the World Food Situation." *Proceedings of the Royal Society of London* 241: 232–244; Rosenzweig, C., M. L. Parry, G. Fischer, and K. Fohberg, 1993. *Climate Change*

and World Food Supplies. Environmental Change Unit, University of Oxford, Oxford.

37. Lovins, A. B., and L. H. Lovins, 1991. *Drill Rigs and Battleships Are the Answer! (But What Was the Question?): Oil Efficiency, Economic Rationality and Security.* Rocky Mountain Institute, Snowmass, CO; see also Heede, R., and D. Houghton, 1990. "Assembling a New National Energy Policy," *Building Economic Alternatives* (Winter): 10–17; Pimentel, D., and eleven others, 1992. *Environmental and Economic Benefits of Energy Conservation.* College of Agriculture and Life Sciences, Cornell University, Ithaca, NY; Romm, J. J., and A. B. Lovins, 1992. "Fueling a Competitive Economy." *Foreign Affairs* 71(5): 45–62; Romm, J. J., 1992. *The Once and Future Superpower.* William Morrow, New York; Schneider, 1989, *Global Warming;* Union of Concerned Scientists, 1991. *America's Energy Choices: Investing in a Strong Economy and a Clean Environment.* Cambridge, MA.

38. Lovins, A. B., and L. H. Lovins, 1991. "Least-Cost Climatic Stabilization." *Review of Energy and Environment* 16: 433–531.

39. U.S. Department of Energy, 1992. *Monthly Energy Review March 1992.* Washington, D.C.

40. Romm and Lovins, 1992, "Fueling a Competitive Economy."

41. Ibid.

42. U.S. Department of Energy, 1991. *National Energy Strategy: Technical Annex 2 1991–92.* Washington, D.C.

43. Romm and Lovins, 1992, "Fueling a Competitive Economy."

44. Geller, Howard, *et al.*, 1992. *Energy Efficiency and Job Creation.* American Council for an Energy-Efficient Economy, Washington, D.C.

45. Government of Canada, 1990. *Canada's Green Plan.* Ministry of Supply and Services, Ottawa.

46. Carrier, J.-G., and D. Krippl, 1990. "Comprehensive Study of European Forests Assesses Damage and Economic Losses from Air Pollution." *Environmental Conservation* 17: 365–366; Nilsson, S., 1992. *Economic Impacts of Forest Decline Caused by Air Pollutants in Europe.* Royal Swedish Academy of Sciences, Stockholm.

47. Benedick, R. E., 1991. *Ozone Diplomacy: New Directions in Safeguarding the Planet.* Harvard University Press, Cambridge, MA; Environmental Protection Agency, 1987. *Protection of Stratospheric Ozone and an Assessment of the Risks of Stratospheric Modification.* Washington, D.C.

48. Gleason, J. F., and thirteen others, 1993. "Record Low Global Ozone in 1992." *Science* 260: 523–525.

49. Benedick, R. E., 1991, *Ozone Diplomacy;* see also Jones, R., and T. Wigley, eds., 1989, *Ozone Depletion: Health and Environmental Consequences.* John Wiley, New York. ICF Inc., 1992, *Regulatory Impact Analysis: Compliance with Section 604 of the Clean Air Act for the Phaseout of Ozone Depleting Chemicals: Addendum* (Prepared for the Global Change Division, U.S. Environmental Protection Agency). Washington, D.C.

50. Environmental Protection Agency, 1988. *Regulatory Impact Analysis: Protection of Stratospheric Ozone,* Vol 1. Washington, D.C.

51. Terramura, A. H., and J. H. Sullivan, 1991. "Potential Impacts of Increased Solar UV-B on Global Plant Productivity." In E. Ricklis, ed., *Photobiology.* Plenum Press, New York; Van der Leun, J. C., and M. Tevini. eds., 1989. *Report of Panel on Environmental Effects of Enhanced Ultraviolet Radiation.* United Nations Environment Programme, Nairobi; Worrest, R., and L. Grant, 1989. "Effects of Ultraviolet-B Radiation on Terrestrial Plants and Marine Organisms." In Jones and Wigley, eds., *Ozone Depletion.*

52. MacKenzie, J. J., R. C. Dower, and D. D. T. Chen, 1992. *The Going Rate: What It Really Costs to Drive.* World Resources Institute, Washington, D.C.; Nadis, S., and J. J. MacKenzie, 1993. *Car Trouble.* World Resources Institute, Washington, D.C.; see also National Academy of Sciences, 1992. *Automotive Fuel Economy: How Far Should We Go?* National Academy Press, Washington, D.C.; Office of Technology Assessment, 1991. *Improving Automobile Fuel Economy: New Standards, New Approaches.* U.S. Government Printing Office, Washington, D.C.

53. Konheim and Ketcham, Inc., 1992. *Costs of Roadway Transportation Nationally, for the New York Metropolitan Area and for New York City.* Brooklyn, NY.

54. Pearce, D. W., 1993. *Economic Values and the Natural World.* Earthscan Publications Ltd., London; see also Daily, G. C., and P. R. Ehrlich, 1992. "Population, Sustainability, and Earth's Carrying Capacity." *BioScience* 42: 761–771.

55. Barrow, C. J., 1991. *Land Degradation.* Cambridge University Press, New York; Dregne, H., M. Kassas, and B. Rosanov, 1992. "A New Assessment of the World's Status of Desertification." *Desertification Control Bulletin* 20: 6–18; Hellden, U., 1991. "Desertification—Time for an Assessment?" *Ambio* 20: 372–383; Pimentel, D., ed.,

1993. *World Soil Erosion and Conservation*. Cambridge University Press, New York; United Nations Environment Programme, 1991. *Status of Desertification*. Nairobi.

56. Bibby, C. J. *et al.*, 1992. *Putting Biodiversity on the Map: Priority Areas for Global Conservation*. International Council for Bird Preservation, Cambridge, U.K.

57. Lindley, J. A., 1989. "Urban Freeway Congestion Problems and Solutions: An Update." *ITE Journal* (December 1989): 21–23; see also Konheim and Ketcham, Inc., 1992, *Costs of Roadway Transportation*.

58. Ibid.

59. Myers, N., 1993. "Environmental Refugees: How Many Ahead?" *BioScience* (in press).

60. Haq, M., 1992, *Human Development in a Changing World*.

61. Turner, S. K., 1990. *The Debt-Trade Linkage in U.S.-Latin American Trade*. Overseas Development Council, Washington, D.C.

Bibliography

Julian Simon

Aird, John S. *Slaughter of the Innocents*. Washington, D.C.: AEI Press, 1990.

Anderson, Terry L., and Donald R. Leal. *Free Market Environmentalism*. San Francisco: Pacific Research Institute for Public Policy and Westview Press, 1991.

Baden, John, ed. *The Vanishing Farmland Crisis*. Lawrence: University of Kansas Press, 1984.

Bailey, Ronald. *Ecoscam: The False Prophets of Ecological Apocalypse*. New York: St. Martin's Press, 1993.

Balling, Robert. C., Jr. *The Heated Debate*. San Francisco: Pacific Research Institute, 1992.

Barnett, Harold, and Chandler Morse. *Scarcity and Growth*. Baltimore: Johns Hopkins Press, 1963.

Barrons, Keith C. *Are Pesticides Really Necessary?* Chicago: Regnery, 1981. This excellent book delves into a variety of subjects related to the present volume but for which there is no space.

Baxter, William F. *People or Penguins: The Case for Optimal Pollution*. New York: Columbia University Press, 1974. An excellent short introduction to the relevant theory.

Beckmann, Peter. *The Health Hazards of Not Going Nuclear*. Boulder, CO: Golem Press, 1976.

Beisner, Calvin. *Prosperity and Poverty: The Compassionate Use of Resources in a World of Scarcity*. Westchester, Ill.: Crossway, 1988.

Bennett, M. K. *The World's Food*. New York: Harper & Brothers, 1954.

Bennett, Michael J. *The Asbestos Racket*. Washington, D.C.: Free Enterprise Press, 1991.

Block, Walter E., ed. *Economics and the Environment: A Reconciliation*. Vancouver, BC: Fraser Institute, 1990.

Cohen, Bernard. *Before It's Too Late: A Scientist's Case for Nuclear Energy*. New York: Plenum Press, 1983.

Deacon, Robert T., and M. Bruce Johnson, eds. *Forestlands: Public and Private*. San Francisco: Pacific Institute for Public Policy Research, 1985.

Efron, Edith. *The Apocalyptics: How Environmental Politics Controls What We Know About Cancer*. New York: Simon & Schuster, 1984.

Engels, Frederick. "The Myth of Overpopulation," from *Outlines of a Critique of Political Economy*, reprinted in Ronald L. Meek, ed., *Marx and Engels on Malthus*. London: Lawrence and Wishart, 1953.

Fumento, Michael. *Science Under Siege: Balancing Technology and the Environment*. New York: William Morrow, 1993.

Hayek, Friedrich. *The Fatal Conceit*. Chicago: University of Chicago Press, 1991.

Hazlitt, Henry. *Economics in One Lesson*. 2nd edn. New York: Arlington House, 1962.

Idso, Sherwood B. *Carbon Dioxide and Global Change: Earth in Transition*. Tempe, AZ: IBR Press, 1989.

Isaacs, Rael Jean, and Erich Isaacs. *The Coercive Utopians*. Chicago: Regnery, 1983.

Jastrow, Robert, William Nierenberg, and Frederick Seitz. *Scientific Perspectives on the Greenhouse Problem*. Ottawa, IL: Jameson Books, 1990.

Kasun, Jacqueline. *The War on Population*. San Francisco: Ignatius Press, 1988.

Kwong, Jo. *Protecting the Environment: Old Rhetoric, New Imperatives*. Washington, D.C.: Capital Research Center, 1990.

Lebergott, Stanley. *The Americans: An Economic Record*. New York: W. W. Norton, 1984.

Lehr, Jay, ed. *Rational Readings on Environmental Concerns*. New York: Van Nostrand, 1992.

London, Herbert I. *Why Are They Lying to Our Children?* New York: Stein and Day, 1984.

MacCracken, Samuel. *The War Against the Atom*. New York: Basic Books, 1982.

Maurice, Charles, and Charles W. Smithson. *The Doomsday Myth*. Stanford: Hoover Institution, 1984.

Michaels, Patrick. *Sound and Fury: The Science and Politics of Global Warming*. Washington, D.C.: Cato Institute, 1992.

National Center for Policy Analysis. *Progressive Environmentalism: A Pro-Human, Pro-Science, Pro-Free Enterprise Agenda for Change*. Dallas: NCPA, April 1991.

National Research Council, Committee on Population, and Working Group on Population Growth and Economic Development. *Population Growth and Economic Development: Policy Questions*. Washington, D.C.: National Academy Press, 1986.

Olson, Sherry. *The Depletion Myth: History of Railroad Use of Timber*. Cambridge, MA: Harvard University Press, 1971.

Osterfeld, David. *Prosperity Versus Planning*. New York: Oxford, 1992.

Ray, Dixie Lee, with Lou Guzzo. *Trashing the Planet*. Chicago: Regnery Gateway, 1990.

Schultz, Theodore W. *Investing in People*. Chicago: University of Chicago Press, 1981.

Simon, Julian L. *Population Matters: People, Resources, Environment, Immigration*. New Brunswick, NJ: Transaction Press, 1990.

———. *The State of Humanity*. Boston and Oxford: Basil Blackwell, forthcoming, 1994.

Singer, Max. *Passage to a Human World*. New Brunswick, NJ: Transaction Press, 1988.

Singer, S. Fred. *Global Climate Change*. New York: Paragon House, 1989.

Wattenberg, Ben. *The Birth Dearth*. New York: Pharos Books, 1989.

Whelan, Elizabeth M. *Toxic Terror: The Truth Behind the Cancer Scare*.

———, and Frederick J. Stare (edited by Stephen Barrett). *Panic in the Pantry*. Buffalo, NY: Prometheus Books, 1992.

Whitmore, T. C., and J. A. Sayer, eds. *Tropical Deforestation and Species Extinction*. New York: Chapman and Hall, 1992.

Wildavsky, Aaron. *Searching for Safety*. New Brunswick, NJ: Transaction Press, 1988.

Further Reading
Norman Myers

Abernethy, V. D., 1993. *Population Politics: The Choices that Shape Our Future*. Plenum Press, New York.

Benedick, R., 1991. *Ozone Diplomacy: New Directions in Safeguarding the Planet*. Harvard University Press, Cambridge, Mass.

Brown, L. R., C. Flavin, and H. Kane, 1993. *Vital Signs 1993: The Trends that are Shaping Our Future*. W. W. Norton, New York.

Brown, L. R. et al. 1994. *State of the World 1994*. W. W. Norton, New York.

Costanza, R., editor. 1991. *Ecological Economics: The Science and Management of Sustainability*. Columbia University Press, New York.

Daly, H. E., and J. B. Cobb, 1989. *For the Common Good: Redirecting the Economy toward Community, the Environment, and a Sustainable Future*. Beacon Press, Boston.

Dasgupta, P., 1993. *An Inquiry into Wellbeing and Destitution*. Cambridge University Press, New York.

Davis, K., and M. S. Bernstam, editors, 1991. *Resources, Environment, and Population; Present Knowledge, Future Options*. Oxford University Press, New York.

Durning, A. T., 1992. *How Much Is Enough? The Consumer Society and the Future of the Earth*. W. W. Norton, New York.

Ehrlich, P. R., and A. H. Ehrlich, 1981. *Extinction: The Causes and Consequences of the Disappearance of Species.* Random House, New York.

Ehrlich, P. R., and A. H. Ehrlich, 1990. *The Population Explosion.* Simon and Schuster, New York.

Ehrlich, P. R., and A. H. Ehrlich, 1991. *Healing the Planet: Strategies for Resolving the Environmental Crisis.* Addison Wesley, New York.

Ehrlich, P. R., and J. P. Holdren, 1988. *The Cassandra Conference: Resources and the Human Predicament.* Texas A & M University Press, College Station, Texas.

Ekins, P., 1992. *Wealth Beyond Measure: An Atlas of New Economics.* Doubleday, New York.

Elkington, J., J. Hailes, and J. Makower, 1990. *The Green Consumer.* Viking Penguin, New York.

Gore, A. *Earth in the Balance: Ecology and the Human Spirit.* Houghton Mifflin Co., Boston, Mass.

Grant, L., editor, 1992. *Elephants in the Volkswagen: Facing the Tough Questions about Our Overcrowded Country.* W. H. Freeman, New York.

Groombridge, B., editor, 1992. *Global Biodiversity: Status of the Earth's Living Resources.* Chapman and Hall, London.

Harrison, P., 1992. *The Third Revolution: Environment, Population and a Sustainable World.* St. Martin's Press, New York.

Holmberg, J., editor, 1992. *Policies for a Small Planet.* Earthscan Publications, London, and Island Press, Washington, DC.

Leggett, J., editor, 1990. *Global Warming: The Greenpeace Report.* Oxford University Press, New York.

Lovins, A. B., and L. H. Lovins, 1991. *Drill Rigs and Battleships are the Answer! (But what was the question?): Oil Efficiency, Economic Rationality and Security.* Rocky Mountain Institute, Snowmass, Col.

MacNeill, J., P. Winsemius, and T. Yakushiji, 1992. *Beyond Interdependence: The Meshing of the World's Economy and the Earth's Ecology.* Oxford University Press, New York.

Meadows, D. H., D. L. Meadows, and J. Randers, 1992. *Beyond the Limits: Globel Collapse or a Sustainable Future.* Chelsea Green Publishers, Post Mills, Vt.

Meffe, G., and R. Carroll, editors, 1994. *An Introduction to Conservation Biology.* Sinauer Associates, Sunderland, Mass.

Miller, G. T., 1991. *Living in the Environment.* Wadsworth Publishing Co., Belmont, Calif.

Mungall, C., and D. J. McLaren, editors, 1991. *Planet Under Stress.* Oxford University Press, New York.

Myers, N., 1979. *The Sinking Ark.* Pergamon Press, New York.

Myers, N. 1984. *A Wealth of Wild Species.* Westview Press, Boulder, Col.

Myers, N., 1984. *Gaia: An Atlas of Planet Management.* Doubleday, New York.

Myers, N., 1990. *Future Worlds: Challenge and Opportunity in an Age of Change.* Doubleday, New York.

Myers, N. 1992. *Population, Resources and the Environment: The Critical Challenges.* Banson Books, London, for the United Nations Population Fund, New York.

Myers, N., 1992. *The Primary Source: Tropical Forests and Our Future* (expanded edition). W. W. Norton, New York.

Myers, N., 1992. *Tropical Forests and Climate.* Kluwer Academic Publishers, Boston.

Myers, N. 1993. *Ultimate Security: The Environmental Basis of Political Security.* W. W. Norton, New York.

Nash, R. F., 1989. *The Rights of Nature: A History of Environmental Ethics.* University of Wisconsin Press, Madison, Wis.

Ness, G. D., W. D. Drake, and S. R. Brechin, editors. 1993. *Population-Environment Dynamics: Ideas and Observations.* University of Michigan Press, Ann Arbor, Mich.

Norton, B. G., 1991. *Toward Unity among Environmentalists.* Oxford University Press, New York.

Odum, G. E., 1993. *Ecology and Our Endangered Life Support Systems.* Sinauer Associates, Sunderland, Mass.

Oppenheimer, M., and R. H. Boyle, 1990. *Dead Heat: The Race Against the Greenhouse Effect.* Basic Books, New York.

Ornstein, R., and P. R. Ehrlich, 1989. *New World, New Mind: Moving Toward Conscious Evolution.* Doubleday, New York.

Pearce, D. W., 1993. *Economic Values and the Natural World.* Earthscan Publications, London, and Island Press, Washington, DC.

Pearce, D. W., A. Markandya, and E. B. Barbier, 1989. *Blueprint for a Green Economy.* Earthscan Publications, London, and Island Press, Washington, DC.

Pearce, D. W., E. B. Barbier, A. Markandya, S. Barrett, R. K. Turner, and T. Swanson, 1991. *Blueprint 2: Greening the World*

Economy. Earthscan Publications, London, and Island Press, Washington, DC.

Pearce, D. W., and J. J. Warford, 1993. *World Without End: Economics, Environment, and Sustainable Development*. Oxford University Press, New York.

Pearce, D. W., et al., 1993. *Blueprint 3: Measuring Sustainable Development*. Earthscan Publications, London, and Island Press, Washington, DC.

Pearce, D. W., and E. B. Barbier, editors, 1994. *Blueprint 4: Sustaining the Earth*. Earthscan Publications, London, and Island Press, Washington, DC.

Peters, R. L., and T. E. Lovejoy, editors, 1992. *Global Warming and Biological Diversity*. Yale University Press, New Haven, Conn.

Piel, G., 1992. *Only One World: Our Own to Make and to Keep*. W. H. Freeman, New York.

Pimentel, D., editor, 1993. *World Soil Erosion and Conservation*. Cambridge University Press, New York.

Ramphal, S., 1992. *Our Country, The Planet*. Island Press, Washington, DC.

Raven, P. H., L. R. Berg, and G. B. Johnson, 1993. *Environment*. Harcourt Brace Jovanovich, New York.

Romm, J. J., 1992. *The Once and Future Superpower*. William Morrow, New York.

Romm, J. J., and A. B. Lovins, 1992. *Fueling a Competitive Economy*. Foreign Affairs 71(5): 45–62.

Schneider, S. H., 1989. *Global Warming: Are We Entering the Greenhouse Century?* Sierra Club Books, San Francisco, Calif.

Scientific American, September 1989. *Managing the Planet*. Scientific American, New York.

Scientific American, 1990. *Energy*. Scientific American, New York.

Soule, M. E., editor, 1986. *Conservation Biology: The Science of Scarcity and Diversity*. Sinauer Associates, Sunderland, Mass.

Tolba, M. K., et al., editors, 1992. *The World Environment 1972–1992: Two Decades of Challenge*. Chapman and Hall, New York.

UNICEF. 1993. *The State of the World's Children 1993*. UNICEF, New York.

United Nations Development Programme, 1993. *Human Development Report 1993*. Oxford University Press, New York.

United Nations Environment Programme, 1991. *Environmental Data Report*. Basil Blackwell, New York.

United Nations Population Fund, 1993. *The State of World Population 1993*. United Nations Population Fund, New York.

Western, D. and M. Pearl, editors, 1989. *Conservation for the Twenty-First Century*. Oxford University Press, New York.

Wilson, E. O., editor, 1988. *Biodiversity*. National Academy Press, Washington, DC.

Wilson, E. O., 1993. *The Diversity of Life*. W. W. Norton, New York.

Woodwell, G. M. 1992. *The Earth in Transition: Patterns and Processes of Biotic Impoverishment*. Cambridge University Press, New York.

World Bank, 1993. *World Development Report 1993*. Oxford University Press, New York.

World Commission on Environment and Development. 1987. *Our Common Future*. Oxford University Press, New York.

World Resources Institute, 1992. *World Resources 1992–93: A Guide to the Global Environment*. Oxford University Press, New York.

Index